Playing
Joan

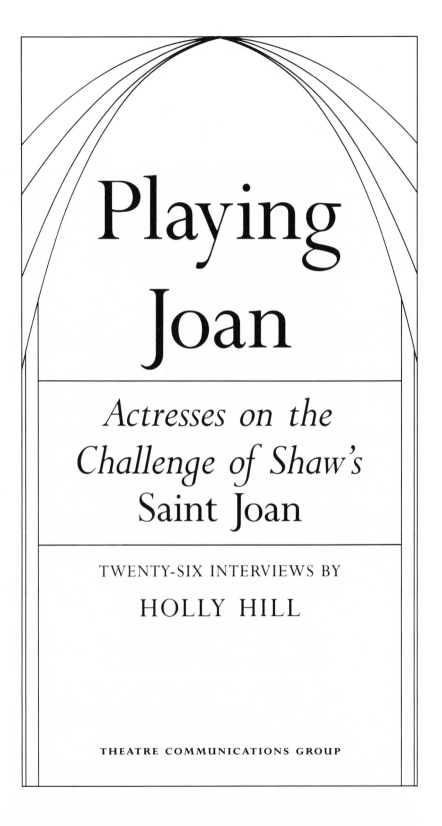

Playing
Joan

Actresses on the Challenge of Shaw's Saint Joan

TWENTY-SIX INTERVIEWS BY

HOLLY HILL

THEATRE COMMUNICATIONS GROUP

Playing Joan: Actresses on the Challenge of Shaw's Saint Joan is published by Theatre Communications Group, Inc., the national organization for the nonprofit professional theatre, 355 Lexington Ave., New York, NY 10017.

Distributed in Great Britain by Ianmead Ltd., 15 Stoatly Rise, Haslemere, Surrey GV27 1AF.

Earlier versions of interviews with Eileen Atkins, Judi Dench, Wendy Hiller and Barbara Jefford appeared in *The Annual of Bernard Shaw Studies*, Vol. 6 (University Park and London: The Pennsylvania State University Press, 1986), and with Jane Alexander and Elisabeth Bergner in *American Theatre* magazine.

Library of Congress Cataloging-in-Publication Data

Playing Joan.

Includes index.

1. Shaw, Bernard, 1856–1950. Saint Joan. 2. Shaw, Bernard, 1856–1950—Stage history. 3. Joan, of Arc, Saint, 1412–1431, in fiction, drama, poetry, etc. 4. Actresses—Great Britain—Interviews. 5. Actresses—United States—Interviews. 6. Acting. I. Hill, Holly.
PR5363.S33P5 1987   822'.912   87-10051
ISBN 0-930452-64-X (pbk.)

Design and composition by The Sarabande Press

Cover photograph: Siobhan McKenna as Joan.

First Edition: June 1987.

For all the doers
and the watchers
who love the art
of acting.

Contents

CONTENTS

Acknowledgments

In addition to the actresses who discussed playing Joan, I give special thanks to:

In the U.S.: at Theatre Communications Group, my editor, Elizabeth Osborn, and Terence Nemeth, Jim O'Quinn, Laura Ross and Herbert Scher; Dennis L. Behl, Norma T. Brady, Bonnie Brown, Adrian Bryan-Brown, Saraleigh Carney, Dorene R. Castle, Freda Diamond, Bernard F. Dukore, Richard Kornberg, Susan Rusinko, Stanley Weintraub, Patricia Woodard and Janet Young.

In Canada: Marie Brewer, Anne Goluska, Katherine Holmes, Glen W. Hunter, Stephanie Kerr, Heather McCallum, Joan Warman-Moss, Herbert Whittaker and Angela Winter.

In Britain: Michael Billington, Antonia Bryson, Bill Clancy, Michael Coveney, Margaret J. Cox, John Elsom, John Higgins, Anthony Masters, Michael Owen, Jerry Rickwood, Ann Marie Thompson and Irving Wardle.

In Ireland: Joe Dowling and Christopher Fitz-Simon.

And the special correspondents: Marilyn Allen, Mibs Bainum, Helene Baker, Paul Baker, Judith Barcroft, Dee Barron, Henry G. Burke, Susan S. Cole, Joseph Daubenas, Rebecca D. Des Marais, Deborah G. Dixon, William Dodds, William Patrick Finnerty, Al Ksen, Stephanie Kerr, Miller Lide, Clark S. Marlor, Jack Melanos, Lynda Miles, Linda C. Miller, Mary Betten Mitchell, Paul Myers, Marlis Nast, Rita R. Neal, Flemming Nyrop, Jackie

O'Shaughnessy, April Shawhan, Phillip J. Smith, Caldwell Titcomb and Kate Wilkinson.

Playing Joan was researched and written with the partial support of a grant from The City University of New York PSC-CUNY Research Award Program.

Preface

As a young actress, I did my favorite passage from Shaw's *Saint Joan*—the loneliness speech in the cathedral scene—for an acting class. I was so awful that all memory of the experience vanished except my rationalization for my failure. I felt that Shaw had written a booby-trapped character with contradictory qualities: farmer's daughter, soldier, cajoler and inspirer, religious visionary, and precocious intellectual speaking ideas a young country girl couldn't possibly conceive. Even after I learned that Shaw had used the transcripts of Joan of Arc's trial, I thought the role unactable.

Then I saw Eileen Atkins in *Saint Joan* in 1978 (the only subject in *Playing Joan* whose performance I did see, I regret to say), and knew that Joan could be a transcendent experience for actress and audience. I met Miss Atkins briefly two years later, and her replies to some questions I asked about playing Joan left me thinking, "That would make a good article about acting."

The opportunity to do an article for *The Annual of Bernard Shaw Studies* came in 1983. In research on Joan of Arc and on Shaw's play in order to form my questions, one of the books which excited me was Brian Tyson's *The Story of Shaw's Saint Joan*. Tyson recalls Shaw's 1934 statement: "It is quite likely that sixty years hence, every great English and American actress will have a shot at 'St. Joan,' just as every great actor will have a shot at Hamlet." I realized that it was centuries too late to record the reflections of many great actors who had played Hamlet, but none too soon to start a record of Shaw's Joans. Except for the originals—America's Winifred Lenihan and Britain's Sybil

Thorndike, plus Katharine Cornell, Diana Sands and Celia Johnson—most Joans of international to regional stature were alive.

My failure to come close to *Saint Joan* as an actress is one thread that led to *Playing Joan*. The other is the closeness I have felt to Joan of Arc since childhood. Perhaps she was my first recognition of heroism and of tragedy in the world. She lived up to the best in herself even unto death—what more could one hope to achieve? Though her best was extraordinary, beyond the reach of most, the heroism she personified helped me to set and work towards my own goals.

I have loved Joan and wanted to live up to her. My friends and detractors would probably agree that I have succeeded in emulating at least her quality of doggedness. One professor on my dissertation committee said at the dissertation defense that I shouldn't have taken on one aspect of the work; when asked why he hadn't spoken up earlier, he answered that he knew I'd do it anyway. He was right. Another long-suffering dissertation advisor broke into guffaws when I told him I was starting this book, commenting: "It doesn't surprise me that you're drawn to *Saint Joan*. You're mounting your high horse and waving your flaming white sword again."

If I have any sword in hand, my aim is to defend actors from such all-too-common attacks as *New York Times* television critic John J. O'Connor's, reviewing a January 3, 1987 new talk show: "It confirms the long-established fact that actors without a script generally don't have all that much to say." This is merely a recent example of the attitude that "actors are dumb," a prejudice that has persisted long after the formal social and religious barriers against the profession have been breached.

Allowing for some stupid and some intelligent or intuitive but verbally unskilled people in most professions, both as an actress among colleagues and as a journalist I have found performers to be perceptive and articulate. One actress wrote in answer to my request for an interview:

> You will just have to put me down as a coward! I do not wish to talk about my performance of St. Joan. I have a God-given gift for acting, but He has not included rational analysis or objective criticism.

According to my father my St. Joan made him forget I was his daughter!—and if I can do that—that's all I want to know. But how? I've no idea. Forgive me.

Many actors do not want, or feel unable, to talk about their work, sometimes in fear of being laughed at for trying to describe a process which makes great demands on both body and soul. Only two of the St. Joans I approached actually declined to be interviewed. Several did not respond to my requests (and possibly, through changes of agents, addresses, etc., never received them). With some reluctance, largely because it meant I couldn't request interviews from two exceptional embodiments of Joan in Anouilh's The Lark—Julie Harris and Dorothy Tutin—I decided to confine the interviews to Shaw's play. Critics and scholars argue over the status of Saint Joan in Shaw's canon and in world literature, and over his interpretation of Joan, but few disagree that his Joan is one of the great classical roles for an actress. I also concluded that exploring only one role would be a unique opportunity to demonstrate the variety of viewpoints and approaches actresses take towards doing the best job they can (and, sometimes, can't).

Shaw wrote Saint Joan for Sybil Thorndike, whose observations on and experiences with the role have been widely documented, and whose influence on and graciousness to her successors is noted by many in Playing Joan. Dame Sybil is so identified with Shaw's Joan that it is often forgotten that Winifred Lenihan actually originated the role. When the British production was postponed due to a prior commitment of Dame Sybil, Winifred Lenihan appeared in the world premiere for the Theatre Guild on December 28, 1923.

Katharine Cornell had been approached to play Joan but was under contract to another management. Eva Le Gallienne was approached but, as she related in a letter to Brian Tyson:

. . . with the temerity and arrogance of my 24 years, I refused the offer. I had been brought up in France and my ideas of "Jeanne d'Arc" were not those of Bernard Shaw. I remember saying . . . that the play should have been called "St. Bernard Shaw"—since I felt it was Shaw speaking rather than Joan.

Interviewed after the premiere, Winifred Lenihan sounded many of the notes struck by succeeding Joans. She told journalists that no part had ever fascinated her like Joan, that she had been frightened of it and had wanted to hide and weep during the rehearsals, that she had done no research because she felt it obstructed an author's idea, that she felt Shaw himself sometimes intruded upon Joan and the actress playing her, that the cathedral scene was her favorite, and that she considered her record high if she was able to give four good performances out of eight a week. Katharine Cornell, before playing Saint Joan in 1936, traced Joan of Arc's life on a trip to France, and during rehearsals she wore a riding habit to foster a boyish stride.

Saint Joan is developing its own theatrical traditions, anecdotes and memorabilia, beginning with the American star Maude Adams lending Winifred Lenihan the helmet she had worn as Schiller's Maid of Orleans. Elisabeth Bergner, who played the first continental Saint Joan in 1924 for Max Reinhardt, gave a performance which inspired Uta Hagen to want to be an actress. Katharine Cornell's biographer Tad Mosel notes:

> [When Miss Bergner] saw Kit's Juliet . . . [she] at once told her she ought to play Saint Joan . . . . It was rare in the theatre of that or any other day for one star to press her favorite role on another. The suggestion was sincere homage, and Bergner backed it up with charming notes and telegrams and even offered to delay the release of her projected film version of the play until after Kit's production, should she decide to do it.

This generosity in spirit and deed characterized my encounters with the twenty-six actresses interviewed for Playing Joan, with their colleagues, friends and relations, and with mine. Most of the actresses welcomed me into their homes and one even came to mine; others gave me time between performances or rehearsals. The interviews were conducted between the summer of 1983 and spring of 1985 in New York, Massachusetts, in or near London, in Dublin, and in Stratford and Niagara-on-the-Lake, Canada. The story linking the two interviews I was unable to do myself I consider the par excellence example of the generosity I encountered.

Heather McCallum and her staff in the Theatre Department of the Metropolitan Central Library in Toronto were invaluable in helping me locate representative Canadian St. Joans. Through them I met the Toronto critic Herbert Whittaker, who suggested that I include a Montreal Joan, Marjorie Brewer. She lives now in Andorra, and answered my questions on tape, adding a complete handwritten transcription of her interview.

When I was compiling the actresses' biographies, the Toronto librarians suggested I call Marjorie Brewer's brother in Montreal. His wife, Marie, answered, and after I told her about Marjorie Brewer's handwritten interview, there was a gasp and pause. "Marjorie has suffered from terrible arthritis in her hands and has not written anyone for years," Marie said. "She must have made a tremendous effort to write out her answers for you."

We talked about the book, and I told her of my frustration in not being able to include the Stratford Festival's St. Joan, Pat Galloway, due to schedule conflicts during my trip to Canada. "I've worked with Pat and I'm going to Stratford in ten days. Would it help if I did the interview for you?" Marie asked. I mailed my questions, Stratford press officer Angela Winter tracked down taping equipment, and Marie Brewer interviewed Pat Galloway in her home. I couldn't have done it better.

I have often experienced magnanimity working with theatre people, but I would like to feel that the extra helping I received in countless instances preparing Playing Joan was in part due to the spirit of Joan herself. Shaw felt that spirit, and directed in his will that his ashes be scattered at the foot of the statue of Joan of Arc in his garden.

The interviews in Playing Joan have been written to read as if the actress is talking directly to the reader, not as if they were English essays. I have tried to preserve the individual personalities of the speakers; I only wish the reader could actually hear the variety of accents and registers, the beauty of the voices, the intensity with which the actresses spoke, and their laughter.

Reflections on Shaw's Joan touch upon aspects of social, political, and religious history, upon biography and legend, upon work and life in the theatre. Among the actresses who have spoken to the challenge of Shaw's character was Winifred Lenihan in the May 11, 1924 issue of the American. To the first actress who experienced playing Joan, the last word in this introduction:

> Joan of Arc is an international religion. It wasn't just a sentimental song-writer who put into the mouths of millions during the war a song calling upon

Joan. He voiced a mass emotion. Something was needed beyond ourselves. If we couldn't all reach up to God, we could to one of His workers, Joan of Arc, her history, legend, idealization, root in our childhood. Each member of the audience comes to the theatre with an ideal, not cerebral, but emotional. That is why I say the actress is given an almost impossible task to fill. . . .

The lines the actress speaks show the girl wise, courageous, far-sighted, intensely human—but the lines themselves don't show the saint. The inner vision, the spiritual surge which lifts the role to the plane of the audience's ideal are not in the lines but behind them. To play the one and let the other shine through is the most difficult task in the world.

Holly Hill
New York
April 1987

Playing
Joan

Elisabeth Bergner in the Max Reinhardt production.

Elisabeth

Bergner

Elisabeth Bergner was born in Vienna. At Shaw's insistence, she played Joan in Max Reinhardt's 1924 production, at the Deutsches Theater in Berlin. For Shaw's birthday she performed the role in English at the Malvern Festival in 1938. She died May 12, 1986.

When I was a young girl, a real heroine for me was Schiller's Joan. I suppose because she was far more emotional than Shaw's Joan, and at that time that was the important thing, to be emotional. I did not ever play Schiller's Joan, or Brecht's. But Brecht was a very dear friend.

Saint Joan was my first work with Max Reinhardt. I believe it happened because Shaw's translator, Siegfried Trebitsch, was a great fan of mine and the things he said about me influenced Shaw, who gave Reinhardt the German rights to the play on the condition that I would play Joan. Reinhardt had wanted to cast Helen Thimig, the actress who became his second wife. I know this because Trebitsch told me. I wish that he hadn't, because it made working with Reinhardt more difficult for me, though he was very kind and patient.

I don't remember any details from the rehearsals except that, at that time, I had a rehearsal phobia. Though I knew not only my lines but the entire play by heart before we began, I still carried my script in my hands until the dress rehearsal. Isn't that silly! I don't believe my phobia went away until much later, when I did *Long Day's Journey into Night* in German.

Reinhardt made many cuts in Shaw's script, which we discussed. We thought it would be far more dramatic with fewer words and, you know, that was Reinhardt. He knew where it was better not to say anything and where the situation is the thing. He did not make a spectacle of the coronation at Rheims. That takes place offstage. The less you show, he believed, the more you have in your imagination.

Never, never did I have any trouble with Joan's voices. I just heard them. I promise you. I have a feeling she never thought about some things. She needed a soldier's clothing because she knew she couldn't go about in women's skirts, which she very intelligently explains in the trial scene. But her intelligence is not something that thinks it out. It is her instinct which is intelligent.

The epilogue is sad. This is the sadness: she is dead and knows more about life than she did before. You mustn't forget, here speaks Joan who isn't alive anymore and doesn't judge anymore her own time and what happened. Here speaks a Joan who is above it all. She is looking back to what she has experienced.

On our opening night in Berlin, there was a great, long applause before intermission, after the tent scene between Warwick, Cauchon and De Stogumber. We were all waiting for this applause at the end of the trial scene, and none came. None at all. I thought I had spoiled everything. Reinhardt put his hand in mine backstage. I told him it was all my fault. No, he said, that was the greatest success we could wish. After that, I was prepared for silence after the trial and expected it. I don't remember if it happened again or not.

I remember the actors I played with, but I mix them up. The Germans that I played with first were very important, because they were selected by Reinhardt, and Reinhardt studied and had a musical ear. That wasn't the case at Malvern, not at all.

I agreed to play Joan at the Malvern Festival because Charlotte, Shaw's wife, called and asked me if I would do so to make Shaw happy on his birthday. I should have known—later Charlotte told me that it had been Shaw's idea. I was doing a film and going on location in two weeks. My husband agreed to do the location shots with a double, and the close-ups of me later in London. Max Ayliff, the Malvern Festival director, promised to accept all of Reinhardt's cuts—at least for my role—and Reinhardt's blocking, and to rehearse without me until a week before the opening. I agreed to appear at rehearsals with my role learned in English. I have always been able to learn lines easily, but it is much harder to learn an old role in a new language than a new role, even in a new language. In the very beginning—it was a long time ago—I think I was terrified of acting in English, but eventually it became as normal as everyday language to me. So I knew my role fluently when I went to Malvern. But the others had not done their part.

The entire set at Malvern was exactly opposite to the one in Berlin, all the cuts had been put back, and all the blocking was new to me. Max Ayliff explained that the sets were old and could not be rebuilt, the actors had done this same production before and were used to it, and if I didn't cooperate he would have to cancel all the performances, which were already sold out. And disappoint Shaw on his birthday.

A crazy nightmare comes nearest to the shock and despair of not knowing what to do because it was different from what I had imagined. Perhaps I should have left, but I stayed. Then came the dress rehearsal. I had my own costumes from the Reinhardt production, but the rest of the actors had the Malvern production's, and I didn't know who was who! I don't remember the opening, except a friend told me I lapsed into German twice. It must have come over well because everyone was very nice and congratulated me, but I was exhausted.

Still, Shaw had not seen it, and I was doing it for him. I thought he might come the evening after the opening—I knew he would not be at the premiere—so I decided to save my strength and my emotions for the evening. I had made him swear not to come to a matinee, and I believed his promise. But he didn't keep it. He came to the matinee the day after the premiere, when I was already so exhausted and had forbidden him to come.

He left after the cathedral scene, saying "Not even the bell speech." And he was right. That was not cut from the Reinhardt version, but for that matinee, I cut it because I wanted to be perfect in the evening, when I thought he would be there, damn him!

Even afterwards, when Shaw tried desperately to make me play Joan in London and I didn't want to because I was so angry with him, we still quarreled about cuts. You see, I gave him the Reinhardt cuts. Reinhardt thought it was better, less many words. Shaw wanted every word and I didn't, because Joan sort of grew in me with cuts, you know, the cuts of the German production.

My copy of the English *Saint Joan* is full of Shaw's comments. In Scene One he wrote, 'You must make the most of Joan's flashes of common sense, instead of cutting them all out." Isn't this amusing: "Don't you dare to do that" and "Besides, I should kill you." He could not have been too mad at me, because he wrote, "You better come to dine with us." He begins, "My dear Elisabeth," and his signature is "Implacably, G. Bernard Shaw." His meanest impertinences were always kind. That is how he was.

Of my roles, Joan stands alone . . . except there is one part that, after a long interval, became as important to me. That was Mary Tyrone in O'Neill's *Long Day's Journey into Night*. Very different characters, and yet each asked all I had to give.

I would say *Saint Joan* stands even with everything that is great in world dramatic literature. Shaw is right to say that Joan is the kind of part that everyone wants, but I do not think she is a fair comparison with Hamlet. I can't say why. You know, you feel something; you can't always explain it. Sometimes you don't want to.

The only advice I would give to a young actress playing Joan is to live totally in the script and what comes out of the script. That is individual. With every great part and every great author—whether it be Kleist or Shaw or Shakespeare—it is your desire to know it from the inside and make it alive, to make it become you or you become it, that is important.

Wendy
Hiller

Wendy Hiller was born in Bramhall, Cheshire, England. Accepting Shaw's invitation, she played Joan at the Malvern Festival in 1936.

My St. Joan, from your point of view, stands quite alone. Six rehearsals, with no money. But the privilege of GBS there, standing in front of me when I'm introduced and saying, "My goodness, Wendy, what's the matter with your hair?" And me, propped up with my armor at a dress parade, absolutely terrified, "Well, it's curly, GBS." And he says, "It's positively immoral."

So I stuck it down with bay rum. But with the lights, and the heat, it began to curl up, and there was no time to get a wig. I thought I'd got it all down, but it began to move. And, of course, he wanted it classically straight.

I was invited to play St. Joan by GBS himself, who had seen me in London in *Love on the Dole*, my husband Ronald Gow's play. Then, when I was doing it in New York, I had a cable: "Was there any chance of my coming over and playing in *Saint Joan*?" Barry Jackson was putting it on at the Malvern Festival to celebrate Shaw's birthday. Tiny festival compared with the ones they do now, but I think it had the highest reputation.

I was released from *Love on the Dole*—I shouldn't have been, it was doing very well—and when I got on the boat to come home, I got another cable: "Would I also play Eliza Doolittle?" So that was two plays of Shaw. There were always several plays done at the Malvern Festival in a month's rehearsal. Not a month's rehearsal each; six days per play. Which one took entirely for granted. Young people look at me today and obviously find it difficult to believe when I tell them it was six rehearsals and, if you were lucky, you got through half a dress rehearsal.

In *Saint Joan* we were very blessed, and did a word rehearsal in an empty swimming bath. It was supervised by GBS, who told me "to hurry up and get on with it; there was no time to try and act with it." We managed half a dress rehearsal. But it went on too long, so GBS, who'd brought out his great big gold watch and timed the Inquisitor's speech, as he always did, snapped it closed and went home.

So I fell into the production. Six rehearsals then for *Pygmalion*, and I wasn't in the other productions. Shaw invited me to go and see the Restoration play. I sat in the first circle with him—he flirted outrageously—and Charlotte Shaw had a box.

Then Gabriel Pascal appeared, saying that he was going to raise the money to make a film of *Pygmalion*, and GBS said—I didn't know, at the time—that I must play it, so I waited for the film to be made. I always remember London Management asking me to play *Saint Joan* in London, and me answering, "Oh, I say, couldn't I do something else? I've done *Saint Joan*." This is when you're twenty-two, you know. The stupidity! The hair-raising stupidity! That was why I was right for Joan. I mean, I was as stupid as she. That's how she did it— youth and inexperience. How could an actress of, say, thirty-five know she was going to do *Saint Joan* and *Pygmalion* on six rehearsals each? No, never. Gibber, gibber, and hysteria.

What do I remember about the Malvern production? Don't be silly, dear, nothing. It was 1936. The thing was to learn your lines, not bump into the furniture—well, there wasn't much—not bump into anybody else, and get on with it. Fortunately, the wonderful actor Ernest Thesiger had played the Dauphin in Dame Sybil's great production, and he just went on. That was a wonderful centerpiece because he knew exactly, wasn't going to alter one jot or tittle, and how could he, and why should he? And we got on with it as best we could.

When I said one day, "GBS, we only have six rehearsals," he said, "It's a very good play, dear. If you can't have six weeks, six'll do." In other words, "Get on with my play. And shut up." He was a man of the theatre, entirely practical. Entirely practical. I think he'd be rather staggered at the self-indulgence today of sitting round and talking about what you feel. You get on. His attitude was, "I have written a play. Get on and do the best you can. With my play. And I want to hear every word."

I knew that Joan was a whacking great part to play because Sybil Thorndike had done it. She wrote me a letter telling me she was so glad I was going to do it, and warning me to "get away from the stained-glass image and make her an ordinary girl." I'd never seen Sybil. She was the great one, and afterwards *Saint Joan* had been done and knocked about a bit, and when they asked me to do it at Malvern I was the first sort of big public one. So that was a hideous responsibility. I was sensible enough to know that I'd got a responsibility on my shoulders and round my neck. But as for starting talking about what St. Joan meant to the Catholic church, what she meant to the medieval church, what she meant to the Church now, and how she stood in history—nonsense. I had six rehearsals, and I had to get on with *Pygmalion*, too. In other words, I was doing a job. You don't sit about and talk.

There's far too much conscious analyzing, which belittles so much. When people ask, "What is the first thing you do when you tackle a large Shaw role?" I say, "Pause at the commas and take a small breath, and take a large breath at the full stops. And say his lines clearly. He's done it for you."

It's the same with Shakespeare. I agree with John Gielgud. You don't have time; it wasn't written in an age of analysis. And that wonderful genius has packed it all there for you, packed it all there for you. I'm not saying that you don't all have to get in on the same beam when a director comes along and says, "Now, we're going to play *Measure for Measure* as Edwardian trollops," or "We're all going to be in the stews in Rome." No, they've all got to get together and do that the same whether they agree with it or not. That is the director's idea of bringing something fresh to a great work of art.

Most of what Shaw wrote was indisputably great. Everything that he wrote was enormously clear, and he never meant it to be overlaid. He always said to me that the best Morell he ever had in *Candida* was a man who didn't know what he was talking about. He was a very personable and physically attractive man—GBS didn't say without a thought in his head, he was far too charming and gentle. Well, he wasn't gentle, but he never would consciously hurt anybody's feelings. Nobody ever thought that. He never hurt mine, however crisp he was with me.

When I played Joan, I had youth, enormous vitality, and a peasant quality. I used a North Country accent. That's because I am North Country. I think it's best when it's done with a slight Irish accent, because GBS is Irish. It's sheer poetry, all of it. It's written in a wonderful rhythm. You can't leave out a syllable. It's like a piece of music. You've got to remember that Shaw was a music critic, and a fine musician with a great, great ear for music. He's not going to have anything legato if he didn't write it legato.

There were things that he was, quite rightly, absolutely adamant about. Like his bringing out the watch and timing that wonderful actor, Cecil Trouncer, with his Inquisitor's speech. I mean, not a second beyond, below or above. Do you know, you heard *every* word, phrasing *impeccable*, and you were getting Shaw's argument clearly. He didn't want a whole lot of false emotion in between his words and the audience.

He used the whole of the transcripts for the trial scene. He got it all documented, in its own language, the language of the time, and he put it into this beautiful prose. Some of the trial really is Joan's own words and thoughts. She was shrewd. But, you know, it is the kind of part, I swear, that *doesn't want* too much thought.

It doesn't need too much thought, because she worked on an entire instinct, because she was one of those unique human beings who are put into the world at the right age and the right time. And she never thought consciously what she was doing when she upped and said, "Look, do you know I'd rather anything than the life of a rat in a hole. My voices were right." That isn't a woman who has

*Wendy Hiller with Ernest Thesiger as the Dauphin in the 1936 Malvern Festival
production.*

thought and thought and intellectualized. There's a different wisdom beyond that. It's the wisdom of the blood. And you act in a certain way with the wisdom of the blood, when you're a certain age.

By that last speech in the epilogue I was jolly tired, I remember. I'd been rehearsing *Pygmalion* all day. I'd raise my arms to my head and say, "How long, oh Lord, how long," thinking, "How long can I stand here without passing out?" I didn't make any decisions about the voices. I think I just played them entirely practically, as though somebody had been talking. I don't think I went off into madness, into "hearing voices." I don't think I fell into that trap; that's a very easy one to fall into.

How you play St. Joan is written down in Shaw's preface. I must have fallen into the trap that three-quarters of the St. Joans do—like Pitoëff did, and Bergner was the worse—of falling all ethereal, and going off into the spiritual and sentimental. I do remember the end of the cathedral scene when she talks about how the common people will be glad to see her, and "if I go through the fire, I shall go through it to their hearts for ever and ever. And so, God be with me!" I probably said "God be with me" in a wishy-washy way, with eyes to heaven. GBS said that the man next to him threw up his arms and said, "Good God!" Because I'd thrown it away by playing it as though I was in a church, instead of saying 'God be with me!' as though "He's on my side. I've got Him, not you lot"—speaking of God as your best chum, the only one you can trust.

I must be one of the last actresses left alive who spoke to GBS and got a whole lot of correspondence from him about the part. He wrote and ticked me off right, left and center, quite beautifully. But *after* the first night, because he knew I hadn't had time to do anything. But he told me exactly what I did wrong, how I did it wrong, and why I did it wrong. And within the performances that came up, I tried to put it right. But that was the only direction I had; except being told at the word rehearsal, "Now, come on, Wendy, there's no time for acting. Come on, speed up," in other words, "Get through the lines, clip onto the cues, girl."

He said in his letter, "Get on with it. She was a peasant girl; she knew what she was doing. She was practical, she was down-to-earth." And then he put it frightfully fatherly, and finished up saying, "Now, I can't rewrite *Saint Joan* for you, dearest."

You know what you are when you're twenty-two—frightfully wise—so when he sent me this long letter telling me I was making all these mistakes, I thought, "GBS can't realize how difficult this part is, and anyway I'm off the stage for all that long time, and it's not really consistent." So I dropped him a note and asked if I could go round to see him in the hotel, and I went round and Charlotte and I talked for a bit. She was a darling, and said, "Now you want to talk to my husband, so I have some letters to write."

There we were in the sitting room, and he said, "Now, Wendy, now what's the trouble? Did my letter upset you?" "Well," I said, "GBS, I do know what you're getting at and I know you're quite right. But," I said, "you know it's not consistent that character of yours." Twenty-two years old. Can you believe it?

"Well, my dear," he replied, "I'm sure you're probably right." He must have been laughing, the dear thing. Can't you imagine, he must have been laughing and laughing. I think I asked him one or two questions. I went back, and tried to get on with it. He gave me about six points, which I suppose I put right—within my limits of being twenty-two, and no director, and no rehearsals.

You see, it's very strangely placed, *Saint Joan*, I didn't find it nearly as easy as Eliza. I just longed for more rehearsals with Joan, and I felt I'd landed on Eliza, although I didn't know how to phrase it. I just felt more comfortable on *Pygmalion* than on *Saint Joan* nights although, as I say, I got better. Well, I couldn't have got worse.

So there we are. The old darling, in spite of ticking me off left, right and center, also wrote this. Somebody had given me this Constable edition of *Saint Joan*, with stage settings by Ricketts, and I took it along to the word rehearsal in the swimming bath. Afterward, he came up to me and said in his beautiful Dublin accent, "I didn't mean to be rude, Wendy, but we've so little time, and I've got to get back for lunch." "GBS," I said, "do just sign that for me." So he wrote under the title *Saint Joan*, "alias Wendy Hiller, G. Bernard Shaw, Malvern, August 1936." So he really didn't think all *that* badly of me.

Sybil was quite unique and the only actress of her time who could play Joan. Nobody could have admired her more than I. I've only heard her—never having seen her—do a couple of speeches, the cathedral or the trial scene, and I thought, "No, I don't think this would do for now." Compared to actresses now, in the sixties, seventies, eighties, Sybil was mannered in her speech. She was superb for her time, but I think she would be considered a little mannered now. Sybil never said God. She always said Go-o-od. She always made it into three syllables.

Everything changes. Except for unique, unique occasions, everything can be contradicted. Somebody's given me a wonderful recording of Ellen Terry doing the "quality of mercy" speech from The Merchant of Venice. Now that was a completely unmannered delivery. It might be a woman speaking in the eighties, and the speed that she uses is entirely modern, not as we think of Edwardian and Victorian actresses, dwe-ell-ing and li-in-ger-ing and tra-ill-ing a-way. No, none of that. There is Ellen Terry, fairly beating along with enormous vitality in the voice. And such beautiful, crisp phrasing. That is a revelation.

Sybil's way of speaking may have been influenced by her husband. Dearest Lewis had a very strange way of producing. He used to produce entirely by sound from behind a screen, and used to make everybody follow his speech rhythm. I never asked Sybil about that. I never dared. We were in the film of Major Barbara together and I acted in a play with her for two years, but I don't ever remember talking about Saint Joan to Sybil.

I feel so lazy. There were telephone conversations with Shaw that should have been written down. There was one wonderful conversation: I'd wanted to play Saint Joan again, having said I wouldn't play in London. He'd promised it to Sybil's younger daughter, Ann, and they were going on tour with it, she and her father. I think the war was still on. Anyway, I remember saying to GBS, "Ah, but GBS, the time is passing and I want to do the play again." He said, "It's all right, Wendy. It always was a good play." I remember saying later to Ronald, my husband, who was listening on the other phone, "We should have put all that down."

I used to go to lunch with him and Mrs. Shaw. Mrs. Shaw was very sweet to me. Looking back now, one realizes that they were an elderly couple and they were delighted to meet somebody young. GBS used to say, "All the actors I knew, they're all dead, Wendy. All dead," and look round for sympathy. He was being so charming and so friendly and we should have asked him to our little maisonette in Bloomsbury.

I think I felt that I mustn't take advantage, I mustn't intrude. I'd been brought up very strictly to believe one mustn't intrude on elderly people. Then the war was quite a disruption in all our lives, and I had a baby—all of that came into it. And yet I did go over when Mrs. Shaw was ill. We cycled. We had no cars in England, except doctors and midwives—emergency people. And so we cycled, Ronald and I, over into Hertfordshire. It was only about forty miles. We spent the night, and came back the next day.

I remember we had a long talk, or rather GBS and my husband did, about Bevin's foreign policy. I remember looking around the drawing room, and feeling really ashamed to look because Charlotte wasn't there and it seemed so rude. But looking at Charlotte's portrait over the mantelpiece and one or two other things, and hearing Ronald, who was very political-minded, talking to GBS about foreign policy. We should have put all that down.

Once we went over to see him when he was alone, and we took the movie camera and took film of him and me. Then Ronald spoiled half of it by letting some light in. GBS was very old and a little bit deaf then. But when I was much younger, I could have taken a good deal more—he obviously held out with both hands to offer. He was a dear.

Marjorie Brewer as Joan of Lorraine in a 1947 Montreal Repertory Theatre production of the Maxwell Anderson play. She wore the same costume in the 1939 Everyman Players production of Saint Joan.

Marjorie Brewer

Born in Montreal, Marjorie Brewer was Joan in an Everyman Players production staged in a local church in 1939.

I was born in Montreal on April 23, 1914. As the 23rd is not only Shakespeare's but Cervantes's birthday, as well as St. George's Day, I obviously had the choice of theatre, fiction or the slaying of evil. I chose the first, and while my adult acting life was relatively short, I started fairly young and, at the age of twelve, joined the Montreal Little Theatre (little, in this case, meant Little People both in the audience and on the stage).

There I was given such eminent roles as Father Bear, the Big Bad Wolf, Pierrot, and, oh bliss, a female part—a Fairy Princess. I remember that for her I tried to pitch my voice higher, but it sounded so odd that I shoved it right back where it belonged. Later I did Romeo in the balcony scene and Sir Peter Teazle in the quarrel scene, but the Little People in the audience were so utterly bored and fidgety that we dropped that sort of nonsense.

Then I went to the Montreal Repertory School and that started off my short, but passionate, affair with the theatre. I played many roles with the Montreal Repertory Theatre—our own group, the 16–30 Club, and a couple at McGill University.

Canada in the thirties had no professional theatre—mostly because of the Depression. Even the Montreal Repertory Theatre didn't pay its actors except when they had to miss a radio program. So we were all amateurs on the stage and professionals on the air. And what remuneration we received on radio! Eight dollars for a half-hour play and twenty dollars for an hour if it was on the independent station which had commercials—this was big money! We were pretty good, too. I remember being bitterly disappointed when I saw my first New York show. I don't know what I expected; "Why," I thought, "they aren't any better than we are!"

There was no television in my day, but I did a lot of radio work. The only awards I ever had were two Best Performance by an Actress in the Montreal Dominion Drama Festival entries. I once played Sarah Bernhardt in a Canadian original play called *Divinity in Montreal* (the co-author was Herbert Whittaker). I had done a fair amount of research and came up with a flamboyant, excitable egotistic actress. Unluckily for me, the adjudicator had *met* Sarah, who had spent half an hour with him talking gravely and knowledgeably about sheep-farming in Tasmania. His views on her character obviously differed from mine. I must say, this rather put me off research for awhile.

I'm afraid I cannot pretend ever to have had Joan as a childhood heroine. If I thought of her at all, she was simply a military leader who saved France and who happened to be a woman—until I read the play. As for the voices, they just added to the romanticism of the tale—until I read the play. Why exactly the play should have changed this I can't say, but it did. I came to accept the voices as fact, unquestioningly, as Joan did. Don't misunderstand me—this was not a profound religious experience; it just was.

Our production of *Saint Joan* started when my father and I saw a superb production of *Jedermann* at the Salzburg Festival in 1932. On leaving, Daddy—who was the organist at the Church of the Messiah in Montreal (as well as at Temple Emmanuel, on Fridays)—said he had always wanted to do such a show in the church, with Riches popping out of the pulpit and Everyman's voices coming from the organ loft here, there, and everywhere. So I said, "Why not?" Thus began the Everyman Players.

There were certain difficulties. For instance: because of the more conservative members of the congregation, Courtesan in *Everyman* became Ladye, and even several years later in *Saint Joan*, the English were spoken of as the English and not as the Goddamns, and Dunois as Dunois, not as the Bastard. Though I'm afraid I myself slipped several times. No one seemed to notice.

Our production of *Joan* had no sets and no decor because it was done in the body of the church, which was decor enough and lent itself admirably to exits and entrances.

The only amusing thing that happened was not so amusing at the time. That was the bat. The famous bat, which swooped down the spotlight from the organ-loft onto the stage. I remember feeling very smug because I didn't duck as some of the cast did. And it was during the "They told me you were fools" speech, my preferred of all. People said afterwards, "Did you see—Marjorie Brewer was so rapt in her role that she didn't even notice that bat." What nonsense, I thought of nothing else but. Proof? The tears didn't come. Fortunately, the bat left the actors soon to swoop down on the audience. I was perfectly aware, still spouting forth those superb words, of the sea of bobbing heads before me.

This all happened almost fifty years ago and I really can't remember details about the interpretation of Joan except that in the beginning, as the country girl, while she was uncertain, eager and hesitant in her dealings with people, she was always, always confident when she mentioned her voices and her God-inspired mission. With the Dauphin, coaxing and wheedling as a mother might be with her child until, finally, aggravated, she exhorts him to stand up for himself.

Sexuality—none. It never crossed my mind, and I don't think the play gives any hint of it. Femininity, yes; motherliness, yes, but sexuality, no.

The most difficult scene for me was the one with Dunois where Joan attempts to explain her voices to him and chants them to the sound of the cathedral clock chimes. I am almost tone deaf, and though I hear tunes in my mind perfectly, I think, I can't voice them. I was given the note on the organ each time, and each time I went flat.

I consoled myself, saying that a peasant wouldn't have perfect pitch, but this was specious reasoning and I knew it. And when the scene was over, I thought "Phew, the worst is over and the best is yet to come."

I wonder if others have found, as I have, that Shaw is remarkably easy to memorize? The ideas flow into one another easily, logically, and one can't help but follow. The glorious language is almost biblical in character and dignity, and I wonder if Winston Churchill, who had the same facility, did not sometimes borrow from Shaw.

In the cathedral scene, with nearly all her mission accomplished and her voices' predictions come true, confidence gains the upper hand and she has become, as the Archbishop admonishes, "stained with the sin of pride." "But I do know better than any of you seem to. And I am not proud. I never speak unless I know I'm right."

Later, as the realization of her aloneness sinks in, and she knows that she can expect no help even from her most ardent followers: resignation—but only for a moment. Then up again, defiant, proud—and alone. And there she is triumphant, triumphant in her faith, triumphant even in her loneliness, for "What is my loneliness before the loneliness of my country and my God?" And, throughout, sadness and disillusionment. Was this her innate intelligence? I don't know.

I've just been rereading the trial scene, and I think it is perhaps only now that I understand what a great privilege was mine to be given the role. Possibly, going back to the Greek plays, you may find a scene that gives an actress the same scope. Possibly. Here, there was confidence and protestation, bewilderment, pathos and disenchantment, heartbreak, and finally the last outburst.

Who, with any intelligence, any sensitivity, any voice, could fail to do something with this magnificent speech? It plays itself and to my mind compares, to its advantage, with Hamlet's "To be or not to be." It will live on, as Shaw says, and the part of Joan will be a coveted one, I believe, for many a long year. You can see that I quite liked the part.

I played Joan again in Maxwell Anderson's Joan of Lorraine, which was great fun to do, more fun than Shaw's. Was this possibly because, being ten or so years older, I took things less seriously? Or was it the difference between the two plays? I'm inclined to think the latter. I enjoyed the sudden transition between actress and Saint Joan, but somehow one never reached the heights as one did with Shaw.

I once saw a production of Shaw's *Saint Joan* in Paris, with a well-known French actress whose name I can't recall at the moment. I was not impressed, but I think largely because Shaw's fluidity of language does not lend itself to translation. Imagine having to end the play—the epilogue—with "Dans combien de temps, mon Seigneur, dans combien de temps?" instead of with the cadence and sonority of "How long, oh Lord, how long?"

There is a growing theory in France that Joan, far from being a simple peasant maid, was, in fact, the illegitimate daughter of Queen Isabeau of France and the Duc d'Orléans. Two books have come out fairly recently and almost simultaneously propounding this idea and proffering, I must say, pretty cogent proofs. As a Princess Royal, Joan could not be burnt, so a substitute, already condemned by the Inquisition, took her place. And Joan, after all, spent five years "shut out from the light of the sky and the sight of the fields and the flowers." She was released in 1436, married the Chevalier Robert des Armoises, and died in 1446. All this information is in the books, accompanied by many authenticated documents. It rather takes the romance out of the tale, doesn't it? Let's be credulous and stick to the old story.

A page from Constance Cummings' scrapbook, showing her in the 1939 Old Vic Company production.

Constance Cummings

Constance Cummings was born in Seattle, Washington. With Shaw's approval, she first played Joan with the Old Vic Theatre Company in 1939. She then performed the role on BBC radio in 1941 and 1947, and on BBC television in 1951.

I often think of the marvelous bit in the Dauphin scene, when Charlie says, "One good treaty is worth ten good fights. . . . If we can only have a treaty, the English are sure to have the worst of it, because they are better at fighting than at thinking." And every once in a while these reports come back from the EEC about where England has ended up, and I quote that and say, "Well, there you go. Shaw was quite right. The English are better at fighting than thinking."

Joan of Arc was only a name to me until I knew I was going to do the play. Then I began to study and learn about her. I don't suppose there is anybody else of such an early date, except possibly Julius Caesar, about whom there is so much verbatim. The Church has it all written down. It's amazing. I wouldn't say that I used a great deal of research in playing the role; it just confirmed what Shaw had written.

You see, a lot of people say that Shaw is an intellectual who cannot write things that are emotional or moving. About *Saint Joan* they say, "Well, he's just a cool, intellectual chap who doesn't understand about God and about how to write a saint." But, of course, he does. Much better than most people.

I think there is no doubt that he has written a portrait of a saint in this play. This is a pure, a very pure person, and I think she's made herself what saints are made of. I think Shaw understood that kind of purity. He understood Joan's belief that she had a direct line to her God. He must have had some sort of direct line himself.

It is hard to elaborate on that because one is talking about things that are very hard to describe. I don't believe I have played another character who had a direct line to a power outside or within themselves, except possibly in Arthur Kopit's *Wings*. I don't think that character thought of herself as having a line to God. But she certainly was a woman who believed in repairing herself, not in a religious but in a very strong way. Again, I don't think you could describe it in words, but I think that the urging which moved her to try and find her way out of the blackness of a stroke was something very akin to the drive that Joan had.

When the Old Vic Theatre Company asked me to join them for a season to play Juliet and Joan, I was told that Shaw must approve me for Joan. I was given an appointment to go to his apartment in Whitehall Court. That was wonderful, meeting him. I suppose I never would have otherwise, and it was a lovely experience. Wonderful blue, blue eyes he had. They were like aquamarines, they were so blue. And they twinkled.

I was so starry-eyed, and the half-hour with him went so quickly, that I can't remember an awful lot about it, but I did have the impudence—he laughed and called it impudence—to say that I was pretty sure I knew how he wanted Joan played. Though I hadn't seen Sybil Thorndike's performance, I had seen much of her other work, and thought I understood how she might have done it.

Sybil was a lovely woman. And she was very straightforward. She had no false pride. I always thought she had no pride at all, really. She had none of the attitude that some actors and actresses have of thinking of the effect that they're making in the part, and wanting to be center stage. She was a dear, lovely, warm, direct woman who really almost never thought about herself.

In that way I felt that she couldn't have helped playing Joan very much like Joan herself was. It must have been a lovely, direct, straightforward, moving performance. I have seen other actresses who have played around with it, given "performances." Sybil never really gave a performance in that sense. Of course, it was a marvelous performance, but that was not what she meant to be doing or what she was aiming at.

That was the only time I saw Shaw. I did write to him and ask, "Why does the Church mind so much that Joan wore soldier's clothes?" because it did seem to me, as it did to Joan, very sensible. He replied with one of his famous postcards, which had a photo on one side. His reply was a bit of a joke, because in the photo he was looking a bit quizzical. On the other side of the postcard he wrote, "Well, as you can see from my expression, I don't remember very well."

He said the reason that the Church objected was that people like St. Francis and John the Baptist cast off their conventional attire, and then their followers sometimes threw off all their clothes and went naked. This is why the Church frowned on it. But I suppose it probably was a naive question, because for a woman to wear men's clothes in those days was, according to the clergy, very wrong. There were the sumptuary laws about the clothes that belonged to your class and your sex.

Esme Church, who directed the Old Vic production, was a very good actress. She was marvelously sensitive, and sensible, about the play. She had no high-flown romantic ideas about how it should be presented. I remember her saying, when we began rehearsals, that she'd been in France not long before, and she remembered going to some church, simply to see it, and there was a service on.

She said there were little French children in the church who were scampering around and playing in the background while the service was going on. And she said, "Those children felt they were in their Father's house. That is the feeling that we want to get in this play. Everybody must feel that the religious side of it is not remote at all. All the people in the play, in that period, talk of their feeling about the Church and talk about God as if they were 'in my Father's house,' and cosy." It set a nice theme.

It was a very simple, straightforward production. The sets were not elaborate; things were suggested. The costumes were of 1429 or whatever the date was. Andre Morel played Cauchon, and he was marvelous. He was terribly moving, especially in the dream scene at the end, when he came on and said, "Well, I did what I thought was best." Oh, he was so moving. Cauchon still didn't understand, you see.

Max Adrian played the Dauphin, and he was lovely. He got all the shrewdness, the meanness, and the charm, because the little man was not a battler; he was really in a job that he wasn't quite up to. But shrewd, a shrewd Frenchman. Not really mean, I suppose, but he had to borrow money; he wasn't a rich king. Maxie was wonderful. He was the best Dauphin I've seen. Well, there's one I've seen since—John Standing. He played it at the Oxford Festival about five years ago. Julia Foster played Joan, and she was very, very good.

Joan was very much of a whole. She was such an uncomplicated person, because everything was so simple for her. I didn't find it difficult, although there was none of it about which I could say, "Ah, yes, I recognize this because I am like that." Perhaps that sounds rather too self-confident.

I have trouble with accents. I'm not good at them at all. And I don't know how good I was with hers. Robert Donat helped me. He wasn't in *Joan*, but he was in the Old Vic season. We did *Romeo and Juliet* together. He said he'd picked an accent which was a little bit like American. So I approximated, I suppose, an English country accent. It had a slight roughness to it, which helped, because obviously she was a rough farm girl, not a refined city lady.

The best scene in the play is the tent scene between the three men: Cauchon, Warwick and De Stogumber. Absolutely marvelous. The Loire scene is a beast, making it believable. I think wherever you are, even if you were by the side of a river, it would still look like a stage. Well, I don't know, if you really were by a river—but I've never seen the scene convincing. I don't know why.

We didn't have a real river when I played Joan on television. It was done inside. It was one of the first televisions done in England, I think. We did *Saint Joan* and *Cyrano de Bergerac*. Leslie Banks played Cyrano, I played Roxanne, and an unknown young man—a very good-looking young man named James Mason—played Christian. That's an impossible part.

Between the Old Vic and television productions, I had played *Saint Joan* on the radio for Val Gielgud. I think the television was filmed, but the radio was live, and I insisted on doing it without the book. I had done a performance on the stage at the Old Vic, and we were doing the whole play on the radio—I think we made one or two tiny cuts—so I just did the performance that I had done on the stage.

I stood up under the microphone and tried not to move as much as I had on the stage, although there wasn't that much movement in the Old Vic production. Val Gielgud told me afterward that he had two or three people, with books, placed strategically so they could throw the book in front of me if I dried. I think *he* believed that I was all right, and was going to get through it. But the crew who were recording it said, "It's unheard of. It's crazy." They were terrified of my drying up and saying, "What's the line?" Val Gielgud told me this when it was all over and there had been no terrible disaster.

I don't think that knowing people would be listening but not watching made any difference to the interpretation. It is a play to listen to. Shaw's plays are, aren't they? And I think there are moments all through the play that are so moving. I suppose it depends on how it is done, but the end of that first scene, when she goes off, having got the horse and the uniform, and the little servant comes rushing in and says, "The hens are laying like mad." And De Baudricourt crosses himself and says, "She did come from God." You see, even thinking about that, the tears come. I find that terribly moving.

Now, sometimes that is played as a gag, and the audience laughs at it. I don't think it should. I think, if that's played properly, it should send a chill down your spine. You really should feel, in the theatre, the presence of God. It should strike you with awe. If it is thrown away as a joke, I think you're belittling the play. You're not doing what Shaw really meant. All through the play there are moments like that.

It is a marvelous play and a great part. I think actresses will always want to do it. Compared to Hamlet, though, I would have thought him much more complicated and difficult. I think Joan is pretty straightforward. I think there is only one way to play her if you're going to play it right, whereas there are thousands of theories about Hamlet, and people have played it different ways. There's almost no limit to what you can do with Hamlet. I think that's a pitfall. People very often play about, and mess it up with over-elaboration.

Joan, I just feel, is somebody I know very well. I can remember great slabs of the play, but maybe that's because I was younger then, because I can also remember pages and pages of Juliet, which I did at the same time. A play that I did ten years ago I would find very difficult. I would have to start from scratch if I were going to do it again.

It is often said that Juliet and Joan are roles you shouldn't play until you're too old to because of the technical difficulties. I played both during the same season, and I think that is possibly true of Juliet. I don't think I was very good as Juliet. To begin with, I really didn't know how to speak verse. I'd had no training in it. And if you can't speak verse, you shouldn't do Shakespeare.

This is a criticism I would make of a lot of modern Hamlets. It's no good tearing the thing apart and making it sound like mundane conversation. You've got to speak the verse first. You can't even get the proper sense if you don't speak the verse. Unless you're really trained and you can speak it beautifully, you shouldn't do it. So, from that point of view, because Hamlet is in verse and Joan is not, I would have thought that Joan was the easier part of the two.

I don't know how good I was as Joan, but it never presented any great problems to me. I felt that I knew her. She seemed to be a simple girl. I don't mean simple/stupid, I mean simple/uncomplicated. To her, everything was so clear. You just listen to God and do what He says. She really was as simple as that. I don't think it presents any psychological difficulties.

Ann
Casson

Ann Casson, the daughter of Sybil Thorndike and Lewis Casson, was born in London.
With Shaw's permission, she played Joan at the Bristol Old Vic, at King's Theatre,
Hammersmith, and on tour through England, Scotland and Europe from 1944 to
1946. She also did Saint Joan on BBC television in 1946,
and with the Canadian Players in 1954–55.

Joan of Arc was a tremendous figure to me. But, of course,
she was always connected with Mother having played it. I
don't remember very much about when she first did Joan, but
I did go to see it a great deal.

When my brothers and sister and I were little and people
came for dinner during the London run, Father would say,
"Why don't you come along and play a monk tonight?"
They'd go to the theatre, get a black robe, and Father would
rehearse with them—tell them where to stand and such.
Mother used to say that she'd get awful shocks looking up and
seeing a friend in the trial scene. One night she asked, "Who's
that funny little monk in the black hood?" and it was a woman—a dancer friend. Some friends rang up regularly and

asked, "Do you mind if I come along on Saturday night?" It must have been difficult for Mother to concentrate sometimes.

When we were all small, after *Saint Joan* closed in London, we went on a motoring tour, going to all the places Joan had been. Children are so beastly when they're taken on such trips, you know—we'd all say, "Mind, now, there's another chateau. There's another cathedral. Don't show them or we'll have to get out and look at it." We thought we'd just *had* cathedrals and chateaus. Of course, I could murder myself now for wasting my opportunity, but we were beyond it then. Still, it's lovely to have that in the back of my mind. Then, when I was twelve, Mother took *Saint Joan* on tour in South Africa, and I played Warwick's Page. So the play itself always meant a tremendous amount to me.

Later on, when it came to playing Joan myself, it was a completely different thing. You have to wipe the slate clean. I went back to the sources—not only the trial, but the rehabilitation of Joan, where so many of her relations and friends from her village spoke about her. I hadn't gone into it in such depth until then, when I suddenly met this extraordinary person.

There's a lot in Joan which Mother, I believe, very much got. Joan was an extremely capable woman. Through sheer common sense she could be a great general because she could see what was obvious, whereas a lot of other people had their own axes to grind and missed it. Joan went straight to it, and she couldn't understand why people didn't see it the way she did. Mother was a very tall, very bold, capable person and I—I suppose I saw it slightly a different way. I think it was something to do with becoming a convert to the Catholic church only a year before playing Joan. I was really filled with faith. I still am.

I saw Joan first and foremost as an ordinary person who was taken over by something that she firmly believed, that she knew had got to happen. I think she was directly inspired, and that made her certain, even in the smallest things.

It is wonderful to see in her dealings with people, as in the very first scene with De Baudricourt, not being at all fazed by his authority and bombast, but just simply keeping her feet firmly planted and waiting. She knows he's going to come round. The Dauphin was a person who had to bring out all her strength, because he was so vacillating. But there again, she knew that she had a call to crown him King of France, and all obstacles had to be moved out of the way.

Each situation is completely different, but part of the total way that she had to go. She was part of a sweep of history. There is tremendous energy and concentration throughout, which focuses in particular ways. Always she has this complete confidence that she is doing the right thing, and so it must work out. Doors will open, because she knows it's going to happen. That pushes straight through the changing of the wind, because she knows that through the power of prayer things can be changed.

Then you get to the cathedral scene, which I always found by far the most difficult. I think actually it's got weaknesses in not having a clear shape; that's the only weakness I see in the play. There is a marvelous feeling of everybody being completely exhausted, like at the end of a long dress rehearsal, when things aren't right and you've got to argue it out. I love the way the arguments crisscross each other, out of frustration and exhaustion. But then she realizes for the first time that all these different people have their own ambitions and have not got her faith. She realizes that she is alone.

Even that gives her added strength through to the trial, which she doesn't understand. She simply cannot see how *they* cannot see what she is doing. I think it's wonderful, that line in Shaw's preface: "An irresistible force coming up against an immovable object." That is just what it was. They were both absolutely firm and strong.

To me, the worst possible moment—more than finding herself alone, or being condemned—was when she suddenly lost her faith. After they convince her that she has been deceived in her voices, nothing really matters. I think that complete despair was the worst possible tragedy she could have had.

The recantation and reversal build up in such an extraordinary way, I don't see how anybody could find that difficult to play. They've been hammering at her all the way round, and though she's very quick-witted and gives commonsense replies, things that are common sense to her they think are outrageous. When she replies, "What other judgment can I judge by but my own?" for instance, they find her completely outrageous and dogmatic because she's setting her own judgment against others. But she knows, as a commonsense woman, that you've got to know deep down yourself what is right, and you've got to act on it.

I knew from the trial transcript that she always believed she was going to be freed because she had a vision when she was in prison saying, "You will be released by a great victory." She believed that she was going to be all right. But in the play, Brother Martin says, "Do you not yet see that your voices have deceived you? Have they kept a single promise to you since you were taken at Compiègne?" Brother Martin, who has really believed in her as an honest person, convinces her, and she concludes that "only a fool would walk into a fire. God, who gave me my common sense, cannot will me to do that."

The reversal of her recantation is *absolute fury*, the fury you get into when you have been made to deny everything that you really believe. She thinks she is going to be free. She's only dimly listening to what they are saying at first, and then she hears "to the end of thy earthly days in perpetual imprisonment." That is a sudden revelation of how totally wrong people must be when they can do to another what is against the whole force and beauty of life, faith, and everything else. "My voices *were right* . . . they *told* me you were fools, and that I was not to listen to your fine words nor trust to your charity." That, to me, is her greatest moment. You have complete disbelief, then the sudden realization and absolute fury, and then the freedom. Complete freedom. Death and pain and everything are of the least possible importance. The main thing is that she knows she was right, and that the visions she had were true.

When you're playing it, you can't possibly think how you're doing it. In rehearsal you dissect it, but in actual playing, it is like singing an opera. It sweeps you from one moment to the other.

My playing Joan came about in rather a funny way, because a London management wanted me to do it, and we had Shaw's permission, and then that particular management got booked up by another management who sort of chickened out because it was too much of an undertaking. I wrote to Shaw then and asked if I might have permission to do it with another management. I had a wonderful letter back from him saying, "When I gave permission for the play to be done, I gave the permission to *you*, so wherever you choose to take it, it is yours."

Ann Casson in 1945, on tour as Joan.

When I was in my teens I had met Shaw in his apartment in Whitehall Court, but I don't know what went into his giving me permission to play St. Joan except that he knew I had been specializing in Shaw with the Macdona Players, who did all the Shaw plays for many, many years in England. He had heard of different performances that I had done with them. When he wrote that it was me he had given permission to, I could look around. There was a company that Basil Langton was running during the war on behalf of the Arts Council. I took the idea to him, and he was tremendously excited by it. So we played it first at the Bristol Old Vic, with my father directing and playing Cauchon, and Basil Langton producing and playing De Baudricourt and Brother Martin.

I had another, really wonderful postcard from Shaw during the time that we were rehearsing. It was such a tremendously exciting time working on the play that I just had to sort of explode and write him what I was feeling about it. I did say that I was a Catholic, but a protesting one. Shaw wrote back a postcard saying, "You are in exactly the right mood for it because my Joan is a volcano of energy from first to last and never the sniveling Cinderella born to be burnt that so many, except the first, made her." And he said, "Go ahead with my blessing. Don't tire yourself out before you begin. Not that you could even if you tried. But, anyway, keep always something in reserve."

Basil Langton and I went down to see Shaw at Ayot St Lawrence. He said, "I'm sorry, but I just don't go to the theatre anymore. I'm too old to go now; I haven't been in years." He was pretty frail then. He didn't talk an awful lot about Joan. He talked mostly about playing and about actors he had loved.

The chief thing he talked about was that he had put all of his ideas into the words, and it was the speaking of the words that was most important. He felt that the greatest actors were those he could just listen to, and get it all from the way that they spoke. He tremendously admired Barry Sullivan, an actor who always played in the provinces. He said, "You could sit backstage and listen to him, and the entire character was put into the way that he phrased things and the actual way that they were spoken." Shaw's advice has always been, "All you need to do is speak my words." Of course you've got to know *how* to speak them, you've got to know the tunes. If you understand the way Shaw goes, you know the way he builds things. Obviously you've got to take the higher notes; the way it should be spoken is implicit in the way it's written if you've got a musical ear at all. And, of course, he always thought musically.

Mother played Joan pretty North Country. I didn't do much of an accent. You have to make it rougher, but that's more the voice that you use. I didn't do it in Lumpshire, which is an accent that doesn't really belong anywhere. I decided that Lumpshire was dangerous, so I got it stronger and perhaps slightly like the Americans. You obviously cannot play Joan in a very English, well-brought-up accent. You couldn't speak the lines if you did it like that.

The most extraordinary moment that I ever had during the playing of it was the E.N.S.A. tour just after the war ended. The war finished in May, and in August we went over to Europe and traveled through Germany, France, and Belgium, playing to troops. We were in Hamburg, in a big state theatre which was standing alone, surrounded by thirty square miles of rubble from our bombing. It was complete devastation. The theatre was jammed. I don't know how many it held, but it must have been two or three thousand, all troops.

It was marvelous to have an entire audience of men laughing at some of Shaw's lines. But what completely staggered me was that after the fury of the recantation and saying, "Your counsel is of the devil and mine is of God," the whole audience rose and clapped. It was just extraordinary to see how the spirit really can break through all things, because it was all these people who had been away from home for a long time and had been doing things that they knew were hateful. It was a wonderful sort of recognition, linking Joan with all people who hate imprisonment or being forced to lead a regimented life that they know is absolutely against the spirit.

It was an extraordinary time to play *Saint Joan* during the war, because everyone was in a great state of tension. Many really big plays went better then, as when we toured Greek tragedies to the miners. People were ready to receive the big plays because when you're going through a terrible tragic period you're looking for big answers to it. We had an extraordinary response, all the time.

The other remarkable performance that we gave was at the very end of our tour of Europe. We left from Ostend, and got up for breakfast to the news that the atom bomb had been dropped. Having had all the euphoria of people being released from the long bondage of the war years, you suddenly thought, "God Almighty, is this how it's going to end?" It was like being thrown suddenly into another age.

That night, we crossed over to England and the boat was filled with people who had been away for years and years. We were off the coast of Gravesend, and the troops who had been so anxious to get home were told that it was not going to be possible to land that evening. There was the most terrible electric feeling of frustration, and my father said, "I think we should give a performance of Joan for them tonight." It was incredible because it was completely impromptu.

There was a big hold, which we had as the stage—first time I ever did a spontaneous theatre-in-the-round. We had all the searchlights playing on the hold, with the troops all around. We were all in uniform because you had to be, traveling on the continent in an E.N.S.A. company.

That was the most *electrifying* performance, and of complete immediacy. Everybody coming through a war thinks, "This must never, never happen again," and troops have to force themselves to think that it was a righteous war. But finishing with the atom bomb had shown where war does lead. If you've got to win, you've got to go on inventing more and more fearful weapons of destruction. If you're not prepared to do that, then you've got to find some other way. So the play must have raised all kinds of questions: "Is what we are doing right if it leads to this? Is this the way you have to end?" I've always hoped that I would meet somebody who had actually been at that performance, but I never have.

After the Bristol Old Vic, we toured England and Scotland. Then the E.N.S.A. tour, another season at Bristol, and a season of repertory at the King's Theatre, Hammersmith. We did *Saint Joan*, Euripides' *Electra*, and a lot of new plays as well.

That was over a period of two years, in '45 and '46. It was some years later when I did Joan for the Canadian Players in '54. Instead of the Players making a big production of it, I was in slacks and a big jersey, and we were going straight for the words and the character in the words. There was no superfluous production, which I think was extremely Shavian. In the original production, the rehearsals had been going splendidly when, at the first dress rehearsal, there was this magnificent set of Charles Ricketts's and these wonderful costumes, and Shaw was absolutely furious. He said to Charles Ricketts, "You've ruined my play." He asked, "Why can't Sybil play it in that old sweater she's been rehearsing in?" That's how he saw it, so the Canadian Players felt we were very much on the right way.

The Canadian Players director Douglas Campbell, to whom I was married, was in the original productions that we did in England. He played La Hire, and some of the time Dunois. So he knew from the horse's mouth, because my father had directed us, and he and Shaw had directed the original production.

We had been playing around Northern Ontario to completely isolated communities, which was very exciting. When you play to audiences that are so remote, they just hunger for it. It was like playing during the war. They arranged a date to play to the Cree Indians in Moosonee, a small port town which was originally a Hudson Bay settlement. Well, there was no way of getting there. There were no roads at that time; the only way was by the Northland Railways.

An amazing man who ran the Northland Railways came with us in a special carriage that was added to the train. We were booked to play either at eight o'clock in the evening or an hour after the train arrived. They never knew what time the train would arrive since, as we traveled, we would sometimes stop. If a trapper came out of the bush with his pelts, then the train would stop for him, and he would get on, shove his pelts on board, and then we'd go on. They had no idea of how long the journey would take.

When we arrived, we had all our own lights and equipment, and we played in a Quonset hut. The hall was already packed with Cree Indians, who stayed there the entire time, watching the lighting being set up, and watching us make up our faces. It was absolutely fantastic!

They didn't speak English, and could not understand a single word we were saying. It's very funny how, automatically, you change your ways of doing things when you know that somebody can't understand what you're saying. I don't know what Bernard Shaw would have thought of it, because we did quite a lot of pantomime.

They did do the tent scene, and I can't remember if they did much cutting. I know there were hurried talks backstage, saying, "I think we'll have to cut from there to there because that might not hold," and "Would they think the Executioner is funny if he wears the black mask?" A lot of it had to be extempore, which was very, very exciting. They were a fantastic audience.

I suppose I should have been intimidated playing Joan when Mother was so identified with the part, but when it's such an incredible role, how can you possibly not do it? And *you've* still got to do it. Luckily, I was quite small at the time that she played it, so I was able to sweep that out of my mind. Father did direct me, but when a director directs two entirely different people, even if he is saying the same things about the character, obviously it turns out different.

What Shaw said to me in that postcard about sniveling Cinderellas says the main thing that Mother was as Joan—commonsense, capable. She didn't think of herself as a saint. I think she knew that Shaw wrote the play to get away from that idea of a stained-glass-window saint.

After Mother had played Joan, Madame Pitoëff, the great French actress, did it in Paris. Then she played it in England, in French, and Shaw hated it, because she was everything that he had written the play to get away from. It was very pathetic and saintly and weepy. She was a marvelous actress, so in her way she would have played it wonderfully, but it was a completely different conception from what Shaw had written. He didn't want to speak to her, he was just so mad about it.

Well, there was a big luncheon, and Mother was sitting between Shaw and Madame Pitoëff, and in her French she was having to translate things that Madame Pitoëff said and repeat what Shaw said to her. She was a great diplomat, so I think she must have managed it very well. But Madame Pitoëff put forward an extremely good defense. She could not stand Shaw's silence, and said, "Look, I know you hated it, but why did you hate it? You've got to speak about it."

So he said that he had written to get away from this sort of saintly, sniveling Cinderella, but that was the way she had interpreted it. Well, she said, "Any great role can be interpreted in a number of different ways. What about Hamlet? People have played Hamlet in completely different ways. And the same must be true of a great role like this." And he said, "No, there's only one right way, and that's the way that the author wrote it." And when she said that about Hamlet, he said, "There's only one right way."

Most actors would not agree with him, except I suppose that there is one way that Shakespeare saw it. Each actor who does it, if he's honest at all, is not trying to think of a different interpretation. He is trying to discover what Shakespeare meant, and playing as near to that as he possibly can. But because there are so many different people, there are so many different ways that they see it.

I think Madame Pitoëff probably saw Joan from the point of view of a religious person, doing it as a sort of act of faith. But that doesn't mean you have to play Theresa the Little Flower, because Joan is a different character. There are an incredible variety of human beings, and Joan was not a weepy little creature. But I think, also, that it does not get the whole of Joan if you play it on a mundane level. I think if you've got no sense of what a spiritual experience is, it must be extremely difficult. One shouldn't be a plaster-cast saint, but there is a dimension to it of another world that is very, very real. St. Joan is charged with the genius of that world.

Uta Hagen in the Theatre Guild production.

Uta Hagen

Uta Hagen *was born in Göttingen, Germany. She played Joan in a Theatre Guild production in 1951–52.*

Every actress I've ever seen play St. Joan has had the same problem of playing the *quality* of saintliness. If one remembers that conflict is the essence of all drama, then what are you supposed to act? If you, as the character, know that you're going to win, you must discover that you still don't know *how* you will win. Most actresses leave the obstacles, the hurdles out of their score. The acting score lies in her struggle to try and win.

In the acting classes I teach at my husband's school, the Herbert Berghof Studio, at least one actress works on Joan each term. The role is almost comparable to that of Hamlet for a man. Most women who want to be serious actresses want to play St. Joan. Sometimes they want to work on *The Lark*, a rather dreary play, as is Maxwell Anderson's *Joan of Lorraine*. Then there are the Joans of Schiller and Shakespeare. The only one I've never seen anyone try, and I think it's because there's no decent translation, is Schiller's, and that's sentimental.

Since I don't direct my students, I try to give them a technique with which they can learn to work on a part by themselves. I don't interpret roles for them. When I see acting, I want to believe there are human beings onstage, not actors. That's my criteria: am I observing the brilliant (at best) performance of an actor up there or am I convinced there is a total human being in action in the given circumstances of the play? And that's the most difficult thing in the world to achieve.

In my opinion, very few people know how to do it, very few. When I remember some of the great actors I've seen—like Laurette Taylor or Albert Basserman, the famous German actor with whom I played *The Master Builder*—I know they have convinced me of that. They are few and far between, actors for whom everything exists at each performance, as though it had never existed before, totally there, *now*, in the present, living in that play, right then and there. That's very, very hard, and the harder the part, the harder that is to make happen.

That leads me to what I think is difficult in the role of St. Joan and what is fascinating in Shaw's writing. I think that in the early scenes he himself had a big struggle which adds to the actress's problem. In his deliberate attempt to deromanticize Joan, to disillusion his audience from sentimental notions, he went a little bit too far the other way in making her a kind of regular "country gal," and not as dimensional a human being as she could have been. I think the very first scene borders on caricature, and it's difficult not to fall into that trap. Other scenes have similar problems.

I doubt, however, that someone will write a better play about Joan, and the problems for the actress in *Saint Joan* can be overcome. I didn't overcome them all, but they certainly can be.

Recently, I got back from France, and while you're there you can't forget Joan for ten minutes. She still knocks me out. What awes me, and always will, is the idea of a faith in something so strong that it is pursued and *served* come hell and high water.

It was seeing Elisabeth Bergner in the Max Reinhardt production of *Saint Joan* that made me want to be an actress. I was about five or six, so I don't remember the performance. I just remember her visually, but then I have a lot of pictures of her and sometimes I wonder if I'm thinking of the pictures or of her. At that age it was a kind of trauma-like experience of "That's . . . where I want to be and what I want to do." After my family moved to America, when I went to high school, I joined the forensics team for dramatic purposes and always used such speeches as "Light your fires."

My Broadway debut was as Nina in the Lunts' production of *The Seagull* for the Theatre Guild. A little later I did *Othello* with Paul Robeson for the Guild, and after I'd played in *A Streetcar Named Desire* and *The Country Girl*, they asked me to do *Saint Joan*. I jumped at the chance.

I did an enormous amount of research, and the research got in my way. I got as many biographies as I could, and I was spellbound by many of the historical effects which Shaw doesn't use. I wanted to jump out of a turret into the moat, I wanted to be in the battles. Often the research which stimulated my acting juices was not what Shaw had in mind. Research put distance between me and the character, so that I could have written an essay on it but I couldn't play it. Now when young actresses ask me what homework to do, I tell them: "You can do any research that makes the character alive to you, but go with Shaw's concept and make that real to yourself and don't dwell on the other things."

The rehearsals were also difficult, because they were conducted in the opposite way in which I like to work. The director, Margaret Webster, had a tendency to choreograph. She didn't really explore the behavior of the characters under the given circumstances; she fixed positions. She made stage pictures. I must say that her approach to the play did not allow for any disagreement because it was a rather brilliant essay of the play, but it was not the kind of direction that stimulates an actor to find the humanity of the characters or the reality of the circumstances.

I didn't have any trouble with Joan's intelligence. I think she had a great human, intuitive intelligence, not an intellectual intelligence. Nor did her sexuality bother me; as a matter of fact, I thought that she was an extremely womanly woman. For her voices, I just used people whose voices were familiar to me. Right now, for example, if

I think of it, I could hear Herbert talking, and I can assume what he would say and how he would say it to me. As Joan, I just assumed that I heard familiar voices saying specific things.

What I loved playing best, what came to me most readily, were the cathedral scene and the trial. I think you can sail in those moments if you have made them specific and real in order to identify with Joan. What made it easy was that at the time I was doing *Saint Joan*, Joe McCarthy was reigning. People were being hounded nigh unto death for their unpopular convictions and beliefs.

I was in trouble politically from 1948 on. I had made a speech in Pittsburgh for Henry Wallace, who was running for President for the Progressive Party, while I was touring in *Streetcar*. The same night there were headlines in the Pittsburgh papers; one was "Get Commissar Hagen Out of Town."

I played *Saint Joan* in 1951, and ran till spring of 1952. Then I was supposed to tour it. There were many letters of protest from all over the country threatening to picket me. I wasn't called by the House Un-American Activities Committee until 1953, I think. But it was always threatening—I was called twice, actually, and once it was cancelled because the person who was my main accuser turned out to be a perjurer.

Why did the Theatre Guild cast me? Well, they were considered to be "liberal." In any event, the whole notion of heresy and loneliness and having your beliefs challenged was terribly easy for me to identify with. Also, this is the way I work: using substitutions from my personal life so that the character becomes one with me. For example, when I played the speech of loneliness in the Cathedral of Rheims, it was as if, instead of saying, "I thought France would have friends at the court of the king of France; and I find only wolves fighting for pieces of her poor torn body," I would be discovering, "When I came into the theatre, what had been my ideals and what was my disillusionment in confronting the existing Broadway powers-that-be?"

The most difficult thing in Shaw's *Joan*, with which I'm sure every actress would agree, is the epilogue. I'm not sure I would know how to play that even now, although I think I've learned a lot and could solve many of the earlier problems. When I said to Peggy Webster, "I don't even know where to start with the epilogue. What do I do with it?" she replied, "Oh, well, you see, you start with the spirit and then you become flesh and then you end as the spirit again." I said, "Gee, that's wonderful."

By the way, the epilogue is often cut in European productions. I still think it would be wonderful to play the epilogue separately sometimes, like *Don Juan in Hell*, even though it's much shorter. I also think that the tent scene could be cut in *half* in a playing version. Many passages are exciting intellectually and lovely to read, but in terms of really making the play *pow* home, they interfere.

I also think that very few producers realize that *Saint Joan* is an ensemble play and not a star vehicle (this is true of *all* Shaw's plays). The producers always begin with a star and then try to flesh it out with "whomever." The Theatre Guild was guilty of this. I auditioned with many actors because I thought it was a way of getting in more work. And I would overhear the talk at the back of the theatre, "Well, what did you think of him?" "Well, he's awfully good, but so-and-so is cheaper." Literally. That's how the production was put together, and I think it showed.

Margaret Webster wanted the best actors, so it wasn't her fault that she didn't get them. The only extraordinary actor in our production was John Buckmaster, who played the Dauphin. He was superb. Interestingly enough, his rehearsal procedure was the exact opposite of mine. He started with a totally external, wild illustration of what the character should be, and as we rehearsed it got simpler and simpler and simpler and more and more and more human, so although it had all the wit that the part needs, and the comedic elements, it also had pathos and was human. It's the only time I've ever seen that approach work.

I also had strange problems with my costumes. For example, in the trial scene I ended up wearing the handwoven tunic from Eva Le Gallienne's *Hamlet*. The tunic was perfect—but it had to be borrowed.

With enormous to-do, they made real armor for me, and it wasn't ready until the opening night on Broadway. In the meanwhile, in the New Haven and Boston tryouts, I had to play in that horrible stuff that looks like knitted chain mail and is sprayed silver. All the extras wore it and so did I, although everybody kept saying how terrible it looked.

When the armor arrived on the opening night in New York, Margaret Webster quite rightly asked me, "What do you want to do? How are you going to work in this for the first time?" I paraded around in it, and all I kept remembering was that everybody had insisted the other stuff looked silly, so I said, "Well, let me try." During the Loire scene, all I could think of was trying to make the hinged legs work. The armor made noise. It was *agony*—my upper body, the legs—it was hard to think of the acting. For the cathedral scene they put me in a white satin *shmatte* with gold fleur-de-lis painted on it. It was supposed to look like a painting of St. Joan, but it looked more like a rented costume. *Horrible.*

They ran out of extras, so they used the ladies-in-waiting from the court to double as the Inquisitors, and put cowls over them. Sometimes, the girls were too lazy to take their false eyelashes off. I'd look up to see who was accusing me, and I'd see girls flapping false eyelashes at me under their cowls. It was *tacky*. Somehow we got away with it. During the run, I got better and better. I'm never ready to open, and I think that my performance didn't make any real impact until I was weeks and weeks into the run.

I was thirty when I played Joan. About twenty years later, I remember meeting Dame Sybil Thorndike and her husband, Sir Lewis Casson, at Sardi's. She was in her seventies then, and she was lovely. She asked me, "When are you playing Joan again?" and I answered, "I would play it tomorrow, except now I'm too old." And she said, "Oh, no, my dear, no. You can never be too old to play *Saint Joan*. Only too young"!

Herbert and I went to see Siobhan McKenna's and Barbara Jefford's productions, and I remember saying to Herbert, "Was our production this bad?" And he said it was *exactly* the same! We had the same tent, the same wind machine trying to make the flag turn, the same chain mail.

I'm talking about old-fashioned theatre, and it's like old-fashioned opera. *Saint Joan* could be the most modern play *this split second* if people would play it for real instead of copying old-fashioned British productions, which are usually imitation Shakespeare. That's how we're doing Shaw now? It's pathetic. It's a miracle that the play has survived.

Someday, somebody's got to do a remarkable production of *Saint*

Joan. God, wouldn't it be wonderful? But it must start with the assumption that this is a play needing eight stars, or rather eight experienced, fine actors with star radiance, major actors to make those scenes really fly. What roles those are. What wonderful parts. But it's a communal work, not a solo fling. We understand it in ballet—if you've got a rotten partner, he's going to pick you up and you're going to fall and break your neck. It's funny that people don't see it in the theatre.

If you want to be a serious theatre artist, you have a problem. I could talk eighteen tapes full of why I believe that, but I can't deal with it superficially here. But it is heartbreakingly difficult and frustrating. Herbert and I work continuously on plays at the HB Playwrights Foundation, but I want to play for big audiences. Not just for eighty people. I know that's better than nothing, but I don't feel I'm an elitist or that what I want to communicate is weird or too avant-garde for large audiences.

When people say to me, "Well, what do you want to do?" and I *tell* them what I want to do, they leave the room and shut the door and that's the end of that, because they're not interested in the things that I want to do. But I sure as hell haven't given up, otherwise I would stop teaching and just bury myself. The only thing I get mad at is when people say, "Oh, you're so choosy," as though I didn't want to work. That's *not* true.

I still think that somebody's going to see that there is another kind of theatre, not just for businessmen on an expense account at a Broadway musical, and that stimulating theatre has enormous communicative powers and is substantial food for the soul instead of "fast food" or for diversion, and *that* will be of service to a nation. I keep plugging away.

Siobhan McKenna as Joan in New York.

Siobhan McKenna

Born in Belfast, Siobhan McKenna first played Joan in 1952 at An Taibhdhearc, the Irish theatre of Galway, translating the play into Gaelic herself. She went on to play the role in English at the Gate Theatre in Dublin (1953), the Arts Theatre and St. Martin's Theatre in London (1954–55), the Phoenix Theatre and Cornet Theatre in New York (1956–57), and on European tour. She died November 16, 1986.

I'm sure she was quite difficult to put up with. But very lovable, I find her. I fell in love with St. Joan as a person when I was about eleven. I was studying European history, and we had done Book One. Then we came to the last chapter, where they said, "Thus started the Hundred Years War, which was not to end until a young girl called Jeanne D'Arc from Domremy . . ." and it didn't say much more. One didn't have much pocket money in those days, but with my pocket money I went down to buy Part Two, my school book. I was intrigued by a girl who could do that, and at that age.

Really, if people think about what they were like when they were seventeen or nineteen, one can be quite extraordinarily mature and brilliant in the mind. I remember when I played it in New York, and by that time I was thirty-six or something—certainly not seventeen or nineteen—and Albie Marre, our director, said one day at rehearsal, "Siobhan, would you like to cut those lines, when he says 'How old are you' and she says 'Seventeen, or so they tell me. It might be nineteen. I don't remember'?" And I said, "Why? That would be awful. The whole point is that this girl achieved this at the age of seventeen or maybe nineteen." And I said "I don't mind if they laugh, but Shaw put that in, and he meant it to be in."

People used to tell me very funny stories. When I played it at the Arts Theatre in London, someone told me they were in the foyer and there was a terrible argument about me going on between a man and his wife. She said, "Goodness, would you ever think that she was married and has a child of four!" "A child? Don't be ridiculous, woman. Didn't you hear her saying she was seventeen or maybe nineteen?"

I've always believed that if you say something with total conviction, the audience are like children and will believe you. Which reminds me of Frank Royde in London. He played the Archbishop. He was a dear man, a very great friend of mine. Frank was about six foot four, a magnificent-looking man with a most wonderful head, and white, white hair which he had allowed to grow and swept back for the Archbishop.

In the cathedral scene, her wonderful "I am alone" speech depends very much on his speech "You stand alone: absolutely alone. . . ." Her following speech answers practically everything he has said. It is during his speech that Joan changes from still being the attacker, saying "We must take Paris" and all that, and that's the only time she has for her transition. I always played it looking up at him, with my back to the audience, and then, about two-thirds of the way through his speech, finding out there isn't any use—he doesn't know, he doesn't understand. To let the audience see that she has got the message that they have turned against her, I think I used to turn away from him, rejecting him as he has rejected me. His speech is her diving board to go into "I am alone."

When we were in Oxford, I was looking up totally trustingly at Frank with his very authoritative air, and Frank suddenly said, "Prompt, please." I almost died! The prompter started to prompt and I thought, "No, don't prompt." I always say to actors, "Don't prompt. It puts you out of character. Say something yourself, but never prompt. Don't say anyone else's words." But the prompter came closer and closer, until she practically came on the stage and shouted the lines at him. And he said, "Can't hear you"! Then she really came on the stage and said it out loud, and he looked at her and said, "Thank you," and went on.

Afterwards, the actors had a great meeting, and they said, "Siobhan, it was the luck of God that it happened now. It could have happened in London on the first night." I said, "Oh yes, I'm always very grateful for things like that."

But then, first night in London, I was looking up as Frank came to the famous speech, and I could see, I could feel something awful was happening. He looked down at me and, with total authority, he said, "Joan, you stand alone . . . . . and so on and so forth." And do you know, not one critic mentioned that. People say, "You made that up." No. Kenneth Williams, who was with me, tells it in his one-man show.

I think that translating Saint Joan into Irish probably influenced my performance greatly. I started off at the Irish theatre in Galway, the Taibhdhearc, while I was at university. Then I came up here to Dublin and was with the Abbey, and then I had done some films and other things. The Taibhdhearc asked me if I would come back, as it was slightly in the doldrums.

At that time, Ingrid Bergman was playing Joan of Lorraine and a friend of mine sent it to me. I read it, and said, "Well, it's interesting. But why do this when one can do the real thing?"

I took Saint Joan, and I knew I would be free only for a certain amount of time, so I had to do it very fast. I thought I would never associate Shaw with the Irish language and yet, when I was translating, it went so freely into Irish. Afterwards, in a first edition I have, I came across a cutting from somebody who had owned it before I did. It was Shaw talking about Joan's dialect. He had written to someone in the North of England for samples of North Country dialect, and he said a very mysterious thing to me: "My own, which is Irish, is unfortunately unavailable." Whether he meant that none of our writers had written country dialogue up to then, I don't know.

When I played it in Irish, I used Connaught Irish myself, and the

English used Munster Irish. We differentiated, and that worked wonderfully well, because we had all of the French playing in the Galway Irish and the English, the enemy, playing in Munster Irish, which is not as rough-edged as the Connaught. Then one had to make a decision when doing it in English, where one didn't do it with a French accent.

Of course, Dame Sybil, whom I didn't see but heard was absolutely wonderful and extraordinary, played it with Lancashire. When Shaw wrote it, he had just a few "Eh, lads," and things like that, and that's what Dame Sybil used. But I thought, "It is quite ridiculous for me to do that, because Lancashire, nowadays, is more connected with factory girls, and why should I look for a country when I have my own country accent here in Ireland?" So I thought it would be more West of Ireland with perhaps a little touch of Longford, but it was just a country accent to establish the fact that she was a country person rather than anything else.

When I was going to London to play it, people here begged me to drop the Irish accent. They said, "Oh, please. You will be such a success, but they will slaughter you for doing it in Irish." I said, "I'm not doing it in Irish. I am doing it with vowel sounds that are country." And I said, "Look, for better or for worse, this is the way that I have seen it." Actually, the conductor Sir John Barbirolli came to see me and said he'd seen it six times, and that I was a musician. I said, "I'm afraid I can't take any credit. I can't play a note. That's Shaw. If the notes are there, that's what I put."

But translating it was a difficult thing to do. You really have to capture the essence of what he means to get it into another language. I felt terribly close to Shaw all the time I was translating it. I felt a great desire to meet him, and yet I have never wanted to meet writers or actors or people like that; I prefer to see them through their work. I know that the Taibhdhearc wrote to him at the time about the royalties, and he was very, very keen on getting his royalties. They got a little card back, saying that anyone who is mad enough to translate my play into that godforsaken language deserves not to have to pay any royalties.

We did it with . . . amateurs, really. Some of the actors were in the army, and the others were university students, and this was a very great experience. I think they formed my performance because they *really* believed in it. They believed every word. There was no acting on the stage. It was a triumph in Galway.

It was an event. The Galwegian people made the costumes, and they made wonderful flags, and some extraordinary Welsh man arrived in Galway and came into the theatre and said, "Have you got a set design?" Well, we hadn't thought of that. He built this amazing set—we had great fun doing that. Then somebody wanted to get a bit of realism in, and we borrowed a coat of arms for Dunois. Dunois was rather short and this coat of arms was rather large, so naturally I got rid of that coat of arms. I've always loved my Dunoises, but I've always had trouble with them because they do like rattling around during the best speeches.

The Taibhdhearc brought it to Dublin for one night, and that was a great success. Then I did it in English at the Gate Theatre with Hilton Edwards directing, with Micheal MacLiammoir playing Warwick and Jackie McGowran, who without any question is the greatest Dauphin. I loved Kenneth Williams, who played it in London, but Jackie McGowran was just special. He *was* the Dauphin. Whenever there was a choice of getting a laugh or a thought, Jackie would get his laughs, but he would choose the silence.

On the line "Come. Let me see thee sitting on the throne," Jackie used to take a lot of time to go up there. He didn't want to, but he made the effort. And when he sat on the throne, and turned around, most Dauphins play for a laugh: "Here's the king for you!"—point, "Look your fill at the poor devil"—laugh. Jackie looked with *hope* in his big, round hazel eyes, and thought, "Well, if this is my last chance, here is the king"—hold—"Look your full at the poor devil," and there was no laugh. I would collect a warm laugh on "Thourt not king yet, lad." But just a warm laugh, not a great big laugh.

Jackie was extraordinary. He was very funny, but he was also enormously moving. And beautiful. One felt so close to him, and therefore so desperately hurt in the cathedral scene when she says "Sire: I have made you king," and he doesn't say thank you. It's like us in real life: for want of something better—I'm sure she didn't mean it—she says "I am going back to my father's farm." And he says, "Well, that will be very nice."

I remember Mendy Wager—Michael Wager—who played with me in New York, whom I also loved as Dauphin. Mendy said, "What do you think of every night that makes you cry?" I said, "Mendy, I listen to your line. It is *awful*." I said "I don't think about"—you know, there was the fashion that you had to think of Christ dying on the cross or your mother or something—I said, "If you listen, you have absolutely no problem about reactions. To me it is shattering."

Well, as I say, I loved Joan from childhood. I just found her extraordinary, and I shared my love of my country with her. This I understood completely: that she *loved* France, beyond herself, beyond anything. I never saw any personal ambition in her as I studied either her story or Shaw's play or any of the other plays. And, by the way, I think that there is no comparison with Shaw's.

My father was a university professor, but my mother was born in the country, on a farm. She was very much a country woman, although she traveled and was a very elegant woman. But there was always that marvelous kernel of earth and reality and truth, and also she was wonderfully imaginative, as people I feel are who are born close to nature.

My mother had an astonishing faith. She totally believed in God, spoke to Him frequently, and actually would astonish people who weren't used to her. I remember her saying, "Well, I have never asked You for anything. I've always done what You asked me. And I've asked You this one thing, and You will not do it." There was a friend of mine there, looking around to see who this person was. There's a lot of my mother that I recognized in Joan. Her purposefulness—if she set her mind to do something, she would do it. The rocklike faith. A wonderful simplicity, and yet a marvelous brain.

Then, of course, I spent a lot of time in the country—my grandmother's place in Longford—although I was born in Belfast and then grew up in Galway, from the age of five. That I knew country people I found terribly important. I feel that any actress who wants to play Joan—I don't like the word *play* in a way—I think that, even for a day, she should walk the fields of a farm or someplace, because country people are different.

I remember, during the Second World War, the immense interest the country people took in the war. In Longford, when my father said "It doesn't seem to have any end," and they were asking "Who would win?" this older man—a farmer—said, "I'll tell you now, Owen, who's going to win this war. General Hunger." And that's exactly what happened, because going deep into Russia the Germans had plundered, and then there wasn't a harvest. Country people have this amazing curiosity—perhaps because they're more isolated—so that they have to think things out. In some of the books about Joan, they said her military judgment was superb but, of course, it was common sense, which a lot of women have to a great extent.

I think she was totally good. If she hadn't become a saint, she would not have been an oddity or anything like that. I think she would probably have got married and had quite a number of children. She wouldn't be sexless. Some of the things she says about wearing the trousers are not the words of someone who is sexless. She's very aware of her own sexuality and danger. I couldn't imagine any country person being sexless. I find her relationship with Dunois so warm, and with the Dauphin it is almost that of a mother. I'm sure she was a strong girl—she would have had to help on the farm—but I don't think she's in any way masculine.

I was always amused by the breach of promise suit brought against her. I love that. Also her mother fascinates me. When you hear that her father and brothers went to the coronation and that Joan rented a house for them and they got marvelously drunk, I thought, "Well, how Irish!" The mother stayed at home to look after the chickens and the cows and the sheep. But her mother must have been an amazing woman. I cannot understand why no one has written about Joan's mother, even though they know little about her. When Joan was burned, it was the mother who started this great crusade to prove her innocence. And we have, I think, some of the things she said in the rehabilitation. I think this could make a wonderful play. With Joan never appearing, with the mother hearing of Joan, or hearing from her, and defending her.

I think in the trial and the epilogue, Joan is very much the country girl of Scene One. During Scene Four, I would never let anyone come into the dressing room. I would get into my armor and lie on the floor, and actually go to sleep—with, of course, instructions that I be aroused. Not so much for the cathedral scene as the trial, because before the trial you sort of have to drain yourself mentally. She has been in prison, and I think her thoughts would go back to who she really was.

I remember somebody saying about the "Light your fires" speech that I put poetry into it and that Shaw was such a dry old stick, which is absolute nonsense. Somebody also said about the "wind in the trees, the young lambs crying through the healthy frost" that it was unworthy of Shaw, it was very sentimental. But, of course, it isn't.

When I was about eleven or twelve, I got some sort of thing in my throat. It was glands. They swelled out and they were drained, which was extremely painful. I could hardly swallow and was on liquids. I was a whole year in bed, and I really didn't see the fields or anything; I was totally confined.

The first day I was allowed out, my mother brought me for a walk in Galway. It was a beautiful day, and it must have been spring because there were lambs. There was a lot of warmth in the air and this field was just full of daisies, and these lambs. And past that, down the red lane were birds. My mother told me afterwards that I kept saying, "Oh, Mummy, look at the daisies, look at that bird, it's got—look!" And I kept exclaiming and saying, "Look! Look!" And she said, "I was just hoping you would not look up into my face." Because she said that she was so moved by the wonder and delight of someone who had not seen these things for a year, and that she felt totally ashamed of any feeling that she—well, she did love life, but she felt ashamed that she had not always seen things as if for the first time.

The trial scene really is, in a way, like going on trial, and yet one must always remember that Shaw was absolutely right about his balance. Again I remember Albie Marre, whom I love as a director, but when we were doing the trial scene we had a very, very funny D'Estivet and Albie said, "Siobhan, I think we'll cut these lines"— you know, about the Bishop's horse and all that. I said, "Albie, they're so important. Joan has to laugh. And the audience has to laugh. We have to have a release. Otherwise it's just too much. "And," I said, "I need it because it's part of her character—I mean, these fools, saying these silly stupid things—she would laugh."

In Italy, a very funny thing happened. Generally, when we were touring in Europe, one couldn't possibly bring all the monks from Ireland. So we brought the main cast, and then we picked up the nonspeaking parts in each city—the monks for the trial scene. Always I was at rehearsals, and would go though the whole trial scene so that they would understand everything that happened.

When we arrived in Florence, we were very late and everybody was exhausted. Hilton ordered me to rest, and I asked, "What about the actors?" He said, "We will explain." "But," I said, "it's much easier to explain if we do it for them." Anyway, I couldn't. He said I'd have to rest. So I went on the stage that night, and everything was going fine. We came to the trial scene, and when the soldiers were ordered to take me off to be burned, they refused point blank. The Italians are terribly emotional and very Catholic and all that. They were totally involved and *no way* were they going to burn Joan. They all got terribly excited and started to speak in Italian, "No, no, no!" "It's awful," I thought, "how are we going to finish the play if they won't take me off?" Eventually, doing a Marcel Marceau, I took them off pretending they were taking me off, literally hissing my little bits of Italian and saying "I must go, vamos, vamos."

In the trial scene, as I said, she's gone back very much to the Joan of Scene One. I remember getting laryngitis when I was at the Arts Theatre because we played twice nightly on Saturday and twice nightly on Sunday—which is totally brutal. It was one of the reasons that brought me around costume-wise, though I think I had it at the back of my mind. I started the play in the so-called peasant costume, the country girl, with the kerchief and the red flannel dress. Traditionally the epilogue is always done in armor. There was no time, however, in the Arts. The curtain came down, and it went right up on the next performance, and one had a cup of tea while the other actors were playing the beginning of Scene One.

I said, "This is ridiculous. Anyway, *Saint Joan* is a circle. She starts off and she goes through the armor, and she would always wind up as Joan of Domremy." So I played the epilogue just as I played the opening. She comes back to Charlie as the country girl instead of in armor. I think Shaw would have agreed with me if he were alive. Sometimes out of necessity come good things. I was awfully glad, because it gave the epilogue a wonderful simplicity. Her final line is a mixture of faith and longing, with a little more emphasis on the longing. I know I emphasized the second "how long," because she knows it's not going to be immediate.

I'll never forget the epilogue on the first night in the Phoenix in New York. It had been magic when we played it at the Saunders Theatre in Cambridge, but at the Phoenix Albie had decided that Hell was a trap door under the stage. Peter Falk was the English soldier let out of Hell for one night, and when he went back down under the trap door, his cape caught.

My light for the last line went on, and I knelt down on the trap door, looked up and said, "Oh God that," and Peter started tugging his cape and the door bounced. ". . . Oh God that"—tug, bounce—"madest this beautiful earth"—tug, bounce—"when will it be ready"—tug, bounce—"to receive thy saints? How long"—I thought I'd never get through. He was tugging his damn cloak off. On opening night. It wasn't Peter's fault. He didn't realize. We should never have put her spot there, in case a thing like that would occur. But we had quite extraordinary things happen.

We were playing at the Gate Theatre—I think it was New Year's Eve—and Hilton Edwards was playing Cauchon. He was wonderful. He had the great big purple robes and these great big purple tights. Now underneath the Gate Theatre was a dance hall. We could hear the music but, generally speaking, it was not so loud. But this particular night, just as I started, of all speeches—everything used to happen through that speech—"Yes, I am alone on earth," up came "Rudolf the red-nosed reindeer, had a very shiny nose." The percussion, the cymbals clashing—well, there I was and I went on. Cauchon, my director, rushed out of the theatre in full regalia, ran through the street with his skirts up, rushed into the dance hall downstairs, rushed up to the bandleader while all the people were dancing, and said, "Look here! Don't you know that Siobhan McKenna's trying to be alone on earth upstairs?" And there was dead silence. They were petrified. They didn't hear "Siobhan," they just saw an archbishop in full purple regalia.

I didn't worry about Joan's voices at all. I just believed that they spoke to her and that she heard them. I don't think she imagined them, but if you imagine something you are creating that something, and that something exists. It never bothered me. I don't think we have to worry about the words—words are formed in order to communicate thoughts. They're only secondary to hearing, in one's mind and heart. I know there have been controversies, did she really hear the voices? But other people have heard voices; I would sometimes hear my mother's voice calling me, and I would forget that she's dead for about thirteen years.

One of my favorite poems is Wordsworth's "Ode to Immortality." You see, I believe that we always existed; that nothing starts; that everything was, is, and shall be, and goes around in circles. I don't think formally about reincarnation or anything. I feel that the whole universe is in some extraordinary way connected. I think because we've been educated and closed up and told, "That's nonsense," "That's not rational," we have got rid of a lot of senses that we have.

Animals have it. I totally believe in telepathy. I had a Norwegian Elkhound who was a great womanizer. I would go away, and Rory would go off. I would have written my husband from America saying, "I'll be back some time next week. Don't come to the airport because if something comes up and I don't go on that day then you'll be at the airport and I'll get upset." Also Denis had developed arthritis, so I said, "I'll take a taxi. It's much easier." But Bridgid, who was my housekeeper at the time, would say, "Mrs. O'Dea will be home tonight." "No, she said sometime. . . ." "Oh, yes." Rory would have come back from his womanizing and would be on the top of the steps, and I would come that evening. He always knew.

I also did Joan in Brecht's *Saint Joan of the Stockyards*, which I love. I played her here for Hilton, and in London for Tony Richardson, when Vanessa Redgrave got ill. The interesting thing is that of all the people who wrote about Joan, and this includes the French writers, the only two who called her St. Joan were Shaw and Brecht, so-called atheists. Now, as Shaw's St. Joan was a country girl, Brecht's St. Joan is a city girl. Absolutely city. And she isn't St. Joan; he's taken St. Joan as an image. They aren't related except, I suppose, this marvelous courage that they both have. I know I'm not a mousy person, but I saw Brecht's Joan as a little mouse, and I tried to be a little mouse in my mind. Oh, I love her seesaw speech. I think she's adorable.

Shaw's St. Joan has so many facets to it. I did dare to attempt Hamlet once, in the DeLys Theatre in New York, with Joyce Ebert as

Ophelia. I love Hamlet as a person, and he is complex, but Joan has far more facets, I think. Joan is more difficult.

They were both, I suppose, politically involved. Most people looking at *Hamlet* don't think about that, but there is a political situation in the play and it's sometimes drowned, but I think it's a very important point. I think Hamlet was very ambitious, personally ambitious, whereas I don't think Joan was ambitious at all. She had a purpose in life, but it wasn't for herself. I think, and rightly so, that Hamlet in his thirties should be keen.

I just feel that Hamlet hasn't the complications of the spiritual life that Joan had. I think Joan had a very, very strong spiritual life, which sometimes warred with her ordinary life, and her upbringing would have been to obey the Church. All through history there have been, and I hope always will be, people who have minds of their own. But, knowing country people, I would say it is much more difficult, because the community is so small and close, for them to stand up and be counted. One is very community-minded if one is a country person. But Hamlet didn't have that complication. He believed in ghosts, and he has some of the most wonderful things to say about the hereafter, but I don't think spiritual life worried him all that much, whereas I think it was very, very important to Joan.

I try not to think of Joan now, because she actually took up an awful lot of my time. At times, I have resented the fact that I would do a wonderful Lady Macbeth and a beautiful Viola and Sarah Bernhardt, and they'd all say, "You know, I never forget your Joan." "Oh," I'd think, "listen Joan, leave my life." But she was very much a presence with me when I was doing it, as was Shaw, because I hadn't met him, and weird things happened where Shaw was concerned.

When I was in the Arts Theatre, I came in very early one night. There were stacks of letters, really stacks of them. I was strangely depressed because I didn't know what Shaw thought. Then—and I never do anything like this before a performance—I found myself picking out a letter—it wasn't on the top—and opening it.

It was from someone who dealt in manuscripts and things, and he said, "I saw your Joan last night, and it was so wonderful that I felt that you ought to have this." It was the second page of a letter that Shaw wrote somebody, and it was only a little bit, but it said, "Nonsense. Get in touch with Siobhan McKenna." His spidery writing was S-i-o-b, with the dot, which was the old Irish, a-fartha, with the accent, -n McKenna—and something else, and signed "Bernard Shaw." And I said, "Well, there's your little message. He had been thinking of you." It was written before I had played it, because he died just as I was finishing the Irish translation.

Perhaps it was when they were thinking of doing the film, and this letter probably could have been written to Gabriel Pascal. Pascal came over here to Dublin and wanted to put me under contract. I wouldn't do that, and then he came over and talked about *Saint Joan.* I remember him saying that I was perfect; then, a month later, I went off and married my husband, Denis O'Dea. When I met Gabriel Pascal again, he said, "Oh, this is awful! This is awful. You can never play St. Joan now. You're no longer a virgin." I thought, "My God, the way people mix up physical with spirit." He started looking for another Joan, so I was very naughty then. I went around saying, "You know, Pascal is testing virgins."

Dame Sybil I never saw, but she came to see me, with her husband, Sir Lewis Casson. She came into my dressing room, and she was so warm and generous. And she said, you know, how wonderful I was. Sir Lewis then suddenly went down on one knee, took my hand and kissed it, and said, "The greatest St. Joan ever," and she took her program and smacked him on the head and said "Too much." I love that. And I remember having a beautiful letter from Wendy Hiller, who had gone with her children. One thing I remember she said, "You were every single thing Shaw asked me to do, but I couldn't do." Which was an amazing thing, because she's such a wonderful actress, Wendy Hiller.

I haven't seen many Joans, because I find it a bit painful, which I don't find about other parts. But I suppose I have rather a fixed idea of some of the things. I suppose now I will start going to see St. Joans. There is a young girl I've seen recently that I think is going to be a wonderful St. Joan, here in Ireland. I think we're all very personal about Joan.

Frances Hyland with George McCowan as the Dauphin in the Canadian Players production.

Frances
Hyland

Born in Saskatchewan, during the 1955–56 season Frances Hyland played Joan with the
Canadian Players, on tour throughout Canada and the United States.

My St. Joan was for a group called the Canadian Players,
which was founded by Douglas Campbell. Dougie had
decided that it was all very well having the Stratford Festival in
Ontario, but it wasn't a bunch of use to the population that
wasn't going to get there. So he formed this little company
called the Canadian Players that traveled, and eventually we
traveled all the way from coast to coast in Canada. The year I
joined—I was the Players' Joan after Ann Casson—we also
traveled throughout New England and as far down as Georgia,
Kentucky and Texas.

We rehearsed at a camp called Lake Kashagawigamog up in
the North Province. We got it because the family of a woman
who had helped found the company owned a summer camp
for little girls called Camp Gay Venture there. We all went up—
Willie Hutt, Bruno Gerussi, George McCowan, Douglas Campbell, Amelia Hall, Johnny Horton, Jack Hutt—all names from

the early Stratford days, and while we rehearsed we stayed in cabins called Elves, Loons, Brownies, Dwarfs, and Kings. There was this wonderful central lodge with a huge fireplace where we ate. It was the most beautiful setting—blue, blue water, fine birch trees, and very cold.

It was a particularly wonderful autumn. The maples were all scarlet and purple and gold. It was a heavenly place to rehearse a play when you wanted to get inspiration, but a large number of the company came down with the flu. Everybody else got over the flu, but I kept on having it, I thought. And more flu and more flu and more flu, and finally I said to George McCowan, to whom I was married at the time, "George, I don't think I've got the flu. I think we've got a baby," and we did. So there I was, rehearsing St. Joan and Lady Macbeth—two of the more notorious maternal figures in the theatre—and I was pregnant.

We did it anyway, of course, and fortunately I'm a very small, scrawny person and as Joan I wore jeans and a floppy corduroy sort of shift. The men were in very nicely cut gray suits. When Max Helpmann was the Archbishop, he wore a purple scarf with a collar on it. When he came on as someone else later, he took the scarf off. George McCowan as the Dauphin played in his shirtsleeves without a collar or tie, and when he put on his tie he was the Inquisitor.

I think we did it truly just for economics and because we didn't want to travel with a lot of stuff. I believe we had two tables, maybe seven chairs, a few stools, and a funny little broom handle with a pennant on it for the wind change. I had seen maybe two productions before and I've seen three since, and each time I find all the armor and panoply gets in the way. I prefer it simple. I remember our tent scene so vividly. That must have gone on for twenty-five minutes, and there was nothing but the passionate argument of the script, and it didn't matter whether you were playing to Cree Indians in Northern Ontario or a high school audience in Texas. They never failed to be riveted, to laugh and to be still at precisely the moments that Shaw had in mind.

For reasons that eluded us all, the man who was responsible for booking us into various places in the States had booked us into, I think, Cleveland as the after-dinner entertainment for a bunch of businessmen. I mean, three hours of Saint Joan? When we started—

we were playing on a funny little platform in the middle of the dining room—they were still serving liqueurs and everyone was chatting away and they kept right on chatting; they couldn't have been more bored.

We didn't blame them, so we all kept cutting furiously ahead. Best of all was when George said, "If you had seen as much of heresy as I have," gave a large sigh, and finished with, "Do you have anything further to add, my Lord Bishop?" He cut the whole Inquisitor's speech. That got us done a good ten minutes early by itself.

We played in a black college outside Birmingham, Alabama, and nearly ended up in the Birmingham jail because we went to the party afterwards and we all had a good time. The next day an absolutely typecast sheriff arrived to tell us, "Now, you all are strangers around here so you don't know, so I'm just pointing out to you that round here we don't like to have to do with our colored folks. They prefer us to keep by ourselves. So when I hear about you pretty little girls from Canada dancing with our Negroes we don't think that's a very good idea," at which point all the other male members of the company had to seize upon Douglas Campbell, who was about to kill him. We left town very hastily.

I had read about the historical Joan when I was a girl, and how could she not affect you, particularly as a girl? I had read a good bit about her before we began to rehearse, and I had tried to visualize to myself very clearly what it would be like to be in that cell. When I finally did see a picture of it, which was sometime after the tour, the actual cell was very similar to what I had imagined: tiny, tiny, and utterly empty.

What I like about Shaw's Joan is her brilliant intelligence—her courage one takes for granted—and her enormous appeal to the best in people, which Shaw's heroines and heroes nearly always have. Some years after, I played *The Lark*, which I found quite boring after Shaw. It was so pitiful. It seemed to me to be a play about a poor little girl who had the misfortune to be burned to death. I found it hard to play her as the leader.

I hadn't played other Shaw heroines before Joan, but I have since. I seem to keep crashing up against Lady Utterword, whom I adore. She is great fun to play because she is so silly. She has that glorious third act where she just swings back and forth in a hammock and has all the funny lines and is never obliged to move. It's heaven. I've done Candida a couple of times, and I had an enormous pleasure playing Prola in The Simpleton of the Unexpected Isles, in a splendid Shaw Festival production by a brilliant director named Denise Coffey.

I played Eliza—I didn't think very well, actually—and two or three years ago I graduated and played Mrs. Higgins, in another superb production by Denise Coffey. It had no set; it was costumed fully, but all we had onstage were five bentwood chairs. There's a lovely story about the lady who, after she saw it, said, "Oh, I loved the scene with the chandeliers," and of course there weren't any. There was the ballroom scene with Eliza and five actors on stage, not even bentwood chairs, but she saw the chandeliers.

Shaw's heroines and heroes always make an appeal for you to listen inside your own brain and your own heart: don't listen to other people's twaddle, but harken to your own inner voices. As Joan does to her voices, however you choose to construe them. Witness her relationship to the Dauphin, when she's always telling him that he has a brain and a heart and courage and strength and should use them. And, for a while, he manages to.

I pictured the voices as a couple of very beautiful ladies who might have come from church windows, because I think that's probably how Joan saw them in the fields. What other experience would she have had of them except the church? I think I didn't want to embarrass her, so I didn't stare into space a lot. St. Michael was all in white, and glorious to behold. Probably with golden hair, which I think she would have known a little of, though I think blonds in her area would have been a rarity.

Probably because of where we were rehearsing, I used what was around me, which was the staggering beauty of the landscape of Northern Ontario. I do remember thinking, "My God, if ever I were gifted with hearing voices it could be in this place because it is so beautiful." It was untouched—very old land. I'm a prairie girl, or was a prairie girl from Saskatchewan. It borders on North Dakota and Montana, in the real flatlands. Like a lot of Canadian artists, I think landscape features largely in my sense of self.

There, transcendental experiences are quite commonplace. One of the great things that happens on prairies is that the landscape is completely flat. It's the land of the big sky, where you can see the bowl of the sky from east, west, north and south. There's nothing to impede that, and sometimes you get in the middle of a very bright sunny day, usually when it's windy as well, and you get an enormous shadow that crosses the land. I still don't quite understand, but it's as though the mountains—which are about six hundred miles away—suddenly throw a shadow and it rolls right across the land.

It's one of the most thrilling things you can imagine to be standing in a bright sunny field and see this great black tide which seems to be hundreds of miles away come at you, roll over you, and leave you still in the sun. It's as if, for a moment, your self just gets out of the way, and that was one of the means I used to get out of myself, as it were, for Joan.

Perhaps that was what happened to her the moment before the voices came, a real loss of self. I used to think of that when Joan was thinking of standing in the fields and listening to those bells. That took away her self and opened her up to what was to be said to her. One had to be very grateful to Shaw for giving one an opportunity to investigate that part of oneself which reminds us that there is an immortality of a sort.

I don't think that I'm anything like the right type to play Joan. I'm 5'2" and I think she ought to be bigger and stronger. Otherwise you're in danger of it being entirely inspirational. Siobhan McKenna's a wonderful type, with that broad, West of Ireland beauty. Siobhan's a big woman, but she's a knockout—that real County Mayo beauty is just magic.

We used to talk about it when we played at Stratford together. She played Viola and was absolutely ravishing. I played Olivia, and we had a wonderful time together. Tony Guthrie said, "Congratulations ladies, never seen it better done." We had a heavenly time, and we used to reminisce about Joan, but that's years ago and I'm afraid I don't remember what we said.

Of course, with Siobhan being Irish, it's in the blood as it were—this strange quixotic person that was G.B. Shaw. Shaw is always being accused of being rather asexual, but he's not. I think he probably wasn't very much interested in the actual act of love, but he certainly knew an awful lot about passion. Denise Coffey's great determination when she's directing Shaw is just flatly to refuse to let people think his plays happen in drawing rooms to people who talk a lot.

She insists on that *passionate* argument. I mean the passion in that scene between Higgins and Eliza in the final act of *Pygmalion* is extraordinary, isn't it?

I was in Dublin to do Mrs. Higgins in a video production of *Pygmalion*, with Peter O'Toole playing Higgins. He was the best I've ever seen. He brought to it an underlying melancholy. I said, "Peter, that's extraordinary. I've never seen that quality played quite that way before," and he replied, "Well, it's an Irishman, so naturally he's a loner." That is probably a very principal part of Joan. There's a good deal of melancholy, a good deal of loneliness, a good deal of the person who finds that she can't quite get her vision through to other people and persuade them to act on it.

When I was in Ireland, there were parts that in a weird way reminded me of Saskatchewan. The isolation with them is the sea; for us it was the sea of land for hundreds of miles around. I think that, spiritually, that does help put you in the right place for Joan, but I always wished, physically, that I had five more inches and a sturdier form.

I went to RADA with Barbara Jefford, who was much more right for Joan than I. Most of my class was quite remarkable. Too many up and died on me—Bob Shaw, Rachel Roberts (with whom I shared a room), Peter Finch, Stanley Baker—all far too young. Harold Pinter and I are left; we're still hanging in there.

In those days, Harold had terrible, terrible skin trouble, and hair like a Brillo pad. Those were days when we were doing *The Barretts of Wimpole Street* and such. Harold didn't ever get to play in any of those. The first time he came into his own was when a group of us got bored with *The Barretts of Wimpole Street*, *The Second Mrs. Tanqueray* and all that rubbish. Rachel and Harold and Jimmy Grant and a couple of others and I set up a little group of our own. We used to go out and badger union halls, church basements, wherever they'd have us.

We did Eliot's *Sweeney Agonistes* at one point, and I remember Harold was so wonderful—it was the first time that we became aware what a marvelous actor he is. He had a speech — "Every man has to once or needs to once in his lifetime do a girl in. I knew a man once did a girl in, and he put her in a bath in a gallon of Lysol. . . ." Wonderful stuff, and he was blissful in it.

We got along very well, Harold and Rachel and I, because we were all kind of outsiders. Rachel and I were certainly not pretty debutantes who were there to learn how to carry books on our heads or be fashionable or whatever, and Harold was an outsider because this was before Albert Finney's big success, when actors were still trying very much to speak BBC English, and Harold couldn't.

I always flatter myself—I've told this anecdote so many times it shows how proud I am of it—that I was one of the first to encourage Harold to write. We were sitting eating our bread-and-jam sandwiches—it was all there was in London then—and he said, "I've been doin' a bit of writin'. Would you read it?" And I read this perfectly wonderful monologue with an old man in an attic. I said, "Well, what on earth are you doing wasting time in this place? Why aren't you writing what you really know?" So he did; he wrote *The Caretaker* and that was the old man's speech.

I haven't seen Harold for years. The last time I did see him I'd been away from London for seven years and I went back to a little club that we all used to belong to, and this man walked in and my heart went boom. I didn't know who he was; I just knew my heart was so glad to see him, and he said, "Frannie, we've missed you. You've been away so long." We hugged, and I said, "It seems like centuries since I was here. The whole renaissance has happened since I left, with Osborne and Pin— Harold!!!!" His skin had cleared up, his hair was all cut, he was in Savile Row grays, and he was physically gorgeous, utterly transformed. So my eyes didn't know him at first, but the rest of me did.

I had no intention of coming back to Canada. I was kidnapped by Tyrone Guthrie. He said, "Got lovely theatre in your home country. Think you ought to come back." So I did—I mean, you don't turn down a chance to work with Tony Guthrie. I had no intention of staying, but in the meantime I met this fellow, married this fellow, and had his baby.

Fortunately I didn't show. Lady Macbeth's loose tunic robe revealed nothing, and even Joan's little corduroy top—in fact I began to look more like Joan ought to look, sturdier and squarer. I kept going for seven-and-a-half months, and finally I said, "I'm not going to make this whole tour, let's face it, fellas." By that time a fine, fine Canadian actress named Norma Renault had joined us and had worked on the role and was ready to take over. We finished a matinee of *Macbeth* and were about to do an evening performance of *Saint Joan*, and I just looked at Dougie backstage and said, "I can't play Joan tonight. I just can't." So that night the high school principal announced to the assembled audience that, "The role of St. Joan will be played by Miss Norma Renault owing to the bad disposition of Miss Frances Hyland."

Joan ranks very, very high indeed among great roles for women in the English language. One of the great glories of playing Joan, as opposed to the challenges and honors that may come your way from playing a lot of other ladies, is that Joan is not a neurotic, and not an unhappy woman. Joan is a woman with a great mission to fulfill and she does so, including saving her own soul. She is a life force.

I mean, I've played Blanche DuBois; I've just finished, thank God, *The Vortex*. I can't tell you the pleasure of waking up in the morning thinking, "I don't have to play that third act again." And when you're playing Blanche, you go to the theatre every night and say, "Why am I doing this to myself?" So many of the great women's roles are based on having to emphasize all the grunge you're trying to get rid of in life—the selfishness, the terror, all the rubbish that goes along with being a woman. But not with Joan, and not indeed with Ellie Dunn or even, for that matter, Hesione Hushabye, demon daughter as she may be. They are not turned inward in that way.

I would like to play Ranevskya and Arkadina before I'm over the hill entirely, because although they are both selfish and neurotic women they don't know it. They escape suffering by it in a way—not entirely of course, but by and large they do. It's the poor Varyas and Olgas that I always get stuck with.

I have played Mary Tyrone; I have played many Shakespeare ladies. None of them can give you so powerful an affirmation of life and good sense and listening to one's own interior voices and having the superb confidence to act on them that Joan does. I can't think of another female role that's like it.

Sian
Phillips

Sian Phillips was born in Bettws, Carmarthenshire, Wales. In 1958 she played Joan
at the Belgrade Theatre in Coventry.

I had been a Welsh actress until I came to London. When I
played *Saint Joan* in English, I remember wishing that I could
play it in Welsh, because all the visionary part lends itself very
much to the Celtic temperament. It seemed perfectly natural
to me that this girl would be standing there listening to voices,
because this is a thing that is easily accessible to Celtic people.
Even that way of talking. I know it's the fashion to work against
it, but a lot of it is very lyrical and mystical, although Shaw isn't
like that. But in spite of himself, a lot of it is like that, and this is
something that comes very naturally to the Welsh or the Irish.
The mixture of the peasant and the lyricism is a natural
combination.

Peter Gill, who directed me in *Major Barbara* at the National,
says that the Welsh peasant is almost the last surviving piece of
true peasantry in Western Europe, because it's what is called
an educated peasantry. They've only got the Bible or maybe

one Shakespeare to read, in Welsh, and maybe an English Bible, but they can all read and write. I had grandparents, for example, who were very good biblical scholars and wonderful preachers. They were nearly all farm people, they worked on fairly poor land, didn't own a lot of good property, but they were all educated, and they all had this wonderful gift for talking.

I remember listening for hours as a child to preachers, because it was the one treat—there was no theatre, you see. And of course they would get carried away and cry, and their audience would get completely carried away. My great-aunt became a very famous preacher. She ran away from home when she was fourteen to be a preacher, and she was such a success that they had to stand, oh, twenty deep in graveyards because people would come from all over the place to hear her. She toured America twice.

I saw her once when I was a very small girl. Her name was Rosina Davies, and she had this same dual character that Joan had. She was very shrewd and very down-to-earth and a real peasant, but she had this incredible knowledge that she was destined to be extraordinary, bringing the word of God to people all over the world. She simply took off with nothing. She did actually make a fortune in the end, but she didn't know she was going to. For Joan, I thought of people like that, who just took a chance on nothing, but who had the ability to sway hundreds or thousands of people.

I came to play St. Joan through somebody else's misfortune. Valerie Taylor was the leading lady at the new Belgrade Theatre in Coventry. Coventry had been bombed so badly during the war and it was having a renaissance. They were trying to rebuild the cathedral and the center of this terribly bomb-scarred city, and they were beginning the new theatre with *Saint Joan*. Halfway through rehearsals, Valerie Taylor was injured in a car accident.

The entire company and the director of the rather large West End show that I was in had just been fired. They simply canceled the whole thing, and I thought my career had come to an end when I was only twenty-one. I had just come home with my West End career in ruins around my feet, and there was this phone call saying would I go immediately to the Belgrave in Coventry and take over from poor Val. I think I had a week or ten days in which to open. I wouldn't have dreamt of doing that even when I was thirty, but off I went, and I think it must have been a rather rough production.

I thought my quickest lock into the part would be to play it as a Welsh peasant. And, indeed, it helped me a lot to play it that way. I had grown up in the country, and I'd only been in London for about three years, off my mountainside. So I thought that might be my most useful jump into it in a hurry.

Everyone was very helpful, but there's a limit to what anyone can do for you when you've only got ten days. It was a matter of staying up all night and learning the moves. I think it actually took me at least halfway through the run to begin to give a proper performance. I did actually change it every night that I played it, and because there was still so much to do, I think I could have gone on fiddling with it for a good six months. I would like to have played it for a long time, because I like long runs. And I find especially with Shaw that, to get all the points really right, I've got to get it into a state of relaxation, because his plays are so muscular and difficult that you've really got to be on top of them. I have a feeling that I was probably in the thick of it, fighting my way through, all the time I played *Saint Joan*.

The only advantage was that when I was at school I used to do a lot of acting in school plays and as a child actress in the BBC. There was a boy's school nearby which did very good productions, with boys only of course. They were rehearsing *Saint Joan* the year I was four-teen, and my headmaster was rung up by this other headmaster, who said that the boy who was playing St. Joan was ill, and could they borrow Sian Phillips? I actually learned *Saint Joan* in a weekend when I was fourteen. I went and rehearsed it, but the boy got well and he played it. But I did know it, so it wasn't really quite such a feat of memory as all that, I suppose, at Coventry. It was there.

Also, I'd done Joans since I was fourteen, not being one to leave any work wasted. Whenever I had to do anything, like an evening recital, I would always do a bit of St. Joan. Every girl must have done "Light your fires" many times, and the loneliness speech as well. It was strange to get to do the whole thing.

From the time I first learned the play I fell in love with Shaw. Which was just as well, because there are aspects of the play that you don't like unless you like Shaw. I absolutely adore Shaw's plays, and I adore him. I love the language, and I love the way he thinks. I love his badness, if you like, the mischievous, rather irritating quality he

Sian Phillips with Jack Rodney as the Dauphin in the Belgrade Theatre, Coventry production.

has. So, for me, *Saint Joan* was a perfect combination of things.

I've got my program here. I usually try to keep old programs. Frank Finlay was frightfully good as Cauchon. There's Patsy Burn, who's got her own television series now, as a lady of the court, and also—oh no, it couldn't be—*the* Alan Howard, surely, playing a courtier? You understand, I scarcely saw anybody because of this terrible travail I was in.

The program says "Costumes by the Old Vic Wardrobe, furniture by the Birmingham Repertory Company"—they were all helping this new theatre, you see. One of the things I remember about the production is that it was the first theatre that I'd ever played in where the stage management came from the back of the stalls. Hitherto there had always been the prompt corner and the prompter, and all the cues given from the corner. This was the first time that there was a kind of computer arrangement at the back of the stalls. A piece of glass, with this monster inside which, of course, went wrong. It was one cue behind. The morning on the river was all blue, and the cathedral was bathed in morning light, and you just knew it was going to go wrong all the way though the show. And short of taking a hammer to it, nobody could do anything about it. It only happened the once, but when these things go wrong, they go badly wrong. I was very disenchanted with that computer. I said, "That will never catch on."

My own costume was very rough. It was bits of old sacking and it looked grubby. I had just had my hair done by a very, very grand West End hairdresser for the first time in my life—for this play that didn't happen—the hair was just extraordinary. Well, within a day I was on a train to Coventry, and I remember standing in the bathroom of this little compartment with a nail scissors, cutting it off to within an inch all over my head. I only had little spikes left, and I thought, "Oh gosh, that's quite nice really."

I think I played a very down-to-earth Joan: she really did look mucky. And probably quite soldierly. I think I would have been very pleased as the young athletic character. That end of it would certainly have been all right, full of youthful enthusiasm and quite rough.

Oddly enough I did get to be frightened of the scene in the

cathedral, because I had read too much about Sybil playing it. Being rather young, I lost my nerve a bit because I was afraid. For me to play it truly Welsh and emotional would have been very simple, but I thought it would not be Shavian enough, and I had got very fond of Shaw.

I had become aware that Shaw might find that too soft, too soggy. So, in a way, I made problems for myself. It was an easy emotional reach, at the time, being young, and I think I bogged myself down with a few intellectual scruples. From time to time, I wouldn't bother, and the play used to be much easier if I didn't put the brakes on. I think the audience preferred it when I didn't. But I think I like Shaw more than I like the audience in the end.

I know what people mean when they say, "I don't like Shaw but I like Joan." Because it doesn't quite fit in. I think that's the problem of playing it. However you do it, you'll never get it right to everybody's satisfaction. You won't get it right for Shavian people if you play it just as you read it on the page, without any thought about Bernard Shaw. If you play it with a great deal of awareness of Shaw, you can miss the play easily because I do think that Shaw is very emotional, and that he covered it up less in Saint Joan.

I found with Man and Superman, for example, that it wasn't until one played the scene at the end extremely emotionally, almost like Wagner, that one actually got the laughs. It wasn't until you actually played it for full drama, as this huge love scene, that the laughs came. Now, that's the perfect combination, the emotion and the humor. For a person like me, Shaw is tricky to play, even at twenty-one, when it should have been much simpler, because I shouldn't have been worried about all those rather fine aspects of it.

I think I was at my best when Joan gets beaten. I felt comfortable when she was really ground down in the trial scene. And I liked doing the epilogue. It's such a relaxed thing to do, so good-humored. That whole finish does have a kind of serenity and a knowledge in it that the play doesn't have, and that the girl doesn't have before. So her "How long, oh Lord" wasn't a wracked, anguished, driven question. It was more of an accepting question; it wasn't rebellious. I think people do come out of the play feeling quite good. Having been through all that, the epilogue is very, very important. Because there's humor. You've got to get all that humor into it.

Having learned Joan at fourteen, I was desperate to play it from then after. So I started to look around. But I realized, I think rightly, that there's no point in doing research into Joan of Arc. If you're going to do Bernard Shaw's *Saint Joan*, you jolly well better do just what's there. It's pointless doing anything else. It's a bit like playing Livia in *I, Claudius*. You're playing Jack Forman's version of Robert Graves's version of a little historical skeleton. There's absolutely no point in reading Suetonius or anything. That's not what it's all about. Shaw's *Saint Joan* is not just about Joan of Arc.

I do quite a lot with music. I also look at pictures. I find there are pictures that give me the mood in plays. I remember in *Night of the Iguana* Hannah's long speech where she describes this embarrassing incident in the boat, looking over the Strait of Malacca. It is one of the great, great speeches, and it goes on forever. When I was playing that, I always used to think of a painting by a Japanese artist who loved Turner. He had painted some pictures out in the East— Singapore and around there. You could hardly tell there was a painting there at all, just sort of a faintly beige water, maybe with a boat. You couldn't really tell what it was. A really lovely modern painting with very, very faint sprays. That was how I did the speech. And I always like Mozart when I'm playing Shaw. Not for St. Joan, but I think Mozart goes terribly well with the gaiety and sparkle that you've got to have for Shaw.

I think if you don't observe Shaw's stage directions meticulously you wind up not able to do the play. I've been in productions where people have said, "I don't think we need to do this." But Shaw is quite right when he tells the actor that you absolutely must pay attention. Because if you do exactly what he says, you will find that you are in the right place at the right time all the time, and when you finish talking you can get off quickly, which is another thing that's very important to do in Shaw. Brian Bailey, the Coventry director, was very good, and I think the stage directions were followed meticulously.

I think Shaw's English is so wonderful. It is intoxicating when it is properly done. It's terribly difficult to speak; it takes an enormous amount of muscular energy to speak Shaw properly. But unless you do, you miss half the play, and there's no point in trying to do it unless you're willing to take that job on.

I think Shaw's own directions are the best—that you think, you act on the line, in the line, through the line. *Never* between the lines. You observe the commas, the semi-colons, the full stops, and in that way it becomes very easy, in fact. And you've got to keep going fast. The minute you start pausing or acting in between sentences, you're pretty lost in Shaw. You don't gain anything at all. You need a lot of vocal punch to keep going. You also need to be running up and down twelve notes of the scale without anybody noticing, otherwise it gets boring because the speech is often long and the thoughts are very, very quick and very difficult. Unless you are actually running up and down the scale all the time, people get tired and they can't take the ideas in fast enough.

In "Light your fires," for example, if you observe the punctuation itself, there is no problem: it actually does follow from the punctuation. It was easier for me to do then because I was still very much in the tune of my own language. We run up and down maybe fifteen notes all the time in Welsh.

Oddly enough, when I came to do Shaw again, lots and lots of him in *Dear Liar* and then *Major Barbara*—one for Frith Banbury and the other for Peter Gill at the National—they both had to remind me about this. I had to work terribly hard to get back to running up and down the scale because English isn't really spoken like that often, and Bernard Shaw wasn't an Irishman for nothing. If you get into a mess with Shaw, a good trick is to do it in an Irish accent. Then you can hear the rhythm and it starts flowing again. You've got to be able to hear his voice somehow, and make it your own. But it's his voice all the time.

St. Joan is one of the great parts. I certainly think it's a part every youngish actress, if she's got any aspirations, should measure herself in. I don't think it's quite on the scale of Hamlet, but it's definitely one of the big ones. I think it is important to play it reasonably young, because there are certain things about the character that are young. From a purely physical point of view, there are very few women's parts that you have to be that fit to play.

Nearly all the Shavian women are pretty exhausting to play, even roles that are not rewarding. They knock you out. Mrs. Clandon in

You Never Can Tell is the most exhausting part, and you get no jam at all. You drive the whole play. You sit there, and you work like a piston engine from the minute you're in the theatre for about three hours until you leave, but you get nothing. It is just not one of those parts. At least you get a lot back, playing Joan.

I've always wanted to play Cleopatra, but I've only played it on the radio. Vocally that's very demanding. It's very showy; you get back lots of jam. It's difficult because it starts and stops so many times, it's hard to make it work. The play actually seems to finish, and then start again. At the end you're having to work a lot harder than you ever were at the beginning. But Joan does progress in the most wonderful way. It carries you. Although it's tiring to play, *Saint Joan* is jam all the way through.

Barbara Jefford in the Old Vic production.

Barbara Jefford

Barbara Jefford was born in Plymstock, Devon, England. She played Joan at the Old Vic Theatre and on international tour from 1960 to 1962.

My very first memory of Joan was when I was about four and we were living in Devon. My mother used to go to a class because she was a frustrated actress, I think. One of the speeches she had to do was, "You promised me my life, but you lied."

As a small child, following her around the house as she was practicing this speech, I had a very pronounced lisp. They said that I used to recite it like this, "You promithed me my life, but you lied. You think that life ith nothing but not being thone dead." I grew up with that speech, not really knowing what it came from or what it was about. But as soon as I became conscious that I wanted to be an actress, *Saint Joan* was one of the things that I wanted to play.

At a very early stage of my career, I came into contact with Sybil Thorndike, and I think that also was an inspiration. I can remember lots of things that she said. One was about Shaw's direction and his insistence on every single line and every single word being given its absolute weight. "Oh my dear," she said, "it was so frustrating. We couldn't wait for him to go away," as he eventually did once they were running. She said, "The night after he went away, we took about half an hour off the play." He was very pernickety. Sybil also said to me—I remember very clearly—"*Saint Joan* without the epilogue is like cutting the last scene of *The Merchant of Venice*. It's as bad as that, like Henry Irving cutting everything after Shylock's exit. It's absolutely essential to the form of the play."

When I joined the Old Vic in 1957 as leading lady, they were still doing exclusively Shakespeare. We were coming to the end of the folio plays in '59, and Michael Benthall, who was the artistic director of the Vic, talked to me about his plans for 1960. He asked, "What do you think about *Saint Joan*?" and I said "Yes!" immediately.

I played Joan at the Old Vic originally, and then we took it on tour to the United States. I played her on and off for about two years. We also took it to Russia, Poland, Yugoslavia, and Czechoslovakia. One of the high spots was playing her in the Herod Atticus theatre in Athens. Stupendous. Quite wrong for the play really, because a lot of it is very personal, with people talking to each other, and it's very difficult if you're in that sort of auditorium not just to stand and deliver as the Greek actors used to do. We simply had to bellow at each other and work out a way of talking, for instance, to Dunois and to the Dauphin, but at the same time giving it a huge amount of power. The last time I played the part was in Cairo at the temple outside by the Pyramids, with the Sphinx in the background. Guns were being shot off because it was Mohammed's birthday. So when I was being set on fire, they were shooting into the air, celebrating in the distance.

I lived with Joan for such a long time. I always used to keep the date of her death in my diary. I have a lot of books about her, some of them dating back to my teens and student days. I think that my girlhood vision of her was very romantic, partly because of pictures of various actresses playing her. In fact, when I first played her, I was more or less accused of being too good-looking to play St. Joan, because she wasn't necessarily a good-looking young woman.

I think the quote about her that I came to realize was the most important one is that saints are very difficult to live with. She is a difficult person; she's always doing or saying the wrong thing at the wrong time. But this is because of her absolute conviction that what she's doing is right. She's an awkward person to everyone in the play and finally, because of her intractable way of going about things, is rejected by everybody.

In that sense, I don't believe that she's complex. Anybody with such a one-track mind, who can risk her life in battle and literally go through fire, has to be simple—this is a word Shaw uses a great deal. This is what they're always accusing her of *not* being. They're always accusing her of being devious. I don't believe that she is. And I find that when I'm an actress approaching a part, if a character is simple, then you've got to think about her in a simple way. If she is devious, you've got to be devious. Your whole attitude to rehearsal becomes different, and your attitude to your director.

The intellectual aspect of it doesn't exist at all. From your point of view when you're playing it, you can't intellectualize it. You *are* a nineteen-year-old girl who has heard voices and who accepts them absolutely. She is a child of God. But saintliness she makes jokes about: "Me, a saint!" She never thinks of herself as a saint. "I'm a soldier," she says right at the beginning.

I did it with a West Country accent, because I come from the west of England, and it all fitted very well. Absolutely down to *airth*. "I'm a soldier," she says, "I want to be treated like a man."

I think possibly the most difficult scene of all is the very first scene, which is when she rushes on as a sort of bright juvenile. A New York magazine critic wrote, "I had my doubts when Miss Jefford pranced on, mutton dressed as lamb, in a red wool dress and a long wig." I think probably I'd play that a little more cool now, although Shaw says she is in a fever of excitement. That's very difficult to do without being a bit—what shall I say—winsome. I think it's the only difficult bit about it.

The scene with Dunois in the cathedral is just lyrical, lyrical, lyrical. I can almost feel tears when I think of it now. She becomes ecstatic, in the true sense of the word. I think she goes into the sort of ecstasy that St. Bernadette was supposed to have. It's a kind of trance. And I think that happens when she recreates it with the bells.

Ah, how do you play that? You bring to it what you can, and you're as well directed as you can possibly be. I mean, how do you play anything? It's very difficult to say. There is a sort of parallel in the way that, when you do Shakespeare, you're not consciously playing in iambic pentameter. That's something that you've gathered during the experience of your life as an actress, which becomes almost second nature, and the sense comes through of its own accord. You don't know you are making line stops, but they are there.

St. Joan is hard to analyze; I can't really explain it. All that I can say is that it's superbly written. Shaw gives her all the right things to do and to say at all the right times. He also gives her the rests at the right times, so that you've got time to settle down before you attack the big scenes. You've also got time to change. These are all practical things I'm talking about now, and they are important factors. It's dreadful to have a terrible rush before, say, the cathedral scene, but there's plenty of time to get into the armor.

The loneliness speech is, I think, even better than the speech in the trial. That's so well known as to be almost hackneyed. I think the cathedral scene is the best in the play for her. I don't as a rule cry real tears on the stage. I usually cry during rehearsal, and then it's all over. Quite often, I think, actors who cry on the stage become less effective, because the more you cry the less the audience does. But I don't think it ever failed—there's something about the music of the way that scene is written, and that speech particularly, which does somehow bring tears.

I remember just before the loneliness speech that the actors were all ranged around the back of me, and they all sort of bore down on Joan and then gradually went away from her as they finished each rejection speech, and there she was on her own. It's just a physical thing of direction and theatrical expertise which puts you in the right place and the right spirit.

There are a lot of different ways of doing the final speech of the epilogue. I think, probably, I played it differently every time. I think the simpler the better, really. The main emotion there is a terrible disappointment. I think it's the only time that there's a hint of pessimism in her character, because she's the perennial optimist, isn't she? And suddenly she realizes that it's not simple, it's not the foregone conclusion that she always thought. They've all run away from her again.

It's not an easy role to play. Physically it's very demanding and exhausting, especially in hot countries. But as far as the simplicity is concerned, it sounds arrogant but at the time it seemed to me natural. I was given the right circumstances, I was given every possible help that I could have. I had a wonderful director, Douglas Seale, for whom I had played Margaret in a marvelous production of the *Henry VIs*. Having a director whom I admired and had worked with before to tackle this big role with was a bonus for me. So was a wonderful set by Leslie Hurry which, as far as I remember, was very simple. The cathedral was suggested by just a great big stained glass window and a lot of candles. The Inquisition scene was—well, I suppose there's only one way of doing the Inquisition scene, and that is to have them all up on one side of the stage in great tiers. I wouldn't call the settings stylized in the Granville Barker sense. I would call them simple. There was nothing to get in the way of the actors.

We played the Loire scene, I remember, very, very close to the edge of the stage at the Vic. In other places we had to rejig the whole thing. In Dubrovnik, we played in one of the auditoria there which is a fort. We did the Loire scene right on a battlement about twenty-five steps up, and one had to nick up there and then nick down again.

I had wonderful people to play with, too. Alec McCowen was the Dauphin and was absolutely marvelous. There was a great deal of experience about, and I had a certain amount of experience myself. It was also something that I'd longed to do for most of my life.

I would say that St. Joan is a woman's Hamlet, but I don't think it's nearly as complex. I don't think there are so many different ways of playing Joan, because Shaw is so specific. You can play Hamlet in many, many different ways. I've seen him played as anything from a scruffy student to the noblest of princes, and everything in between. In a sense, it's almost unplayable because there are so many aspects of him. I don't think that St. Joan is nearly as difficult as Hamlet, but it's an amazing star role. Cleopatra is an obvious Shakespearean comparison, particularly in the last part of the play when she has the most wonderful things to do. Juliet is another.

I've seen ladies play Joan who couldn't possibly, from the physical point of view, have withstood what she had to. She's got to be sturdy, I think, and give an impression of physical strength. She was a woman, but her strength became superhuman because she was imbued with divine power. I truly believe that—otherwise she couldn't have gone on fighting when she was wounded. I cannot quite believe that when I see ethereal St. Joans. I think that's Anouilh's The Lark, not Shaw's Saint Joan. I also think it demands a tremendous vocal range, because she has such a lot to say.

In playing Shaw, I think it's a very good idea to stick to his stage directions. Dougie Seale wasn't by any means a traditionalist. He's a very quirky, very offbeat chap. We kicked it around; in fact, Shaw is so very specific in his instructions that it almost makes you feel Bolshie about it, and you want to do the opposite. And you do. That's what rehearsals are for. We'd try doing it some other way, and then we'd come back, because what Shaw says is the best way to do it.

Shaw is international. Saint Joan played well absolutely everywhere. It holds its place as a great play—I think Shaw's greatest. It's different. Although there are wonderful discussions, particularly between Warwick and Cauchon, where you see the Shaw that you know being discursive and doling out messages and airing opinions, for the most part the play seems to me to be a deviation from his usual approach as a playwright. He's a man who's in love with his subject rather than standing away from it.

Pat
Galloway

Born in London, Pat Galloway played Joan with the Canadian Players in 1961,
and at the Stratford Festival Theatre in 1975.

W hat amazes me is that anybody in the fifteenth century would pay attention, let alone the amount of attention that was paid, to Joan of Arc. To a *woman*, I mean a *girl*. She was clearly special. Not just any old Jane Smith could have got up and said, "I want a horse and I want to go and crown the king." It wouldn't have worked. There was something extra-special about her which she probably sensed without knowing, and certainly without knowing in a conceited way.

She got a bit conceited, at least according to Bernard Shaw, once she got Charlie crowned, when she thinks she's going to achieve everything and she gets ticked off. I don't know how historical that is. But, on the other hand, you can understand that people do get carried away with success. Having done that, she might think, "Right. Today, Europe; tomorrow, the world." But it is amazing that, in the 1400s, she was able to do any of it.

Pat Galloway with William Needles as the Inquisitor in the Stratford production.

At the age of sixteen, I spent some holidays in France with a family who lived very near Rouen. It was there I decided that I really wanted not just to get the hell out of boarding school in England, but to be an actress. We went to see the statue of Joan in Rouen, and in a way I related to her, because I was thin and boyish and a bit of a tomboy.

As a kid, I always thought that my father wanted a son. In fact, not many years before he died, I faced him with it and he denied it. But I always thought he really wanted a boy, and I think I wanted to be a boy. As a teenager, I thought, "Oh, I wish that I was a fella."

As a matter of fact, when I was at boarding school, the first thing I did—at the age of twelve—was audition for the drama department, and both my audition pieces were fellows. One speech I distinctly remember doing was Launcelot Gobbo's. I really didn't understand what on earth I was talking about; it was "Budge says the fiend, budge not says my conscience," however it goes. The other speech was Richard II's "For God's sake let us sit upon the ground/And tell sad stories of the death of Kings." God knows why I chose those.

When I read *Saint Joan*, it had a kind of North Country ring to my mind. My grandparents came from the North. My mother was born there and they moved when she was about two years old. I don't remember their ever having North Country accents, but perhaps there was something Northern about them. Joan seemed to me like a North Country lass, and a boyish, tomboyish girl. And so when I finally managed to get to RADA, it was one of the parts about which I felt, "I understand this, I think." I was a bit mixed up with religion as well, having insisted upon being confirmed in the Anglican church, too young really to understand what it was all about.

As far as taking Joan from my own childhood, I can also think of being brought up during the war, deep, deep in the heart of the English countryside. So I was a country girl, and my life as a kid was totally involved with animals, especially with horses. This is related to her sexuality, too. I don't think she was that much unlike myself at seventeen. I mean, my God, I was a virgin until I was twenty-two. That might be odd today, but it didn't seem very strange to me that at seventeen Joan was bounding about on horses and rallying around with the fellows, and not so interested in Dunois or whomever.

I got to play Joan the first time because of Douglas Campbell. He invited me here to Stratford, where I played Hippolyta in the 1960 season. He was also running the Canadian Players, and at the end of the summer he came to me out of the blue and said, "Will you play St. Joan?" I was absolutely *bouleverse*, and said, "Yes, of course." And everybody in the management of Canadian Players told him that he was mad. They said, "What are you doing? Who is this girl? Nobody knows her. What are you doing, casting her as St. Joan?" However, we did it. We went all over the States, and it was a great success, I think.

Douglas had a good go at me, of course, because there were things that I was sure I couldn't do, and he'd scream at me and say, "Get on, you Canaanite." "I can't, I can't, I can't." "Yes, you can." Finally, there was one high breakdown. It was just before a preview, and I had a dentist appointment at lunch time. He yelled at me so hard that I burst into floods of hysterical tears—really, I mean out-of-control tears—and stamped and screamed and carried on like a maniac. He came up with his big teddy-bear hug and said to everybody else, "Right. Lunch break. Off you go." And in the afternoon, in spite of the dentist, and in spite of the fact that I was totally hoarse having screamed, it was better.

It was a big breakthrough. I wasn't ready to give in to the sort of emotionalism that I think is inherent in this part. That made a difference to whatever I've done subsequently. It was a sort of breakthrough to an emotional freedom which I couldn't, wouldn't, didn't think I could allow myself—the freedom of appearing emotionally naked on the stage. Once that was achieved, it no longer terrified me.

That point, I am afraid, must lead me to the next *Saint Joan* production, the one that we did the summer of 1975 here in Stratford. Bill Hutt, who is a dear, dear friend of mine, was directing. One of his opening speeches at rehearsals was that, I think I quote correctly, "We want no arias in this." And I thought, "Oh, God," because by then I knew the play, and I don't think it can be done without arias. The right sort of arias, but nonetheless, arias.

I don't think you can just do those huge, religious, lyrical passages as if I'm just chatting to you here in the garden. The girl had something else. She was a peasant girl, but she had something which made her special. There was a terrible sort of hush after Bill Hutt's speech, and I said, "Well, um-um, ho-ho, excuse me," and there was a coffee break called while we had that out. In fact, we didn't get over that hurdle until about two weeks after the opening. I always try to do what I'm told, which is sometimes silly, but on the other hand, I think a director directs and you try to follow. It was just one of those occasions where we didn't see eye to eye about some things.

Bill did a very, very sweet and generous thing. It was a rocky production because it got off on slightly wonky legs. We opened to the most ghastly press, and then we got some very good press later on about how quickly the show had changed. One afternoon I came home and found Bill sitting on this lawn here. He said, "I just want to tell you to go back to your original instincts about those things we had problems with, and follow your own instincts and do it." I've never forgotten him for that.

I think that St. Joan is the best woman's part I've ever, ever read or attempted to play. The pity is that I had two shots at it and am too old now. It's always the same with these wonderful things—when you first have a go you're too young to get at them, really.

I think possibly, together with the Duchess of Malfi, that Joan is the most emotionally exhausting part I've ever attempted. More than Lady Macbeth. Perhaps that's my fault; maybe I was a lousy Lady Macbeth. But Joan—that trial scene and the cathedral scene, and the amount of belief that you've got to find within yourself—you just can't make it up. It's got to come from somewhere inside you. I think all parts do. But I did find Joan one of the most strenuous and—this sounds crazy—unhappy, in a way. Taxing. Not the first act, but the trial: I don't think you can go on and do that whole thing at the end without suffering.

I suppose the most difficult scene was the cathedral scene, because that is about the voices. It's the scene where all that has to happen for her in a spiritual way, whereas the trial is more factual. So, although the trial is very painful, it's real and it's something that you can understand—there you are and you're about to be done in; burnt, of all the terrible things. The cathedral scene is something which has got to come from somewhere else.

Playing St. Joan certainly shaped my life for that year, shaped it in a not altogether happy way because, as I said, we went through many trials and tribulations with it. And it is not a part about which you can think, "Oh, well, we don't have to do it till Wednesday." It does live with you. It's a triumphant tale in some ways; on the other hand, it's a tale about a lot of suffering. It wasn't a summer in which I could get up and go out for a joyous picnic and think, "'Isn't it wonderful, we're going to do Joan tonight."

Maybe that's my error. Maybe some people think, "Isn't it wonderful that we're going to do Joan tonight." I found it painful, frankly. Very painful. As parts of any great tragedy are. I found parts of *Malfi* exceedingly painful. I remember talking to Maggie Smith about *Virginia* and I said, "Do you dread it? Do you wake up in the morning and think 'Oh my God, we've got to do it?'" And she said, "I don't only wake up that morning. On the day before, I'm thinking, 'We've got to do *Virginia*.'" I knew exactly what she meant, because I was doing the same thing. It becomes part of one's everyday life even on the day off. And that's why I'm not too keen on working fifty-two weeks a year anymore.

Zoe
Caldwell

Zoe Caldwell was born in Hawthorn, Victoria, Australia. In 1962 she played Joan at the Adelaide Festival of the Arts and on tour for the Australian Elizabethan Theatre Trust.

I've just come back from Australia, playing *Medea*, opening an arts center. I hadn't been back for twenty-five years, not since I played St. Joan. I was amazed that such a lot of people remembered *Saint Joan* and remembered it as a breakthrough in some way. I don't remember it as a breakthrough. It was remarkable for me only because it meant my going back home and realizing how deeply Australian I am.

I was born, brought up, and trained in Australia. I'd been sent away to Stratford-upon-Avon on a scholarship from the Australian Elizabethan Theatre Trust. I'd been away for five years, and they asked me to come back to do *Saint Joan*. So I said, "Sure. That would be interesting. And I would like to do it with an Australian company." As I'd been sent away by the Australian government to learn what I could learn and then come back with it, I felt it only right that I should then play with an Australian company.

But the Australian Elizabethan Theatre Trust, which then was our throw at a national theatre company, unfortunately had a lot of non-Australians in it. I would have preferred everyone to have been Australian; I suppose that was some chauvinistic thing with me. There were Australians in the company, and they were marvelous.

I still have an Australian passport, but I'm not someone who needs koala bears and gum trees and all the reminders, so I felt I was sort of free. When I went home to do *Saint Joan*, I knew how deeply Australian, how chauvinistic I was. I guess Joan was very chauvinistic.

There is not a lot of research to do about Joan. At least, I don't think so. Shaw is very clear about what he wants; almost too clear. He's like Eugene O'Neill. The instructions are extraordinary. You can almost play it with Shaw as the director if you truly, truly observe. But then one can play almost any play if you truly, truly listen to the author. If the author is good enough to do, then he's usually mightily specific. The better the author, the more specific.

The only thing I can remember that blew my mind about Joan is that the artist, George Bernard Shaw, had used things Joan actually said. The best Shavian lines, the lines that you felt, "Ah ha ha ha, this is Shaw making a comment about women, about a certain kind of woman," were not his at all, but Joan's.

I remember all the references for most of the parts that I have played. They were very deep references for anything to do with painting, writing or music, but with Joan—nothing. I was clearly overwhelmed by something else. I'm not sure what it was.

That year that I was home, I went straight from *Saint Joan* into a play by Patrick White which I remember deeply, *A Season at Sasparilla*. I find that suddenly very interesting. St. Joan clearly did not connect with me. A book about the historical Joan interested me only because it made her seem so incredibly Shavian. That makes her an extraordinarily bright, remarkable creature, but I always like it when the character has, in some way, taken a disability that we all can understand and made it into an ability. Joan's voices don't seem to me like a disability. I believe in her voices.

Making her speak like a country girl doesn't humanize her for me.

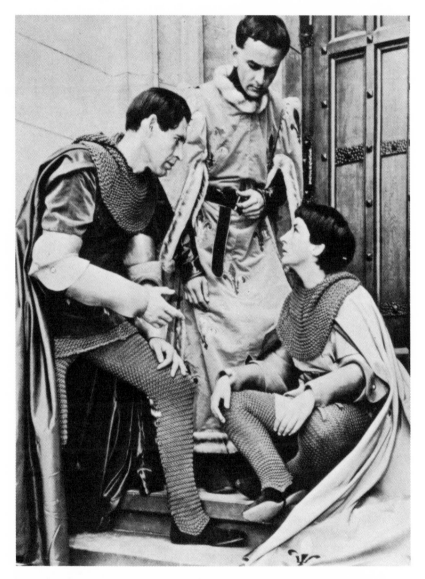

Zoe Caldwell with Ron Haddrick as Dunois and Roger McDougall as the Dauphin in the Australian Elizabethan Theatre Trust production.

What excites me is some innate, human frailty that connects to humanity. The exposing of human frailty in great people and small people in the theatre is what moves me. That's the thing that makes me laugh, makes me cry. I guess I didn't discover her human frailty. Maybe I didn't dig deep enough. I didn't find her very mysterious.

The only thing I'm interested in doing in theatre is something that will reveal to us some facet of a historical character, a shrew, a killer—whatever the category is—that will extend our knowledge or our perception. I realize that consciously as I grow older, but that's always what I've been interested in doing. As a consequence, when I was young and hot and passionate and was asked to play Juliet, I didn't particularly want to explore the role.

I think that maybe there is nothing really unique about our perception of Joan. Now Mary Tyrone in *Long Day's Journey into Night*, who is usually played like a victim, can be perceived uniquely. I did an enormous amount of research on O'Neill's mother, who became Mary Tyrone in the play, and I thought she was not a victim but, indeed, she was the killer. She was a spoiled, Irish Catholic girl brought up by nuns, with all the attendant sexual hangups. She had really just wanted the prize that came into town—the matinee idol James O'Neill—like she'd wanted the prettiest dress and the fanciest dancing master. She had gotten what she wanted except, of course, it wasn't at all what she wanted.

I felt Ella O'Neill was the destroyer. One of those women who are so nice and so dear and so pleasant, and eventually they destroy all of the men around them. It was very interesting because, when her husband died, she and her eldest son went to California. She went into a retreat, cured herself of her drug addiction, came out, and lived in a very pretty house with her son in the kind of nonsexual relationship that she really, I think, demanded. She wanted all the prettiness, but none of the real womanly commitment. Not just sexual commitment, but the commitment that makes you truly involved with your husband and your children and helps them to realize whatever strengths are in them.

I guess Joan is a great role. I don't know. I don't have the normal criteria for the big ones. Lady Macbeth is a big one supposedly—it never was in my terms. Cleopatra is a big one. I think maybe it is

Joan's lack of sexuality that made me not remember her. Maybe I'm not big on heroines. Is she a heroine?

Isn't it funny? This is not mock modesty; this is something that I don't quite understand. I don't know why I don't remember much about *Saint Joan*. It doesn't mean too much. I remember Dame Sybil came and saw me in Adelaide and gave me a little medallion which, if it had meant anything, I should have kept. But I quickly gave it to the next actress playing St. Joan.

In every part I play, I want to examine something about the human condition. I guess there was nothing particularly in Joan, in the way that I explored it, that enhanced or made clearer to me the human condition. I was obviously doing it in a vacuum. I don't know what happened.

Sarah Miles in the Ahmanson Theatre production.

Sarah Miles

Sarah Miles was born in Ingatestone, Essex, England. She played Joan at the Connaught Theatre in Worthing in 1962, and at the Ahmanson Theatre in Los Angeles in 1973–74.

I played St. Joan twice. She was one of the first roles I did when I was in weekly repertory for six months at the Connaught Theatre in Worthing, and I was much better than I was at the Ahmanson in Los Angeles, mainly because I wasn't surrounded by actors who were wrong for their roles. I had a Dunois who was a military leader rather than a wet. You really need a good cast to make it work. It can't work, finally, because Shaw is too critical. He wrote from a skeptic's point of view, digging holes in the character. It's just one of those unplayable plays. I've seen an awful lot of Saint Joans, and I've never seen one that worked. It's a heartbreak, because it should.

I don't think any other author has made it work, either. Mind you, she was a strange character anyway. If it were written by somebody who totally believed, it wouldn't be interesting either. You've got to get the balance. But I think the way Shaw did it, it's tilted, as if it were tongue-in-cheek. He mocks her, playing for laughter.

I like the idea of the lady. I think the lady herself has always thrilled me. Joan of Arc has always been a heroine. Maybe the idea of leading her army and all. I think it appeals to tomboys. When I was a little girl on my horse, I used to think of myself as St. Joan. My father read me the story when I was terribly young, and it left a mark on me.

I did it at Worthing Rep, and I was not bad. I'm a terrible critic of my own work. I never think anything is any good. But when I played St. Joan, I knew on stage that something was happening. It must have been, because my father, whom I respected very deeply and who was terribly anti my being an actress, came around afterwards with tears in his eyes and said, "bbbbSarah, you dddamn wwell can act."

That's all he said. But from then on, in my whole career, the words were always, "Yyes, bbbut it's not sSt. jJoan." And I got that from him echoing through eternity. Everything I did was fine, but it wasn't St. Joan. I never moved him to tears again, ever. About twelve years later, I did it at the Ahmanson just for him before he died. I sent him two tickets, but he never came. Which was very good actually, because it was a catastrophe.

I was asked to do it in L.A. by Bobby Fryer—Robert Fryer, who runs the Ahmanson. I had some trouble before I did it. I was in Arizona, and I had a disaster—my business manager killed himself. It was in the news for weeks, and the people who run the Ahmanson had a general meeting. Someone said, "Look, we just can't have a whore playing a saint." Bobby Fryer stated, "But she's already cast." And someone else said, "Well, get rid of her. We can't have a whore playing a saint." Bobby protested, "But she's not a whore. How do you know she's a whore?" "We've been reading the papers like everybody else." "The papers never tell the truth."

Anyway, they decided they couldn't have me because I was a whore. But Bobby Fryer stood up and said, "Look, I've been running your theatre for I don't know how many years. Either she stays or I go." He went to the door and said, "I'm going unless you keep to your word. She's been signed to play St. Joan, and she's playing it."

So they declared that they loved him and needed him very much, and they backed down and said, "All right, all right. We'll have her.

But we've got to clean her up. We've got to give her a really clean Dauphin." So they come up with Richard Thomas. It was a joke from then on. I'm cleaned up with John Boy, and John Boy simply cannot act classical stuff. They found somebody equally amazing to play Dunois. Quite honestly, it was a farce.

When I played her at the Ahmanson, I did have to carry it all myself. I wept at night because I knew what it could have been. But I would never weep in the day, or let anybody else see that I knew it wasn't what it could have been.

I would never tell anybody else how to act, but I always try to compensate and make them look good if I can by changing my performance to suit what they obviously can't change. You suddenly realize an actor cannot change what he's doing. Therefore you've got to compensate, and change your performance to make it all look better. And I think that in trying to make the other actors look better, I often didn't give Joan her full worth.

I like Arvin Brown, who directed, so much. And I love Joyce Ebert, his wife, who has also played Joan. I think that Arvin had too many cards stacked against him. He just didn't have the cast. It was such a shame. But there you are. It's a tricky play.

I kept one of the reviews from a Los Angeles paper, and it's a classic. It starts off, "This is not one of Shakespeare's better plays." My own personal reviews were terrific, and people came around weeping and all that. But I could only compare it with what I'd done at Worthing, which was magic.

I think there was an innocence attached to my performance that probably wasn't there later. Innocence is something that you have in the beginning, and if you're very fortunate and wise, you can come back and have it again in the end. But in the middle, it's going to be slightly contrived. Given the way that Saint Joan has been written, I think it has to come from innocence more than "a creature from the earth and of peasant stock."

I don't see her like that at all. I see her as somebody who had enormous spiritual potential. And I think she's going to become more and more important as we delve into our inner selves. We've completely lost spirit in the world at the moment, and she does speak to spirit and the powers of thought and of belief, which have been going through a bad patch. I think what Joan was about may be more understandable when we enter a period of spiritual renewal, which may be approaching. I'd like to see a new play written on her. I wouldn't mind having a go myself. I think we should all have a go at what we believe in. I believe in St. Joan, but I don't think anybody who's written about her does believe in her.

Her power of thought was above the level of everyday life. She did hear voices, and lots of people hear voices but either they shut up about them or they're in loony bins because of them. Certain psychic mediums hear voices. I've heard voices. You've probably heard voices, and if you carry it through, it will come true. It just needs you to believe enough to make it happen. All Joan did was hang in there and not doubt her voices. Today we hear our voice— our inner voice, whatever you want to call it—and we go, "Uhhh, mustn't tell my friends that I'm having inner voices. I must shut up and have some more beans on toast or I'll be called mad."

I've never wavered in my knowledge of the spiritual world and my total belief in her as a lady, so when I played her at Worthing it was blessed with innocence as an actress, because I hadn't been on a stage more than a few times. In Los Angeles I still believed in her and her voices. I think I knew that the play wasn't so hot then. I'd studied it. When I first did it I was just total belief in St. Joan. The second time my belief in St. Joan hadn't wavered, but my belief in Shaw's play had.

Spirituality is my whole life. Several years ago, I gave up acting because I had revelations over a period of three years. It put me in a catharsis, because I was brought up as an atheist. Then I found out that it wasn't so. I have no religion. It isn't a faith or a belief. It's a knowledge that we continue on. You really have to back off from life and repattern your whole existence, because it makes a big difference when you know that you don't die. It changes everything. It changes the way you live, the way you breathe, your goals, your fulfillments, your everyday moments.

I had to go through an enormous catharsis, and I left the theatre, I left films. I lived on my own for three years. I did it all through being alone. Even though I was an atheist, and even though I'd had no experiences of voices talking through me, I somehow, going back to my childhood, remembered that I used to have voices. I think that's what St. Joan did for me. Even when I played it at Worthing, it reminded me of when I was a child, when I was very spiritual, before it was sort of killed by what other people said, and growing up, and going to boarding school.

I was brought up deep in the English countryside, and we had no television or anything. I spent my whole first childhood in total aloneness. I don't say loneliness; I've never been lonely. I think because of being with animals and trees and birds and flowers and not having any friends, I lived a very spiritual life. I was unaware that I was doing so, but when I did *Saint Joan*, it connected me to my childhood and inner voices.

Joan could have been any age, she could have been from any class. If she didn't already have a sense of military strategy, she'd have learned it. Because once you hear your voices, you do anything, you just obey. She would have learned to be a great soldier in no time. She did the impossible, so whether it comes from peasant stock or something else, it's still the impossible. We all have it within us, but it's dormant.

I don't think a saint is saintly all the time. I think when playing a saint, you must always emphasize the sinner. If you go out to play godliness, it's a hell of a bore. You've got to find a way of making her flesh and blood by making her wicked. I watched nineteen hours of the uncut *Gandhi* because my husband, Robert Bolt, was doing the film script. And through these nineteen hours Gandhi came out a real wicked, foxy bugger. That's what thrilled me, because the man was a man and not a saint.

I played a lot of energy in the first scene, and a lot of life and a certain cheekiness. And also a strength, so that although she's cheeky, you don't really want to mess with her. I think the strength is so important for Joan, and that can take any color from wickedness to holiness. You can go through all the emotions as long as you keep that absolute energy. Energy is what we are made of, and if God blesses you, you have more energy than the average. If you play Joan as holy, it's a pain in the ass. If you play her really down to earth, I think that's a fault. I think she's more of a Peter Pan than a Mother Earth figure.

There are so few great roles for women, it's pathetic. I think Shaw's Joan would have to be included only because there's such a shortage. That doesn't really say much for it. I think that women want a play like *Hamlet*. Both Joan and Hamlet are talking about the paranormal. He sees his father, and he has somehow to justify what he's seen, and he lives his life completely differently from that moment on. She did the same, except that she always had her voices and she knew the time had come to do something about it. But they're both dealing with the paranormal.

I think we're in for a spiritual revolution. When I can't say, but I think it's beginning to happen. I think that then there will be a huge new burning desire to play St. Joan, and I think that it will take on a different coloring to people once our conscious minds are aware of the potential of spirituality. I wouldn't mind another whirl at Joan. It isn't a burning desire, but if it came up, and it was comfortable, I might have a go. I could play her better than ever before.

Joan Plowright

Joan Plowright was born in Brigg, Lincolnshire, England. During the 1963–64 season, she played Joan at the Chichester Festival Theatre, at the Edinburgh Festival, and with the National Theatre at the Old Vic.

When I opened in *Saint Joan*, Sybil Thorndike gave me this, and I've got to hand it down. It is *Jeanne D'Arc*, by H. Wallon, an 1876 Paris edition about her life and the trial, bound in red leather with gold leaf, and with wonderful illustrations. Shaw inscribed it here, "This is for Sybil Thorndike, 'Saint Joan,' 1924." On the other page, it says "From Sybil Thorndike and Lewis Casson, for Joan Plowright on her first night of 'Saint Joan,' Chichester Festival Theatre, June 24th, 1963." Shaw gave this book to Sybil, and she said she waited until she found a Joan that meant as much to its own generation as hers had meant to her generation. Even though it might be vastly different from the way she played it, as I'm sure mine was.

One's problem in playing St. Joan is how much you deal with Shaw himself and how much you create a Joan that fills in behind the lines. It's very much George Bernard Shaw, and you can be very tempted to play the first scene for comedy, particularly tempted as there are such heartrending scenes later. Obviously even Shaw wouldn't have any idea of what a French girl's humor was. He makes her an English femme—he gives her what we call North Country humor: peculiarly English, no-nonsense, down-to-earth, shrewd. I used a half-Yorkshire accent for her—I'm from the Lincolnshire-Yorkshire borders. Not a full accent, because it would have been too difficult for some audiences and for the "Light your fires" purple-prose passage and the cathedral speeches.

In the first scene, you can choose to be a girl who's been waiting at the gate for weeks and has finally got in; or a girl flushed with success who's only just arrived and pushed her way straight in; or one who is patient, knew she would get in there someday, and is perfectly calm. Does she rush in with tremendous enthusiasm and lean over the desk, with huge energy and urgency, or does she just walk in and say "This has to be"? One tries to find out historically what might have happened with the very brief things that Shaw gives you to do, and what look like fairly simple choices that he's put in that text.

There's really much more choice for an actress than appears on the surface, and for the director. John Dexter directed, and we were into the sixties and were slightly antiheroic. We started saying we would try first to find the peasant girl who had an obsession and belief. We wouldn't play the piety, we wouldn't play the religion and all that. You are playing an extraordinary being whatever you choose. Either the warrior or the saint or the peasant humor—how are we to know what she really had? We're not given any insight into how she behaved with soldiers other than rallying them with great inspiring cries forward. We don't know what sort of camaraderie there was among them, or if there was none. We're told that the soldiers wouldn't have dreamt of touching her as a woman because they were so awestruck. But were they all? Or did they just say it?

I went into all that. I suspected that either she was a moonstruck maiden, with this peculiar listening to voices on a hillside, or she was a tomboy who climbed trees and caught fishes as a young girl. Shaw has her say "I am alone. I have always been alone." Is that just a good line before the trial scene, or was that what she really thought as a child? I thought that she would probably be frightfully good

with everybody in a tomboyish sort of way, actually knowing somewhere along the line that she was different. All the time.

But she would make a great show of being a child in the village to
begin with. And she would get on with them and would have
friends for a bit, but she would perhaps go on long walks and go up a
track, suddenly, off the road and around another way, walking
through woods and fields, having strange thoughts and longings.
She's an obsessive character. Whether she actually hears the voices
or it's her own imagination which provides them, there is no question but that there was an obsession that she had been chosen to
save France. It's an enormously grand idea to choose for yourself,
isn't it?

I remember Sybil saying to me, "Well, of course, darling, she
never had a period, you see. And if you don't have a period, you do
get these kind of visions." Her research had led her to that—that
Joan never experienced menstruation, so that she was some kind of
hysteric. There is no question of the type. But then Kierkegaard
wrote that an essence of an actor tackling the big roles is that he or
she must be partly a hysteric. And you must, because that's what
hysteria does—you believe you're somebody else. You believe it to
the extent that you take an audience with you. It's a kind of mass
hysteria, isn't it? That is a necessary ingredient of Joan and of an
actress playing Joan—to go so far with it. That makes it a very
exhausting evening for you as a person. Though, in a strange way,
exhilarating.

I didn't do it consciously, but the voices became vague kind of
faces. I couldn't say whether they were from illustrations I'd looked
at or what, but, I did feel that they were constant companions or
guardian angels. That doesn't mean that I actually believed right
from the word "go" of rehearsing that that's all there was to it—that
there were these three angels sending messages to her which she
obeyed. I did think she created them, but that she was in more
touch than ordinary people are with a stronger power—whether it's
an afterlife, the other world, the supernatural, or just a higher
power. That I believed.

I used to have great arguments with Kenneth Tynan about how
much the actress must believe. I have a feeling that Sybil probably
did believe, because Sybil was a very religious woman. And I had

moved from a very religious phase into a kind of atheistic or agnostic one, but I was still being tugged. My older brother had become a Zen Buddhist, having been deeply involved in the church and, we thought, going to be a priest, and I went along with him a bit. I was not, as Sybil would have been, steeped still in belief.

I had to find again that kind of openness, a childlike quality in a way, to start on Joan. You can't put any kind of sardonic doubts which you may have as a human being into preparation for that character, because she does not have them. When she doubts or she renounces, it's only through exhaustion, fatigue, desperation. The voices told her wrong and they have gone, or they seem to have gone. But, then, so has her energy gone, everything that made her—her mind, her intelligence, the intensity of her emotional level. Everything was too low to be in touch again.

I suppose I only found how to play the beginning after I'd played the end of the play, and really in a dress rehearsal. After the end, I found a way of still playing the first scene for comedy, but with the charge underneath it that never lets go. You can play Joan funny as long as you, at the same time, play her religious. You do not play the religion, but it is in your bones when you first walk on the stage. I discovered what it was fully by playing the recantation and on to the end of the play. Then I could go back and play the first scene with the comedy, knowing that it was this energy, and the religious belief that was part of it, which set her apart.

The few minutes that Shaw allows—in real life it was days—between when Joan recants and when she says "Light your fires'" is a difficult transition to make because it's a theatrical effect. She makes very pertinent replies in the trial. They're not of a daft girl, they're not of a religious fanatic. They're very shrewd. Very astute. Yes, she is blinded, finally, by those Inquisition gentlemen, but then Shaw has her go into the "Light your fires" purple-prose passage, which is an enormous problem because what you want to keep is the strength that comes from an unwilling martyr, but a martyr nevertheless.

She has decided to be burnt when she tears up the recantation, and the strength that does *that* is more than she has ever had to summon before. In a way, one feels that she's been brave because she hasn't known the pitfalls, and she's miraculously got through all

Joan Plowright in the Chichester Festival production.

these battles fairly unscathed. But to have had the kind of misery and anguish and physical deprivation, and cruelty and horror of that trial, and to reach back to find the strength, that is greater than anything she's ever shown.

At the same time, the passage that you are given can be chokey and sentimental. The lines "the fields, the lambs," and that sort of voice that sometimes comes upon St. Joans—you can't bear it, because she's not going to moan and sing away. But, when you try to play *against* that text in order not to be sentimental, you cut down the size of the text and of the performance. I did that at first. And then I let it go.

Sybil helped. It was Sybil who came around after I'd done *Roots*— also about a country girl, Beatie Bryant, who comes to town and makes it on her own—and said, "You've got to play *Saint Joan*." And Sybil was in this season at Chichester, in the *Uncle Vanya*, and she would come in occasionally to the *Saint Joan* rehearsals. I had a supper with her where I said, "Sybil, I can't get that speech. I try it this way, I try it that way; I do what John Dexter says, then I do what I think, then I do half-and-half, but I'm never, never satisfied." And she said, "Oh, my dear, and you never will be. You never will. One seeks perfection, but one will never quite find it on that speech. But, finally, you must do the best you can in the mood you've risen to. But *don't fight* the text the way you've explained to me. It's not soppy. You've built a St. Joan in whom one will recognize the pain it costs to *agree* that she never had the voices, and *then* what it costs in that her fear of the fire and physical hurt is very great. But," she said, "I'm afraid you have to go all out for that speech and then let it all pour out, whatever fears you have of it."

"Light your fires" is such a set piece now. It's the standard audition piece. The awful thing is the audience waits to see how you do it, not what it is anymore, what happens to Joan. They know what happens to Joan. They're really waiting to compare you with the last three.

So you just have to take off there. You have to take off in whatever way you choose with your director, but take off you must. And there's no way of making it utterly contemporary and thinking between and saying "er-um," and pausing a lot. It has to go like a Shakespearean speech, which you don't dream of interrupting with ums, ers, and ahs, because it's verse. The purple-prose passage is that. You have to believe that her thoughts take on another dimension, that during all those weeks and months in prison something's been singing in her heart and head in that kind of language.

I only managed it the second time round. I was fortunate enough to play *Saint Joan* three times, I mean three openings. I played it at Chichester, and I didn't reach her. I fooled a lot of other people, but I myself knew that I hadn't got her. And you know even if you've done one good night; I would know that on many a night I'd got half the play.

The second time, at the Edinburgh Festival, we were in the Assembly Room, and it was very sort of Scotch Presbyterian. The Assembly Room had a kind of austerity, plus both a religious atmosphere and the atmosphere of a court with all the dignitaries. Somehow, Joan became truer to me there. By the time I opened her at the National Theatre, then I did get her—though not every night, because one doesn't.

You want your concentration never ever to be interrupted when you play *Saint Joan*, and that is dependent on your audience and your fellow actors. You have to prepare. I would be prepared for a *Saint Joan* performance in the afternoon, and I would be in my dressing room two hours before. Because, if your fellow actors aren't particularly in the mood, or forget a line, or move at the wrong time, or the audience eats peanuts, you have to stare through it. In a comedy you can bat your eyes or whisper to somebody else in the cast about how awful they are; there is no way you can do that in *Saint Joan*.

Playing it in repertoire, that trial scene is such a pill, in that several of the men had speeches which started "If the Church tells you," and whenever there was a pause, they all thought it was them, and they would all start "If the Church. . . ." The pauses had been very well orchestrated by John Dexter but, unfortunately, after a ten-day break some of the older ones weren't sure where the pauses were and where somebody had dried. Max Adrian always leapt in and filled any pause by starting "If the Church," and that was as far as he got, because he would get a stern look from somebody else whose turn it was to speak. I had quite a bit of that every time we came back. It did get hard, I must say, because the rest of them would start to giggle.

The audience has to be aware anytime they look at you—particularly all through the trial scene when you're not speaking much and other people are—that that creature is different from everybody else on stage. This difference can be conveyed through total immobility; in fact it's almost better if it is a stillness which speaks volumes. But that can only come from an intensity of feeling which gives you the courage as the actress to do absolutely nothing, because you know something is emanating from every pore towards an audience in silence.

I don't know what to call it, that sort of vibration you give out and get back with a live audience, but it has to be there in force in *Saint Joan*. And with somebody who is going towards martyrdom and sainthood, nobody expects to see an ordinary creature at any moment on the stage. They need to see a creature filled with an intensity, an emotional and imaginative energy that they have not reached, or even aspired to. Or the play doesn't stand out.

Quite a lot of the play is an intellectual argument, so its centerpiece has got to be something that arrests them emotionally and sensually. More than any other part. Of course, one hopes to have that same thing in almost every part, but it isn't *as* necessary. In a Masha, in *Three Sisters*, you want it, but Masha is a human being, she's identifiable *with*. St. Joan is not identifiable with. There are very few saints walking around.

The epilogue, again, is very hard to play. If you're not careful, you can come on very self-satisfied and complacent, and just beam at all those people around the bed. But you do have to suppose that there is a huge difference from the struggle as a mortal being when she comes back as whatever she is. You have to try and suggest some kind of serenity which still encompasses her humor, her background, her struggles, her relationships, but now they are seen from a distance.

It's odd playing that. Quite nice. You do go through a most extraordinary journey, and one is rather glad that one can round off the journey and not go home after the burning, not leave the theatre in that state. You do actually go back to the dressing room, slough that off, and recompose yourself and Joan into a sort of ancient wisdom, which none of us really possesses, but that she must, presumably, by then. You come back on with yet another form, but this time it should be—well, I guess it has to be radiance, but not an effortless radiance, if you can achieve that. It's very hard.

The voice is quieter—or it was with me—without strain, without struggle. And the voice is possibly more mature. I went inward on that final speech, rather than looking up to heaven. You could just say it like she's having a conversation with herself, really. I tried to go in there. I don't know what that means, really, but I know I did try.

I went through a very religious phase as a girl of fourteen, fifteen. I used to sit in our church. There was a huge cross with Christ on it hanging right down the center, above the altar. For about three years, in that very fervent time of wanting to be a missionary or Florence Nightingale or an actress—perhaps they were all bound up, because I wanted to play, not actually be them—I used to imagine that I saw that Christ figure move, and that it moved when I moved.

I remembered that when I started to rehearse. I had a most awful, awful longing that I hardly dare confess to, that if I went into the whole role with such intensity, and did yoga and meditation, that I might conceivably be able to practice levitation at the end, for "How long, oh Lord." I thought, "If I slowly rose off the stage, the audience would absolutely be stunned!" It never came to that. But playing the part gives you those sorts of folies des grandeurs. You say, "Well, if faith will move mountains and I have sufficient faith, why can't I do that? She did."

Shaw has provided a zonking great part for a woman in Saint Joan. What he said about Joan and Hamlet is perfectly fair. They each represent a universal figure. There is not another woman's part, really—one can talk about Cleopatra and the infinite variety and all that—but it hasn't quite got attached to it what St. Joan has. In fact, it isn't dramatically as open to choice, because there are various set things said about Cleopatra that have to be fulfilled to begin with. She has to be a beautiful woman, or be able to appear a beautiful woman on stage. There are many limits to that queen who is a creature of man's desiring. St. Joan's on her own. She doesn't have to live in anybody else's view of a beautiful or a desirable woman. She was probably androgynous, but you don't know what she is. She's a hybrid. She's anything. She's absolutely indescribable apart from what she did.

Hamlet, too, can be any size, any shape, because what people say about him can be taken in many ways. And people say different things about him, anyway. I'm sure the fellows wouldn't like me saying it but, really, Hamlet can be played on technique, if you're brilliant. Joan can't be played on technique alone. Hamlet's speeches are so marvelous that they sort of do it for him. They lead the audience. They've got to be said wonderfully and fiddled and acted, I know, but he can be any kind of different human being. He is different because of his particular problems and dilemma. He's different from the ordinary run of mankind because he's the son of a king and all that, but she is different in that she is supposed to have been in touch with the divine. That is a quality that cannot be in the text. It simply has to come from the person. You know it when you hear it and see it playing properly—it is in the voice, it is in the eyes, and it, therefore, has come from the heart. And if it doesn't do that, you're not moved and the play doesn't work.

I was moved by Siobhan McKenna. And to me, the Irish worked so marvelously because there was a recognition, both spiritually and to do with religion, that one is aware of at church service in Ireland. And there is a kind of music in the voice anyway, in the Irish lilt, that could encompass all parts of the text, suggesting the country girl and having no problem with the poetry.

Among the parts I've played, Joan stands very, very high in my regard. It's hard to choose one's personal favorites, because each creation is a child. Beatie in *Roots* was a kind of Joan, but a normal one. But, then, Masha and Sonya in the Chekhovs are way up there, too. St. Joan has to be special in that it's the girl's Hamlet. That doesn't mean that you would particularly want to play it again. It's almost as though having played it, it's a relief. You've scaled that, and you don't have to do it again. It's like saying "Does a racehorse actually enjoy the race?" I mean, it's in a lather and a sweat and it looks dreadful at the end. It's run a very good race, but did it actually enjoy that while it was happening? I'm sure it enjoys winning. And you enjoy *having* played St. Joan more than you enjoy actually playing her. Because enjoyment doesn't really come into it. It's the audience's job to enjoy. And you do not *enjoy* playing St. Joan. But you enjoy the challenge, and then the achievement. The actual doing of it is an enormous task.

Ellen

Geer

Born in New York City, Ellen Geer played Joan at the Guthrie Theater in Minneapolis in 1964.

Zoe Caldwell probably had a great influence on my getting Joan at the Guthrie. She took over for me as Ophelia when I was too pregnant to finish the run there. We had a lovely vacation in the woods, and I was teaching her Ophelia's songs. We were walking down this country lane singing these weird tunes, and she mentioned something about their doing *Saint Joan* next season. She said, "You should do it, you know." I'm sure she put in a good word for me. She's always been very supportive and marvelous to me.

During that summer, my husband, Ed Flanders, was acting in San Diego. I was eight-and-a-half-months pregnant when Tyrone Guthrie came out, really to see Ed's work, and he invited us to dinner at this famous old hotel, the Coronado. Dr. Guthrie didn't have a tie on, and I was worried they were going to say something. But he was such a huge presence to me that I didn't have the guts to mention a tie, and sure enough the waiter said, "You won't be able to stay." I remember Guthrie pulling out this green tie and throwing it around his neck, saying, "I knew you'd be stuffy about it."

We had this fancy meal, and he invited Ed into the company and told me that I was going to do St. Joan. It was one of those glorious dinners. I was thrilled and awed, and I was scared. I have a deep, deep respect for acting, and I didn't know if my tools were ready, frankly.

I had grown up with a theatrical background because of my father, Will Geer. I auditioned for Ellis Rabb and Rosemary Harris, and got into their APA company at sixteen. Ellis is one of my favorite directors, and I love and adore him. He was my beginning, other than my father. He and Rosemary. She gave me my first architectural work. She would help me take a script and show me where to lift and where to make the marks for pauses, glottal stops. She began me on this training which most young American actors and actresses do not get. I was taught that in order to be free, you must have technique first.

When I was eighteen years old, Rosemary and Ellis said that Tyrone Guthrie was starting a theatre in Minneapolis and they thought I should audition; it was the only company they would let me go to. I used Joan La Pucelle—Shakespeare's Joan—for the audition. She's wonderful in a whole different way, because she's exactly what Shaw's Warwick thought of Joan—this silly bitch with these voices that she says are from God, when all she wants is to get her own way and be a big shot, a ballbreaker. I'm sure that's how he thought.

I first became acquainted with Joan of Arc through Jules Bastien-Le Page's painting of her in the Metropolitan Museum of Art. Mother always took us to libraries and museums, and I must have seen the painting and heard Joan's story when I was about eight. I love that picture. It's before she got into the war; she's not in armor on a horse. Joan's belief in her strength is very, very powerful in the painting.

When I was going to play Joan, I looked around for role models and questioned why there weren't many. I found one in my great-grandmother, Ella Reede Bloor. She was a great suffragette and helped form some of the unions we have today. She did a lot of research for Upton Sinclair. She got disguised as a worker and went down into the meat-packing plants to get the reports for his book. But she didn't get mentioned in the history books because she was a Communist. I got to meet her a couple of times. She was very old, but she was an extraordinarily strong woman who had many children, a couple of husbands, and dedicated her life to humanity. My mother loved her so much and spoke of her and kept her alive for us.

I didn't do any research on the real Joan. I wasn't that smart as an actor when I was twenty. I prepared by reading many plays by Shaw. I felt very behind in my education. A playwright's got to stick his thumb in now and then, especially when you're dealing with such a great character in history. The loneliness speech is really one of Shaw's statements, but I didn't find that hard because I think that if Joan couldn't verbally say it, it's what she felt.

She knew she was going to die. A rebel like that knows, I think. Martin Luther King knew he was going to die; Gandhi knew he was going to die. They know. They speak with a great love and a beautiful simple wisdom. Those kind of people are alone, but they can't stop. They're pushed along by the tide of humanity. It must be very lonely, but oh how gorgeous to have that kind of strength.

The sexuality is an extra-hard question, because everybody will say that Joan has no sex, I'm sure. But it depends on how you feel about it. There are different kinds of sex. There's the hunga, hunga, wham bam, thank you kind. There's an imbedded-for-life kind that isn't even physical; it gets to be spiritual. Joan's love for her God, her saints, and her religion seems very sexual to me because it is strong, deep, and forever.

Her love of battle and her lack of fear were my two waterloos. I hate war. The warrior aspect worried me most. As I said, I started to look for other women heroines in history and didn't find many. If I were looking today, I'd use someone like Sonia Johnson, the ex-communicated Mormon who ran for President. Her belief that the world is going to remain muck until women have their place in the making of roles in society is so strong and powerful; it is a great commitment.

I looked at a lot of pictures to get the warrior, and I went to armor collections at museums. I went through a period of wearing pants

Ellen Geer with George Grizzard as the Dauphin in the Guthrie Theater production.

and boots, secretly in the woods so nobody saw me, to get a strength. I strode. It was the weight that you had to think about, the weight of boots and armor when you were a warrior in that day and age. They made me armor out of fiberglass. It was wonderful, because it was light, so I could act the weight of it.

Then, because I had to work so hard on it, I loved the warrior. I loved attacking that scene with Dunois. I loved the anger she has there. I don't think she had any fear. You had to play it when she found out she was going to be burned. She was a young girl and she didn't want to be hurt. But otherwise, I don't think she had fear because she had so much belief in what she could do. She really knew she was right. But it wasn't just that she knew. It was because she was a funnel.

It wasn't just Joan; it was all people who have that kind of strength to move humanity. When I heard Sonia Johnson speak, it was as if all the great women suffragettes and women's rights people were speaking through her. I've never seen that happen before. When she was sitting down, before she spoke, she was just a human being named Sonia Johnson. Then she stood and started to speak, and she was a funnel of all these other women who were speaking through her. It was so powerful. I believe that when people like Martin Luther King, or Gandhi, or Joan spoke, that they spoke beyond themselves. It's not just them. There are other people beyond.

Joan scared the shit out of me, I'll tell you. I've been around a lot of radicals because of my background, and it's not something that I wanted to be. You want to have all facets of life being an actress, but when you're a radical you've got one line. Joan had one focus. That's why a person that young could have that much energy and raw faith. When you want to act and to be a mirror for life, you've got to be able to encompass all different kinds of feelings, and have a respect and love for any kind of human being in order to play them. So it was fascinating to play her, because it's the very opposite of what I want to do.

Douglas Campbell, who directed, gave me courage. He said, "Ellen, get to the point where you stop worrying about whether people like you or not, because Joan wouldn't give a hoot and a holler," and that kept ringing in my ears. I worked on that—not me/Ellen but me/Joan. I worked on, "I don't care what the hell you think about me. I know this is right and this is the way we're going to do it." He gave me great strength.

We would have our own private sessions. They were long and exhausting and they focused on vocal technique, raising and lowering of the voice. It was not what you'd probably get at the Actors Studio—not "How do you feel?" It was pure technique: how to get variation, how to get across the strength. He would always explain the principle, and from there, once I had a framework, I could begin to take off, because my technique was nowhere prepared for what you need for Shaw. I think you need more for him than for Shakespeare.

I am indebted to Dougie forever for helping me get the epilogue. At age twenty, I couldn't figure that one out for love nor money. It would be like a seventeen- or eighteen-year-old doing the third act in Our Town. You don't know what the hell they're talking about. You have none of the feelings about death that young.

I couldn't figure the epilogue out, and Dougie helped me find the way to get it. I did it with the blacklist. My father was blacklisted for ten years. He was forced to be a beggar, but he wasn't bitter. I learned so much from him. The blacklist was the closest thing to me that seemed outrageous and wrong. I couldn't figure out how you could blacklist people, and so I could connect the killing of people in the Inquisition with the blacklist. I lived through that with my family. I was gifted with an incredible background, with understanding people and the situations that society forces them into. I'm a very lucky human being. So when I met the characters in the epilogue, that is how I was able to be gracious to them.

When Pop was blacklisted, I was laughed at and called "Little Red Commie," and had things thrown at me. I could use all those things for what it's like to be alone. I knew what it was like to be strong. I watched my father cross the country in a trailer with a dove of peace on the side. He had the gall and the guts to say things like, "Well, every actor is in a turkey in his life, and I think that this is the biggest turkey that I've ever been in," talking about the House Un-American Activities proceedings of those awful men.

So as a child I felt what it was like when a society decides that what you do is wrong. I didn't understand it. Joan didn't understand it. That's why, when she speaks during the trial, she makes perfect sense, and she's damned for it. It's like that now. It's exactly like that now.

One of the great elements of the production for me was the designs by Tanya Moiseiwitsch. There were platforms, and marvelous stairs that came down, so there were lots of places to play. My favorite place was where I stood to listen to my bells—it was over on stage right, on a wing where the stage lip comes out.

George Grizzard was the Dauphin. We had a wonderful time and I loved it. We had a great deal of trouble with that damn nose. I think most of the Dauphins do. Is it going to stay on or is it going to come off? I don't really remember a lot of things. I was so busy working on something that was way over my head.

I remember one funny thing that happened. During the trial scene one night, someone in the audience called out, "Joan, could you just shut up." Another thing that happened was a fuss during the trial scene. The actors offstage, some of the people in the court, were noisy. It was becoming difficult for me to work, but I was afraid to squeal on my friends. One night it just became too hard, and John Cromwell, who played De Courcelles, came up and said, "These people need to keep quiet. Has this been going on?" I said yes, and that I didn't know quite what to say to them. He started to bawl me out, and got Douglas Campbell and Douglas bawled me out. He said, "Do you not know what it means to play a lead? You are responsible for this whole production." They scared the hell out of me. I had no idea it was my responsibility. I learned about what it means to be a lead in a production, and after that I had no problem. I was still scared and felt like a squelcher, but I realized it was a responsibility in the world of theatre.

I felt the weight, but also the tremendous honor, of carrying on a tradition with *Saint Joan*. Dougie was married to Ann Casson, whose mother was Sybil Thorndike. Ann had played Joan, and Douglas had been in that production, directed by her father, who with Shaw had co-directed Dame Sybil in the original. Then Dougie had directed and acted, and Ann had played Joan, for the Canadian Players. And in the Guthrie company that season were both Ann and Zoe, who had done Joan in Australia. They were so supportive of me, so marvelous.

I'll never forget Tyrone Guthrie striding across the stage after our final runthrough. I thought, "Oh God, he's going to hate it," and he took me by the hand and shook it and banged me on the back and said "Great guts, girl. Great guts!" I kept thinking, "Does that mean he likes me or what," but I was happy.

I rehearsed and played Joan on basic technique and guts. I remember it was probably about the second week of the run that I was released in the role. I don't even know what happened, but I do know when—it was during the epilogue that suddenly I wasn't worried about getting it right. I started to play it.

Dougie always felt it was mine. His belief was the reason that I had the courage to do it. And whatever it is he saw in me, he made me feel that I will always act. He gave me great courage. Whenever I've thought, "Oh God, I'll never get a job again," I hear him saying, "Oh, Ellen, you'll always work in the theatre and you'll always make money at it." I'm lucky to have had that so young, from him and from Ellis Rabb and Rosemary Harris. I teach and I direct a lot of plays, and I try very hard to pass on to my company and students the things that were given to me.

Judi
Dench

Judi Dench was born in York, England. She played Joan at
the Nottingham Playhouse in 1965.

I believe that at the end of *Saint Joan*, you should have tremendously mixed feelings about her. The epilogue is usually where the play gets holy and soft. I remember doing the last line very angrily and impatiently. Furious, because they'd been so slow about it. I think that the audience should probably feel ambiguous about her saintliness and her holiness, but they should feel it was an extraordinary woman that history threw up at that time, who achieved something very remarkable.

The side of Joan that has always been shown is that she's always right. Because of the saintliness and because of the visions, somehow the right must always be on Joan's side. I don't believe the right is on Joan's side all the time. I think that sometimes she is just doggedly determined and intolerant. Because of the way she behaved, they did achieve a victory, but that is an incident. Out of the incident it's up to you to make up your mind about her actual saintliness, or her being chosen by God, or her being the only one who was right.

My playing Joan happened really by accident. I had done Ophelia opposite Johnny Neville at the Vic. He was running the brand-new theatre in Nottingham and asked me to go there and play *Private Lives*, *The Country Wife* and *Saint Joan*. I never had Joan as a goal. I've never had that ambitious thing of wanting to play certain parts at all. I've always waited for somebody to ask me to do something and then felt, "Yes, perhaps, if they think it is a good idea, then I'll have a go at it." The things that I have wanted to do have not been the things that have been successful, really.

When I was asked to do Joan, I thought, "Yes, I would quite like a go at that." I just believe so strongly that she was a presumptuous, jumped-up girl. Her assumptions are very pretentious indeed; well, not pretentious, but they're arrogant: to assume, for instance, that Dunois is not leading the army correctly. And in the end, they just turn against her. In actual fact, during the trial, they have a very, very good case. She surely can't believe that she's not going to be burned and not going to be imprisoned. She's amazingly naive.

But the *arrogance* of her. I'm sure I played up the arrogance, and I'm sure that if I were going to play it again—which I'm sure I shan't—I would find that more. I think she's an uncomfortable person. Some people who are fighting for the right are not easy to be with. I think people thought she was an arrant nuisance, who must somehow be gotten rid of. There are many pointers to that in the play, but I don't think that's ever been emphasized enough.

The real Joan was interesting and she was a kind of heroine to me. When I was quite young, my father and mother took me to Rheims, where I saw her statue. They told me about Joan of Arc, and I bought a little copy of the statue. I had also been to Domremy before I played Joan, and heard the church bell there. Continental bells have a very metallic sound. People go off on that thing of making Joan's bells sound like Great Peter, the bell at York Minster. But I think that it's a much smaller bell. More in character with the person that she is.

I never do research for anything because then I fall out the hole in the middle. I just get so confused—it's like seeing the play masses of times. You want to take the best of everybody and you want to read, but then you don't do something very instinctive. I'm only an instinctive person, really. I do try to work things out, but I only act on instinct. It's probably very arrogant of me to say that.

I just thought that I'm probably built quite like St. Joan anyway, because I'm amazingly strong and small. I don't know whether she was small, but I thought about that and hoped that it informed the performance enough. I also trained as a designer, so I developed a very clear picture in my mind of what she should look like. I was very, very relieved when I heard Sir Lawrence say that he does that. I have to kind of design it in my mind first. Also I had my hair chopped very, very roughly.

Patrick Robertson did the costumes, and they were very workmanlike. They looked like people had worn them. My armor was made by the same person who made Joanie Plowright's, and it looked battered about. If I were to do it again now, I would want that even more. I would want her to wear an armor made up from something like bits of old metal tied on. It's playing against that thing of being very shining and precise. It was a very black, very simple set—the same set that we did Measure for Measure on. We never brought the curtain down. It was very, very stark, and that was a wonderful help.

I played her with a Yorkshire accent, which is where I come from. It's quite soft and flat, and then when Yorkshire people get heated, it's a very strange sound and not so soft. It worries me a bit actually, accents. There's no way that Joan could come on speaking in a standard English accent, because she doesn't speak like anybody else. So what do you do? I don't know what the answer is.

The Yorkshire accent I played her in is very brusk, very much to the point. I'm not saying that Yorkshire people are intolerant, but the way I played her didn't leave much room for tolerance. She understood with a kind of Mother Earth, basic animal intuition what people were saying, but I think it is ignorance that makes part of her mind so shut off. Not willing to see other people's point of view, and calling a spade a spade. Maybe that's also something to do with her youth. I remember that being the thread all the way through. And certainly not playing, in any way, the saint. I was very,

Judi Dench in the Nottingham Playhouse production.

very matter-of-fact about saying, "I'll ask Saint Catherine. She'll send a west wind." Total assurance that she is on the level of the saints. It must have been intolerable for them.

When she hears the bells and thinks that her voices are speaking to her, it was as matter-of-fact as saying, "We have thirty head of cows." I cut out a lot of lyricism in the play.

I think I made the "I am alone" speech insufferable. I remember taking off any soft corners, so I don't know whether the production made people cry. I don't think I played any of it in an acceptable lyric, compassionate way. I think I played it with a tremendous stubbornness and a dogged determination. I was sure that black was black and white was white, and I never let up on that. I only pursued material, total belief.

Under that canopy also came the saints and my belief that God had sent me. I don't believe that she was a tolerant person, and I didn't allow for any tolerance. In a way, it's like Juliet behaving so badly sometimes. She behaves terribly irrationally and hysterically. It's the intolerance of youth. I hope I wasn't monotonous.

When we did *Romeo and Juliet* for Zeffirelli in 1961, we strove to make them children. Franco was interested in the fact that they were children. Up until we did the play, productions were about these very romantic, very poetical, beautiful, lyric lovers. There's more antagonism in it than that, and that's what I worked for in Juliet and in Joan—that kind of intolerance of youth, of simply lying on the ground with your hands over your ears and saying "Don't!" That dogged determination and stubbornness is also what can go out and win battles.

A lot that happens to St. Joan is, I think, luck. That may be a heinous thing to say, but in actual fact it is luck and drive. She was a catalyst, and that is as important as that maybe she was a saint. Too many Joans make up their minds that she's a saint from the moment she walks in. I don't think she is; I think she's a rebel. People who are rebels are often people who are saints.

What I remember about the performance, strangely enough, is that when the trial came I was always immensely relieved. It was the work done before the trial that I found difficult and more of a challenge, to make her that much of a catalyst.

I think the Dunois scene was the hardest. It is fiendishly difficult to do. Shaw makes Dunois such a charming hero. It is a very lyric scene too, in a way, but when they come on, it should be very prickly and difficult. It is actually a does-the-work scene which precipitates the play forward. We discussed that a lot. Suddenly Dunois sees more in her than a woman because she has that marvelous speech about "I do not care for the things women care for." He begins to accept her when she says, "You think you can win battles with a great noise and smoke. You must have guns, and much bigger guns too." I don't think he accepts her fully until the wind changes at the end, when he comes to total belief. She sees, too, that they are compatible in a way they shouldn't be when they come on.

Jimmy Thompson was Dunois. He was actually there for Lucio in *Measure for Measure*, and he wasn't the kind of person that people would have imagined as Dunois. Simply because of that it was unexpected and different. Ronnie Hines played Warwick. It was a marvelous performance—very, very solid and again, a kind of man who gave the impression that you couldn't move him. The more the people stand firm in the play, the bigger the battle.

We did a joke. This is a terrible, terrible story. Harold Innocent played the Inquisitor. You may know Harold's work from the National Theatre. A big man. Likes his voice a lot. We suspected he was listening to it a bit, and about two days before we opened, the company got together and asked John Neville to call a dress rehearsal of the trial.

We ran up to the Inquisitor's speech, where Harold always started getting slower and slower. About three lines into the speech, Job Stewart, who was playing De Stogumber, I believe, took from underneath his cassock a very small flask and a couple of cups and poured out some hot coffee and passed it along. Then Ronnie McGill, who was playing the Bishop of Beauvais, got from underneath his costume an enormous piece of purple knitting and started to knit. I just remember hearing a thud—it was John falling on the ground he laughed so much. Harold was frightfully cross, frightfully cross, and then we all laughed and apologized, and he was wonderful about it and has told the story often. And he did do the speech marvelously well.

I never had any trouble with Joan's intelligence. Indeed she was intelligent. I remember my husband and I being at dinner with a great friend of ours, Joseph McCullough, who is director of St. Mary Le Beau. At this dinner were the Rev. Tom Carlinsky, who is a Jesuit, and Edward Carpenter, Dean of Westminster. They had a theological discussion, of which Michael and I understood I suppose less than a third.

Now sometimes very, very clever or very sophisticated people speak in a language which is not direct or straightforward. I believe that somebody of as much intelligence as Joan, or maybe even more, could go into, say, an Oxford college and be baffled by what people talk about. In the trial it's sometimes like lateral thinking. I think that there's a genuine country person in the middle of the room with the princes of the Church, who actually does not understand what they say and just pursues her own belief and her own assurance.

I remember thinking that I hoped what I did made her more accessible. We know she was a remarkable person, but playing a unique, remarkable, saintlike person on the stage may leave very little that people can identify with. If you can make her more accessible—if people can understand more about her even through anger or through thinking "what an appalling way to behave"—then somehow, through all those things, the saintlike qualities should be there anyway.

Strangely enough, Joan is not a part I feel that I've put behind me. I feel I've done groundwork on something—as when I played Lady Macbeth with John Neville in West Africa in 1963, and it was the most wonderful groundwork for when I played it with Ian McKellen for Trevor Nunn. I do feel very much that Shaw is like that. You can have so many shots at something and never get tired of actually playing and perfecting and getting something nearer.

I suppose Joan is like Juliet, in that they say when you're Juliet's age you're not old enough to play her, and when you're old enough to play Juliet, you're too old. *Saint Joan* is technically a very difficult play for an actress. If we are going to get somebody of nineteen or twenty, she has to be very, very proficient because you have to have the most incredible energy and driving force to play Joan. That perhaps is the biggest thing you have to get over because, when you get to the trial, in a way you've done your physical work and then have the mental work to do. There's a tremendous relief when they say, "Take her to the fire," and you think, "Oh, thank goodness." The physical and mental resources called on are very considerable for a girl or a woman.

Jane Alexander

Jane Alexander was born in Brookline, Massachusetts. She played Joan at Arena Stage in Washington, D.C. during the 1965–66 season.

One evening a couple of days after we opened *Saint Joan*, I passed by the stage manager's office and saw a dozen or so actors huddled over his desk. They were looking at the *Washington Post* review of the play, which was devastating for me. Now at that time I didn't read reviews, but I came in—it was a five-minute call already—and said, "Oh, what are you looking at?" Their faces were so long—I needed to know what everybody was so unhappy about. So I read the review just before I went on stage, and I recall feeling very, very distressed about that.

Jon Voight, who was in the company, said to me maybe that evening, maybe the next, "Boy, it takes courage to be an actor." And I felt so angry at him. I said, "What are you talking about, courage? This guy can write a lousy review about me, but it doesn't take courage for me to get up in the face of it.

That's not what I was thinking when I went on." And, by the way, it didn't take courage for Joan to do what she did.

Courage is when you're aware of all the pitfalls that can be set. When you're aware that you're going to cross a crevice on one thin wire, and you have to do it standing up and to bring your seventy-five-pound child on your back as well. Joan didn't have to have courage. She didn't know about those crevices. She'd never been in battle.

Jon saying that "It takes courage to be an actor" made me angry in the same way I think that sort of remark would have made Joan angry. "Courage? What are you talking about? God's telling me to do this." Not that I felt that God was telling me to act, exactly. I was going to act no matter what.

I literally knew that I wanted to be a performer when I was six, and an actress when I was about nine or ten, when I couldn't comfortably be on point. I was taking ballet, but my toes were too long. They would have had to have been broken and reset, and I didn't want to go through that.

My father was an orthopedic surgeon, but he was enamored of the theatre, and my mother had become so as well. Dad had done some theatre work himself with the University Players, of which Hank Fonda and Josh Logan were members. When Dad was at Harvard he had been a part of their company in Cape Cod for three summers.

Theatre was my parents' love, and they went to the theatre quite regularly in Boston and would tell me about it. So when I determined at a young age to be an actress, it was a stage actress that I wanted to be. I wanted to play the great classic heroines, and of course Joan was one of them.

I think I first became interested in Joan because of Julie Harris's The Lark. I remember my father and mother saying, "Oh, this is the best thing we've ever seen," and giving me a blow-by-blow description of her performance. I guess I'd been studying Shaw's Joan since I was about twelve or thirteen. I'm not sure Joan herself—the real Joan—was my heroine, but certainly I would say that Shaw's St. Joan meant an enormous amount to me, particularly since my father was a very literate and witty man and I think he admired GBS more than almost any playwright. By the time my sixteenth birthday came along, Otto Preminger was doing the film and I was one of thousands who tried out for it. A young thing named Jean Seberg got it.

I was always looking for a production, so by the time I was twenty-one and I was in some classes here in New York, I was working on Joan all the time. One particular teacher, Mira Rostova, kept saying to me, "You should play this part. You should play this part."

I went to a regional theatre in Boston for a year, and Al Schoemann, the casting director for Theatre Communications Group, called me there one day and said, "Jane, you've got to get down here right away. Arena Stage is having an audition. They're going to start their season with *Saint Joan*, and you're going to do it." Well, I had the audition but I didn't have high hopes for it, because I had auditioned for the Arena's founder, Zelda Fichandler, twice before and she rejected me both times. And at least once I had done the Joan for her, either the "Light your fires" or something from the first scene. This audition was different because Ed Sherin, who is now my husband, was there. He was going to direct *Saint Joan*. And he has told me since that from the minute I opened my mouth there wasn't any question that I was going to be the Joan. I was just twenty-four.

Then I started to work on the role. Well, at that time I was doing reams and reams of research that I felt would give me greater understanding—I was reading books and books about her, and about how different actresses had played her. I remember little details interested me enormously. Somebody had written that Joan wore lots of rings on her fingers; I remember having three or four rings when I played her. I also recall writing at least two spiral notebooks full of details about how I was going to do Joan. I'm sure I still have them somewhere, but they are probably boring as hell.

My ideas were that Joan was not a peasant, that she was certainly of what we call an upper-middle-class family, a more privileged class. She certainly did go up in the fields with the animals, and heard the voices as well, and I think she had time to reflect on things in life.

I did see her as young. I saw her in that kind of prepubescent dream that girls have before men become a part of it. Now it's hard today for us to have parallels with that kind of feeling because our culture wallows in male-female relationships and sexuality—but,

Jane Alexander in the 1965–66 Arena Stage production.

you know, if a girl is interested in horses, she's interested in them right through her teen years, until a man comes into her life. That's how I saw Joan. I don't think that she had a crush on anybody except maybe the saints, and so everything was projected out. It was just a young sexuality that was substituting for what might have grown up later with the love of a good man.

I didn't see her at all butch or dyke. So I didn't see her uncomfortable in women's dress. It's very much like Calamity Jane, whom I played on TV and who was closer to me in time. Calamity simply dressed in men's clothes because she had to do men's work. Riding a horse was the primary mode of transportation for Joan and for Calamity, and it doesn't make a lot of sense if you want to get somewhere fast to be doing it with a skirt and sidesaddle. That was all. It was utilitarian.

I don't know that much about how one conducts battles, but it seemed to me that she was on to something in her analysis of France's lack of confidence and its needs. I had this idea that she had listened to her father and his friends talking about the situation and she made her own assessment. That it was dire, that their fears for France were real. Then she would mull it over and talk to the saints about it and come up with an answer. I think she was astute. Yes. I think she had quite high intelligence in terms of analytical powers.

It never bothered me at all that she couldn't sign her name. It's a matter of established fact that many children, in particular boys at the age of eight or nine or ten, can become chess masters without being able to read or write. That's the kind of intelligence we're talking about here with Joan. It was the ability to analyze situations and a very clear, highly focused and motivated direction. And she had added to that the belief that God was telling her that this is the way to go. So how could she fail? She couldn't, really.

Her situation reminds me of what I learned from Helen Caldicott and the nuclear disarmament movement. Helen has given up her work as a pediatrician to devote full time to going around the world talking, making the public more aware of the dangers of nuclear war. Helen always said to me, "Don't be nervous about jumping in in areas that you think may be covered. You'll find that most things in the world aren't being done, so you might as well go in there and do them." I've discovered that she's absolutely right.

I don't think experience or any person was telling Joan that—but, as I say, she had all the elements to succeed. She had everything going for her. She was coming to France's aid at a time when they were in the doldrums. She wouldn't have succeeded if they were on the crest of success. They were grasping at straws. Joan had this added thing—what God was telling her. That's why I say it's the great role.

I do use pictures a great deal in my work, either paintings or photographs, and I very often use music, too. My father gave me a triptych of Joan in various times of battle, and I had that up on my wall. Somebody gave me a picture of the sculpted head that Shaw thought was modeled on Joan. It didn't, in fact, influence me a great deal because of the haircut—something was not right about the haircut. Prior to playing Joan I had always had a long, full head of hair. At the time I arrived at Arena Stage my hair was down to my ass, and I went out two days before rehearsal, not telling anybody, and I had it all cut off. I needed to experience that as Joan, and I also knew it was the only way we could do the play, because I couldn't put a wig on and leave my hair long.

I could relate to all of that loneliness because of the teenager I had been. I was alone a great deal. I'd also been quite religious. I had turned to the Catholic church in my late teens from an Episcopalian upbringing. I was enamored with the ritual of Catholicism, so I was very directly able to relate to that aspect of Joan's life.

What was so devastating for me as Joan was the utter belief that I was going to succeed in what I set out to do because the voices told me that this was what was going to happen—and then I ended up in prison. It was that schism: "It didn't go the way you said it would; ergo it is possible that you were not voices." So this enormous self-doubt started to invade me. When I recanted it was genuine, with an enormous sense of grief.

I was able to do the recantation with a great honesty and truth and I think it was probably heartbreaking. Brother Martin is very important in that part, and we had Robert Foxworth, who was wonderful. He was so supportive. It wasn't a difficult transition for me from the recantation to "Light your fires," because, as I remember, I thought, "That wasn't the deal. Wait a minute . . . no . . . that wasn't the deal."

And it was just that simple outrage of, "You say that I'm a liar and my voices are lying . . . well, what about you?"

I loved the epilogue. The epilogue is pure Shaw, Shaw at his best. It's Shaw in that dialectical discussion in which he sparkles the most. It is sublime to play it. I was so grateful to be able to play the epilogue. After all that had happened in the play, to be in heaven and to have been canonized. I felt like I had wings. It was wonderful.

I'm told by people who saw it that my final scenes were wonderful, but that I did not succeed in the initial transition from the young girl who went in front of the Dauphin. One of the reasons that I probably wasn't as convincing in the early scenes was that I was not aggressive or demanding. I remember feeling that I had the angels on my shoulders, and if De Baudricourt or anybody couldn't see them, that was really their problem. This is probably not the right way to envision it, because she had to get through something with those guys. It is also very important that your supporting cast communicate an openness, a sense that they can take in this maid.

At twenty-four I didn't have any real experience carrying a show in the professional theatre, and that's what Joan is—one of those roles. Without Joan you don't have a play, but at the same time it is your supporting cast who creates the believability in Joan. I remember having a little trouble with some of the men in the cast, who I felt were doing their own kind of star turn, which wasn't helping my credibility as Joan. But by the same token I must say to you that I did not hold my own.

Joan is one of those roles for which you have to take stage. You have to have the weight, not just equal to but more so than the other fellows. I was coming from a school of work that said, "If you have this inner core it's going to radiate out," and that isn't enough. I know it now because I've done it for twenty years; if I look at this room and it's a stage and I want to take this space you will feel that energy from me. I will make it tangible. But in those days I didn't know about that. All I knew was that somebody had said to me "Be truthful and it will all work." Well, there are a lot of actors who are very truthful, but their presence isn't felt.

Ed Sherin helped me enormously, because I came out of an acting-class situation that, instead of expanding my—well—consciousness, and the joy of performance I had grown up with, had tended to internalize everything and bring everything down. I was really no longer performing for the audience. I was performing for some kind of truth that I was trying to reach in myself. He made me open up again. That was very important.

Joan was a vital turning point in my life. It was the beginning, of course, of a wonderful collaboration with Ed in our work and in our life. It was the first time that I understood—after the play closed—how much I needed to work, how much I needed to take stage, how much I had to learn. I really threw out all my acting training and started all over again, and the audience was my teacher. I stayed at the Arena for three years. The last year that I was there we did *The Great White Hope* and took it to Broadway and then did the film.

The Arena really started me on the road to what was demanded of me as an actress, what I needed to work for. It was the personality of Joan as I finally understood it that I wasn't able to fulfill at that age. I don't think that I was particularly good playing her and I'm not sure that many twenty-four-year-olds could bring it off.

But I think there's an upper age limit, too. I've been asked since to play her, but I think I couldn't play her now. I'm too old. I've seen older actresses do it, but I feel that it's most right if you hit somebody in their early thirties. That would be dynamite. I tell young actresses that I meet—not all of them, but ones that I think are right for Joan—to study it, even if they never play it. It's one of those roles that will click something off in you because of the range you have to experience.

There is no other role around like Joan. Lavinia in *Mourning Becomes Electra* is one of the great roles. Having had the opportunity to play it in Stratford, Connecticut, I can say that that is a marathon and a fascinating study. Certainly some Ibsen would fit in the great category. I've never done *Rosmersholm* but I'd like to, and I'd love to do Mrs. Alving. In terms of heroines I'd say Lavinia is closer to Hamlet than St. Joan, simply because of the psychological affinity. They actually start off with the same thing—revenge for the father's death. But in terms of classical heroines I can't think of anybody other than Joan. I really can't.

I'm very drawn to heroines. I'm developing films now myself, and I'm producing, and I find the stories that I'm drawn to are those about women who are doing rather extraordinary things that have to do with some kind of social consciousness. It's important that we have genuine heroines in the world.

I now won't even do Shaw anymore because I repudiate so much of his stuff. It just makes me angry now, and having played a number of Shavian heroines, I feel that I have a right to my opinion.

I've been in two productions of *Misalliance* as Lina, played Gloria in *You Never Can Tell*, done *Major Barbara* twice. It was when I did Barbara for the second time that I started to get very angry at Shaw, and it happened because Undershaft is given all the great arguments. Just like the Warwick-Cauchon scene in *Saint Joan*; it is the heart of the play.

Shaw's intellectual analysis of society is so universal in theme that it will go on; it will be true whenever. But I realized after my second time around as Major Barbara that no matter what I did, or how I felt, it was still going to be Undershaft who was remembered.

Now that's not to say that when I see the movie of *Major Barbara* I don't remember Wendy Hiller. She was radiant and she was beautiful, but for Shaw that kind of radiance almost verges on a sentimentality compared with his intellectual arguments. And not one of those arguments is given to a woman in any of his plays—even in *Man and Superman*. That's what I started to get angry at. Shaw could talk about women and equality, but I never felt that it was built right into the plays. The life force in Shaw's plays is the word, and he is going to be remembered for his words. God bless him for writing them, because he's a wonderful writer. But the words are given to the men.

Lee Grant.

Lee
Grant

Born in New York City, Lee Grant played Joan at the Morristown Theatre
in New Jersey in 1966.

I came to *Saint Joan* with a tremendous need to do it since I
had been a blacklisted actress and I was a crusader. I felt that
she and I would connect, that I would have an enormous
release for the kind of passion I needed to release. But I found
that Shaw's character did not connect with the neurotic explo-
sion I wanted. She was a much more intelligent, more charming, more social, more together young woman. My need was
to be a totally involved, passionate Joan, and I kept on bumping into parameters that Shaw had set which broke that
involvement.

I tried my utmost to do what I wanted to do. And, of course,
I had to do what the playwright wrote because I had no other
instrument except the words that he gave me. The clash between his strong insistence as to what his play was about and
my strong need to twist it into something else was a very good
lesson for me, because the play was also something that I

respected. I thought it was a fine piece of work, a fine play that I was not in the right place for. I'm a *great* admirer of Shaw. One of the most fun things that I ever did was *Pygmalion*. I had a great time with it and a great empathy and no problem. But maybe I came to Joan with so much darkness that all the piquancy of Shaw's Joan bothered me.

It wasn't the production that bothered me. It was a special production that was put together by a sensitive director, Arthur Siedelman, who got a company of very, very good New York actors. We had only two weeks to work, which was not enough, and it was literally brought to the Morristown theatre—we were not in residence. The reaction was good, as far as the papers in New Jersey and friends whom I cared about; but after I'd done the Shaw, I thought that it was Anouilh's *The Lark* that I should have done. The Anouilh would have given me the outlet I needed at the time.

Of course I had a girlhood attraction to Joan of Arc, but I don't think it was special until I saw Julie Harris bring an incredible originality to *The Lark*. But the idea of Joan, a crusader, alone, at that particular time, so demented that she carried out this incredible fantasy of hers, has always been remarkable to me.

The being burned at the end was a tremendous analogy for me as far as the period that I had come out of, where people around me died for their beliefs—something I felt I had been willing to do. So in many ways, organically, I was very prepared. I didn't do any research for the role. I felt at that time that my own life was the preparation.

I feel that Shaw throws you into Ireland. I don't think there's any escape from it. I think that his was a very fresh and very original point of view. And I think that it's a very big help and a very good base, especially for that transformation for an American actress.

I did use an Irish accent. I think a lilt. As little as possible, just enough to place it. I think if you're playing Joan you have to decide where you're from and then find a way of vocalizing it. I'm not saying indicating, I'm saying from the bottom—because we're all so sophisticated now, you need to be from somewhere that will place you in a much more simple position. I've done this in many other parts in which I've been successful at blocking out all the areas except the one that fits for them, like the Shoplifter in *Detective Story*, my first role.

I think I did look at pictures of Ireland at the time, because what I usually do is write out four or five pages from the character's point of view about where I live, where I came from, what my parents are, who my friends are, what I want, what my obstacles are. I try and fill in all the realities that have to become my new reality when I walk on the stage. I think after finding where I was from, taking it from an Irish point of view—and I don't know whether that worked or not—I didn't have any problem with that. And once I found the boy-Joan, the voice and the movements followed. I didn't have to think about it.

Joan is a tomboy: in particular she's a dedicated tomboy; that's how she starts out. There's a whole putting aside of frills and female things, and I loved discovering the boy in me and in her. I was an only child with a father who wanted a boy, so that part of me was very accessible. There was nothing that I wasn't permitted to do. I was raised in New York on Riverside Drive, and there was country life in the summer. Those were the areas—the country girl, the tomboy, the soldier—that were better.

The trial scene was the one I always looked forward to, because that was where I really wanted to go. That's where I felt the concept of punishment for being good—I always see that concept astonishing people who take political action. People believe they take an action to be good, and then either when it doesn't work or they become pariahs, they're astounded. It's like children who are told, "If you're good, you'll be rewarded." We all have that tremendous belief, and I do think that is the principle on which Joan worked. She really did believe that if she was good she'd be rewarded, and had to cope with the reality of people who were actually punishing her for doing good.

The recantation was very real for me. I wasn't noble when I said "I'm not going to give names." I said, "I'm not going to give names," and they said, "Okay, then you can't work." I must say I never had a temptation on that, and I really acccepted the fact that I would not work except in the theatre because there was no blacklist there.

But if somebody had said to me "You'll be burned alive unless you give names," I would have given names, that's all there is to it. There's no question about it. I accept Lenny Bruce's reality on that. He had a satirical routine called "The Hot Lead Enema." It featured a captured prisoner of war saying "No, sir. I give you my name, rank and serial number. Oh, you're going to put that hot poker up my ass? Yes, whatever you want to know, I'll tell you." What Joan had to give up for recantation was so devastating and so real that I understood. I loved that.

The recantation and "Light your fires" were fine for me. But there was still something about it. The words were more temperate than I wanted. I was ready to go out-of-body and I constantly felt pulled down to a more rational place than I felt that I, as Joan, would have been. It was too charming for me. The need that I had was more Brechtian, harsher and more connected with terrible realities that I knew and wanted to explore. I think Shaw had Peter Panned the picture for me.

I don't think I ever cracked through on the religion. My spirituality is a weak area. Usually in such areas I use substitution. But in *Saint Joan* the problem wasn't the technique of substitution, it was finding substitutions for Shaw's particular choices. For example I never got over the epilogue—her showing up at Charlie's bed. It bothered me enormously. Her being on top of every situation, being so plucky and so Dickensian, almost, in her "Come along, Pip, we're off to find God, we're off to save France." There was something about it which embarrassed me. I felt that the rawness and the passion of Joan just couldn't be encircled by that darling and intelligent woman.

Maybe it's true that if there is a trust that God is with you, you can be very accepting. But what I identified with was the loss of that God. I identified with the fact that those verities had fled, and with the hole that one lives in when the verities which made you strong and made you accomplish things that were impossible don't exist for you anymore. The questioning, the need, must throw me—and it would be me/Joan, not somebody else/Joan—into a terrible place, a terrible void. I felt that I was not permitted to experience that in Shaw's Joan.

The last line of the epilogue, however, I loved because it's very political. One of the things that I loved about the play was that the political line was so clear. That particular cry of "How long, oh Lord" was very close to me at that time and, as a matter of fact, still is. I think it was left a confrontation with God and with the audience.

I don't think there's any question that Shaw's Joan is one of the great roles for actresses. That's why I did it; I just did not feel that I was successful. My best work was in Sophocles' *Electra*, which I did for Joe Papp. I'm attracted to Arkadina, certainly, which I did once and would love to do every five years. Medea, Hedda, Nora—though I think I'm too old for Nora now.

Of American roles, I think I'd like Mary Tyrone in *Long Day's Journey*. I did Regina in *The Little Foxes*, and I did something controversial with her. I felt that a woman in the South was trapped, that Regina's strength was surface. I approached her as a victim of the men in her family—both her brothers and her husband—whose only tool was manipulating and trying to get out of a place in which Southern women were put. Particularly in that period. I just did not believe in all that uncomplicated strength. And while a lot of people didn't agree with it, I think it was an interesting piece of work.

The conclusion I came to was that I'm not Shaw's ideal Joan; I needed to be somebody else's. I certainly found in *Electra* the kind of release that I felt should have been in Joan. I do think there can be an ideal Joan. Certainly my memory of Julie Harris was that she realized her Joan and was in a state of grace.

A state of grace is exactly what I was looking for. It's that place where you transform yourself, and find that your saints are with you, and God is with you, and you can do anything because of it. You're able to soar. You're on stage, and something happens and you go. After the performance you don't really know what you did, you just know that it happened.

Electra would take off every night, and that was the most demanding part I have ever played. I think from the time when my hand went around the door until it was over, it was like opera. The hardest work I've ever done, but once it was set, off it went. I thought that was because of the depth, the confrontation, the sustaining of a kind of tension and power emotionally, vocally—the demand for the use of myself was total.

Joan was always work. It's hard for me to say because I wanted it to be that state of grace. But I was always conscious of the fact that I was working, and that it needed more work. I was using my craft, but that didn't give me the joy of taking off.

Joyce Ebert with Austin Pendleton as the Dauphin in the Williamstown Theatre Festival production.

Joyce
Ebert

*Joyce Ebert was born in Homestead, Pennsylvania. She played Joan at the
Williamstown Theatre Festival in Massachusetts in 1967.*

A remarkable thing happened after I played Joan. My husband, Arvin Brown, is artistic director of the Long Wharf Theatre in Connecticut—we've worked together there for twenty-one years—and we go to Europe every summer. We went to France, and visited practically every place that Joan had been. We went to Chinon, a beautiful medieval town; to Rheims, where she crowned Charles; to Rouen, where she was burnt. On the cathedral at Rheims is an angel that's called the smiling angel. She has this sort of half-smile on her face and is absolutely wonderful. I thought, "That's Joan." The half-smile has the humor of Shaw's character. That angel wasn't "looking up to heaven."

Then we went to Domremy, a really remarkable town. Arvin and I arrived there on a Sunday around 11:00 A.M., and we went first to the church where Joan was baptized. We went to her house, where we saw the room she was born in. She had the second-best room—her brother had the best—and it was a substantial house. She didn't come from poor people—it was like a middle-class family.

We went out into the front garden and were looking at a plaque that said, "On this spot in such-and-such a year at twelve o'clock, I heard the bells of my church ringing and I first heard the voices of"—I can't do this without crying— "of St. Catherine, St. Michael, and St. Margaret," and it was twelve o'clock on a Sunday and the bells rang and we were standing right there. We couldn't move. Arvin and I drove out of town, and couldn't speak. I'm not a spiritual person at all, but I felt the little gal had such spirit and such energy and somehow or other, they were there.

I always wanted to do *Saint Joan*. I wanted to do *Joan of Lorraine* when I was just a kid because Maxwell Anderson's play is, for a youngster, more understandable. I'd like to have done Anouilh's *The Lark*, too— I was always fascinated by Joan of Arc. As I gained in maturity and humor, I wanted to play Shaw's Joan.

Nikos Psacharopoulos, artistic director of the Williamstown Theatre Festival, repeats *Saint Joan* every once in awhile. I've been here at the festival, off and on, for about twenty years, and that was my summer to play it. That year I did everything. I did the Stepdaughter in *Six Characters in Search of an Author*, I did my last Nina in *Seagull*—I've done Nina five times—and it was just my summer to do Joan.

It was a pretty terrific production. Nikos has a genius for putting together a show with music and spectacle. He loves technical rehearsals, which I loathe, but Nikos is in his glory then. You always have wonderful lighting here, and costumes. At first they wanted to dress me like a Valkyrie—you know, the armor with the bosoms on. I said, "No, I don't think that's quite right," and Nikos said no, too. The only problem was the hair. I had long hair and I used it in the peasant scene at the beginning. They finally had to get me a wig for the rest.

Nikos directed it wonderfully. We had a great argument about the trial scene, but that's all right—I won. He'll tell you he won, mind you. He kept saying, "Don't play it sentimentally," and then he would demonstrate, sentimentally. He has a technique of getting you so upset that he can get what he wants out of you.

I had been reading about Joan for years. The trouble with doing a lot of research is that some things aren't going to help you much, because Shaw's Joan is so specific. Knowing things such as the children of the neighborhood had a fairy ring and she sort of belonged in it might get you in the mood for it, but mainly what you have to do is work from yourself and see what is right in you that would fit the character.

I definitely was a tomboy. I was brought up on a farm, so I used those aspects of myself. The loneliness is a lifelong thing with me. I was an only child, and I loved my parents, but we didn't always get along. I went through a bad first marriage, and that summer I was separated from my first husband. He hadn't treated me very well either, frankly, and I was going through a lot of trauma. It was a very unhappy summer for me, so that fed into the loneliness speech.

I didn't have any specific image for St. Catherine or for Michael, but I did for St. Margaret for some reason. She was quite motherly for me. I didn't know I was doing Joan until just before I got up here, and so I had to work fast.

The first scene is extremely difficult because it's almost farcical. I don't think I ever quite got that one. I think I know more what I'd do with it now, and what the other actor should do in it, too. Just play it lighter. I'd have to look at it again, but when my husband directed Sarah Miles as Joan at the Ahmanson in L.A., Sarah had that scene right on, and the guy playing opposite her was terrific too.

I liked the epilogue. Basically it is a tragic comedy, and I think the epilogue wraps it up. It's hard to play, mind you, after you've been burned at the stake, but I like it. Joan is bouncier, more positive, more forgiving—well, she forgives anyway throughout the whole play—less intense. The "How long, oh Lord" I read as a straightforward question to God.

Of course it works as a play. I think it's very involving. If she's done right, people love Joan. I think a lot of Shaw's plays are terrific. Sometimes I get annoyed with Shaw when I see them, but when I play them I have great fun. I've done *Man and Superman* twice. I loved that. *Back to Methuselah*, Hesione in *Heartbreak House*—I really enjoyed myself.

In my hierarchy of roles, I would say that Joan is around third. The first two would be from Chekhov and Shakespeare, since they are my first loves. I think Nina in *The Seagull* is a wonderful role. I've done

Arkadina, but Arkadina is nowhere near as good as Ranevskaya in *The Cherry Orchard*, which I've done twice. It is a great role, hard as hell. I think I accomplished it to a great extent, but I would love to do it again.

Lady Macbeth I've done and I'd like to do that again also, except she fizzles out at the end. That's the only problem with Lady Macbeth; you never see her after the sleepwalking scene. I'd like to do Katharine in *Henry VIII*. Juliet is a great role, of course. I did it in a terrific production with a wonderful director named Allen Fletcher, who was my teacher at Carnegie Tech. Stephen Joyce was beautiful as Romeo. A great Mercutio—Clayton Corzatte—and a lovely character actress named Joanna Roos did the Nurse. Altogether a wonderful experience.

Clytemnestra is among the great leading roles for women, except I never really wanted to play it—funny, that. Andromache in *The Trojan Women* I loved. I learned a lot from playing her for Michael Cacoyannis. He was a pain in the ass, mind you—he would demonstrate and give you line readings. I'd had enough training at Carnegie Tech to know that when you get line readings like that, you're not to imitate them exactly. You are to get the feeling of what he wants and translate it your own way.

Cacoyannis gave me things that I'll never forget—for example, when the Greek herald told me that my son must die, I practically pushed the boy back into my womb, and circled back away. Cacoyannis gave me that movement. I saw a production of *Trojan Women* at Epidaurus last summer and it was nowhere near as good as Cacoyannis's was. Playing Andromache helped me play Joan, helped me use my voice every night the way I had to. Just technically speaking, I orchestrated the speeches and felt them emotionally like I had to do as Andromache.

Andromache goes in the top five roles. It's hard to put them in order. Is there anyone I'd like to do? I've done them all, I really have. I would love to do *Rosmersholm* again. Duse said that Rebecca West is the most difficult role she ever played. I was not successful in it. Really, though, I've had a very interesting career. I've gotten to do some great roles more than once, and that's pretty wonderful, especially for an American. We just don't get that kind of experience. I've been very, very lucky.

Janet
Suzman

Janet Suzman was born in Johannesburg, South Africa. She played Joan
for BBC television in 1968.

I don't think St. Joan is a Hamlet. I think Shaw's wrong. First of all, *Hamlet* is probably the greatest play ever written about death, in all its aspects. If you hold it up to the light, it's a black diamond. Every single particle of it reflects ideas about death. Not as something gloomy in the least, but as something to be considered seriously by people who are alive. I don't think there's a scene in *Hamlet* that doesn't discuss the thing that happens to every single one of us.

Saint Joan is a sort of rogue play. Those things don't happen to people. It's a very simple and weird little voyage she's taking. The hoops of cynicism that she has to pass through are legion. Nor do I think that it is intellectually the equivalent of *Hamlet*. Her expansiveness is untutored, instinctive, simplistic, faithful, cheeky. His is tortured, sophisticated, educated. They couldn't be more different.

But I know what Shaw means: he means that this is a part that every actress must play. As an individual, Joan haunts us from the sidelines, but she's not central to our problems. I don't think the play is formative in the way that some plays are. When audiences watch *Saint Joan*, they believe they're watching a sainted, blessed, peculiar life, but not one with which they can really and truly identify.

Parts for women, compared with those for men, are so few and far between that there are certain touchstone roles. I think Joan is a great part for a youngish actress. It's more spiritual than any of the others. Her love affair is such an extraordinary one. The others—Masha, Cleopatra, any of the girls in Shakespeare—are all too human, and all their involvements are with themselves and their men and their lives.

I have never found that one kind of role feeds into the other. In all great dramatic characters, the conflict is to find within themselves something that either makes them survive, or makes their survival impossible. The desire for life, and the desire to find emotional sense in life, shoots through all of them. That's the only thing they have in common; otherwise they are really very different animals.

Let's put it this way: not to play St. Joan would be foolish, if it came your way. It's not a play that comes up often. It seems to be a play that comes up when the actress concerned is ready to do it, like Juliet or Cleopatra, I suppose. I was asked by Cedric Messina to do it for BBC television. He was in the full flight of doing a lot of major plays. And I was right for it, at that point. The good thing, I think, about my Joan is that I was still young enough to play it. I didn't come to it too late in life, which meant that the young side of her I didn't have to battle with much at all.

I had played La Pucelle as my first part at the RSC when John Barton was directing those French sections of *Henry VI*. I began to pooh-pooh the whole Joan thing then, because I began to believe the Shakespeare one, so persuasive is he. Shakespeare's incapable of writing something that you can't believe in. All La Pucelle's protestations of being pregnant at the end, her terrible lying, somehow rang very true to me, the response of a terrified child. I went into a lot of the witchcraft business in that period. And that, too, began to make sense—the way a young girl could become a prey to voices, and could easily become part of something like a coven and all that strange black underworld. I found that the wiliness and spiritedness of the Shakespeare Joan rather took me. I liked it.

Saint Joan is the better play about her, obviously. And of course one has to remember that Shakespeare was a Protestant writing about a Catholic country and an enemy to boot. I took all that into account. But La Pucelle was a really terrific little thing. She was persuasive and very articulate, and she dissembled a lot, but altogether she did seem to have something—people couldn't resist her.

I think that some of the ideas I got playing La Pucelle carried over into the Shaw, except that I had to abandon the witchcraft side for pure religion. I do remember struggling a bit with trying to make it unsentimental and as real as I could. One is always a child of the decade one is in, in a sense, and in the 1960s nobody was prone to great faith and great belief. But I knew that if I was going to do that Joan, that's what I would bloody well have to do. Find it, somewhere or other. Once I had made that decision, it actually wasn't difficult to believe—totally, completely.

I don't find it difficult, if that's what the character has to do, to do it. In the more cynical, grownup, worldly part of my being it is, of course, ridiculous. But this peculiar dichotomy happens, whereby you've got to stop asking questions. I think Shakespeare taught me to do it. We belong to the post-Freudian age; Shakespeare didn't. If you start acting Shakespeare asking all kinds of psychological questions, you're sunk.

I found this to be true most specifically in the wooing scene in *Richard III*. Ian Holm was playing Richard. I could not understand how that girl could be moved by this monster who killed her father, killed her husband, and whom she loathed in every fiber of her being. At the end of that scene, how could she be at his knees, his for the asking?

I went to Peter Hall, who said, "Don't ask questions. Just do it." And he was right. You're not to ask *why* the wicked duke is wicked in *As You Like It*; he's just wicked. You're not to ask *why* Romeo and Juliet fall in love; they just fall in love. Don't ask questions; just get on with it. The same thing I think pertains to a play with the kind of emotional rush of *Saint Joan*. Don't ask questions. She *heard* the voices. She *hears* the bells. She *believes*. So do it. And it helps, not to ask questions.

I remember weird little things happening. I was mulling one night over Shaw's stage direction, "Joan makes her mark," in the trial scene, when she signs the recantation. I was in my bath—one always thinks best in baths—and I was lying there thinking, "Joan makes her mark . . . what was the mark? What was the mark?" And immediately, instinctively, I eschewed a cross, which I knew was the normal mark. I thought, "I know she didn't do that. I know she didn't. I know what she did: she made a circle!" And do you know, she did. I found that out later. That was the oddest occurrence, because it was so peculiarly instinctive. But it seemed important to me to know exactly the way her hand went on the page and how she signed that unwilling piece of paper.

The clothes, too, I was determined should not be classic, although I think Joan was rather vain at a certain point in her life and there is a lot to be read about that. I consumed books about Joan. And none of them seemed to give the answer. They never do when you're acting a part. All they do is flesh out a background which you're going to leave behind anyway, because you're going to be in the present. But I did read avidly, anything I could lay my hands on.

I think the hangover from *Henry VI* was this: she was a slightly scruffier Joan, a bit more lousy perhaps than the idealized one. I know she slept out in the battles; there would have been no official palatial hairdresser around. She was a bit of a little punk, I think. I remember the hair stuck up all over the place.

I had seen Ingrid Bergman and worshiped her and that beautiful blonde pageboy. I was in love with her when I was nine or ten, but that didn't appeal to me at all by the time I got to the sixties. I remember deliberately eschewing that pre-Raphaelite looking-up-to-heaven thing. I think generally, if one has to say anything physical about it, my Joan would prefer to close her eyes and imagine the saints rather than to gaze up towards some pink-tinged clouds. I thought too, that unless the king had ordered a suit of chain mail to be made for her, whatever she had would be castoffs, and would be slightly too big for her. Baggy. So things drooped a bit. I asked for that.

Whatever she looked like, it seems not to matter, because I still feel that what was inside her was this *glowing* persuasiveness. You always believe in people when they are fervent about their beliefs. I

Janet Suzman in the 1968 BBC television production.

liked also this nice sense of humor that pops up, in both Joans actually, but Shaw's more particularly. That kind of wonderful flat, commonsensical, no-nonsense sense of humor.

John Barton and I were convinced that we should try to find a distinct accent for Joan La Pucelle. It's a totally English play, the *Henry VI*, though the French form a part of it. Most actors find that mid-Wessex or Somerset kind of drawl. It's either sort of Harry Hotspur Northumbrian, or Welsh, or a kind of generalized Mummerset accent. For Joan, John and I were determined to find something a little different. A bit odd. Something that would make your ears prick a bit when she spoke. And so we plumped for Elizabethan. John knows a lot about how the Elizabethans spoke. It was great fun, actually. Joan pronounced, like the Elizabethans did, *all* the vowels—like *airth*, *e-a-r-t-h*—you heard every one of them.

John always brings up what an Elizabethan saying, "Ill met by moonlight, proud Titania" would have spoken like, and it would be, "Eel met by mo-onlicht." The *gh*, now dropped, would have been heard, and also the *mo-on*—they would have pronounced both *o*'s. *Prawd* instead of *proud*. It was those vowel collisions that we were looking for, and found. So La Pucelle spoke in a very weird but still very English way, yet didn't sound like any of the English side.

That worked wonderfully. Doing that rather hard *r*, too, that she would have spoken—that did spill over into the Shaw Joan. Not as fully, because it would have sounded peculiar on television, where you cannot do anything too extreme. People's names and place names are always so wonderful. France became *Fra-ance*, as a sort of Big Name. A kind of resounding sound. The way Shaw uses the word *alone*—I seem to remember drawing out the *lone* part very much.

As I recall, she came from a village where she would have had people around her all the time. But as somebody who had experienced the peculiar events in her life—hearing voices, being given commands—there would be in her something which was just a touch odd, and therefore more perceptive, I suppose. I felt that she was both puzzled by her voices and utterly accepting of them. But the loneliness—well, it's horrible, and I think it's easy to understand. I didn't find that difficult. I found it an awful thing for somebody to come to terms with.

Just to be *alone*—it's a bit like that speech in *Measure for Measure* where Claudio imagines what death is like. To be caged in ice—it's an unthinkable thing to have to suffer. And I think I remember wanting to play it like that. As if the ideas were just coming out of her, at that moment, and it was intolerable. It's an even more extraordinary speech, I think, than Hamlet's "To be or not to be."

I don't think the tomboyishness of it interested me, because what happens when you wear pants or chain mail is that you naturally change. It's a bit like writing on a blackboard and writing on a piece of paper: you don't think when you do it bigger. So when you wear that sort of clothes it just happens. They dictate what you do.

I didn't want her to be a sort of jolly hockey-sticks schoolgirl. She had lived in the country, was very basic and very instinctive, and I suppose most of all I felt it was her instinct more than her intellect that fed her verbiage. As to the way she talks to the king, the Archbishop and the others—I think that if you are being spoken to by saints, then no king, no lord, no officer is going to impress you very much.

The first scene is tricky. It's always fine once she becomes whatever it is she's got to be, which is a crusader, a soldier, a persuader—one of the boys. But when she's neither fish, flesh nor fowl, when she's still in her kirtle and still a peasant girl and has performed no persuasions or miracles as yet, I must say I find that first scene a little mawkish.

Telling Dunois about the voices was like a big secret. For the first time, she just sort of says, 'You will never understand it. I don't even understand it, but this is what happens." I think I was so in love with that speech, with that secret, that I romanticized it a bit. I seem to remember my feeling that she actually saw the saints in her mind's eye, and they were very classic, medieval-manuscript creatures. Always qualities of light. All these things do cross your mind about what is saintliness, and why do better people have brighter feelings around them? And, indeed, the origin of the halo in religious painting, *where* in hell does it come from? It seems obvious that, in some instances, certain people have been blessed with being able to see the kind of electricity that we all let off. In science fiction now, we have the idea of stellar bodies giving off auras. Her saints seem to me similar.

We played the Loire scene on two horses, and there was a camera up on a dolly, on the level of Dunois and Joan. We were beside some English river, and we did see the wind change. That was lovely. I remember the pennant. That's always an emotional moment when the wind changes direction. You know, in a way, there is an essence of melodrama in the play; you sometimes feel that, if you were to do it on the stage, there would be moments when you'd want the audience to cheer. And boo. Take sides.

I remember that Keith Baxter, as Dunois, gave me the baton—a big moment, and the tears were running down our faces, and it was all working beautifully. Then we had to go over the brow of this hill, cloaks flying, towards Orleans. And my horse went one way, and his horse went the other.

I had this vile horse called Kate, who hated me, and she headed straight for a pair of trees that were growing very close together. I knew this swinish horse was saying, "See if you can stay on," and it went straight for the middle of the trees. I stayed on. Don't know how. I went straight to the middle of the trees, and I heard this wild, elfin laughter behind me: it was the camera crew sitting on the dolly, swinging the camera ninety degrees of the compass trying to film both of us. Terribly funny. We had to trot back and do it again; couldn't have the horses flying in different directions to Orleans.

I *loved* the trial scene, because it is, as we know, the real thing. It's so amazing. That made me feel very peculiar, I must say, that voice coming out of the centuries. I found the trial the most emotionally effortless scene. It sort of swung me along in a great wave.

There was a nice bit one day when we were just beginning to rehearse the trial scene. Those sentences of Shaw's are so long. They go on and on and on and on. I remember we broke for lunch, and John Gielgud, who was playing the Inquisitor, came up to me and said, "Do you mind if I say something?" "No, Sir John, no, please do." And he said—the best note I've ever had in my life— "I think you'll find that Shaw had only one stress per line." And walked off, went to have lunch. I stood there stunned: "My God, he's right!"

I went back to my text, and in those long sentences there's only one important word, and you have to find it. I was floundering. I wanted everything to be as important as the next thing. No. I had to let some go, and find that really quite simple mind hitching itself to one particular word or idea. And then those long Shavian sentences became possible. That was an incredibly useful note. An actor's note to an actor. I thank him for that.

We did use the epilogue. I remember fighting about it because, at a certain time in rehearsal, I thought, "Enough! The story is told. We don't need the coda." But the purists prevailed. In a sense, it gives it a happy ending.

In the last line, I wanted to leave the audience with thoughts of Hiroshima. Atom bombs. Sanity. It's a good line, although it doesn't have the humanity at the end of *Uncle Vanya*—that great surge which has such a heartbreaking optimism to it. Shaw is too rhetorical for that, but if one could possibly get that surge into the last line it would be the feeling that we must go on believing. We must go on doing good things, however long it takes.

How long is it going to take? Well, how long are people going to go on being unspeakable to each other? Because the line is constructed like an aria, it's difficult to encompass that. But I think it is there. I also think it is easier on the television than on the stage, because you can make it a soliloquy to the audience. I can't remember whether we did that or not, but there is an opportunity to speak directly to the audience and ask them a question.

Her spirit speaks to us. Tremendously so. I think that's what I meant by saying the trial scene really used to get me. You did hear that voice coming like a knife through the centuries to you, those peculiarly mysterious phrases of hers: "If I am in a state of grace, may God keep me there." I so believed that voice that I felt a sort of little connection there with her. There was something very touching about her, too.

What Joan had was something that I guess most of us, in our most rational moments, envy. She had unthinkingness, absoluteness. Not weighing up both sides of the question, as most of us do. She's perfectly bright, but she hasn't got the time or the inclination to see both sides. A lot of politicians do that too. It's only bad politicians who think too much. Then you have a problem. The narrow-mindedness of great leaders—Alexander, Napoleon, all of them—gives them their fervency. That, of course, is why Joan must be young. She doesn't have experience. She can't see.

Like all really good dramatic characters, she fights to the very end.

I don't think she's a stoic, nor do I think she's very fatalistic. I think she's terrified of being imprisoned, of being alone, and most of all, of being burnt. I think she was never the kind of girl who could see the consequences of her actions. She simply had to do them. So when things blew up in her face, I think she was truly shocked and taken aback by what she had done, and by what other people did. I think that young terror, that shock, and her battle with them, are what is touching about her. If Joan had been in, say, her thirties, it would have been a very different saintly struggle, and far more belonging to those saints who accept their lot, and come through it in some way. But I don't think she was like that. I think she fought like a tigress.

Angela
Pleasence

Angela Pleasence was born in Sheffield, Yorkshire, England. She played Joan at
the Mermaid Theatre in London in 1970.

I played Joan as somebody who had revelations, but they
weren't necessarily a call from God. She could have been a
schizophrenic, she could have been one of a number of
things. Played on that level, the revelations are genuine; once
you have them, you believe it. It's like having psychosomatic
asthma: you may get it for psychosomatic reasons, but when
you're having an attack, you've got asthma—the real, physical
thing. I played Joan like that.

I was at the Mermaid Theatre in London, playing Miranda in
Jonathan Miller's production of The Tempest, which was being
very much acclaimed. Lord Bernard Miles, an actor and director who had started the remarkable Mermaid Theatre, had
been in the original Sybil Thorndike production of Saint Joan.
He said that he had always dreamt of directing the play himself
one day, had seen all the Joans from Sybil Thorndike onwards,
and had waited all his career for an actress to play his Joan.

"I've waited thirty years," he told me, "and you've come along and you're going to play St. Joan."

I read the play, phoned my agent and told her, "I don't want to play this part. I'm not interested." She said, "You must be out of your mind." At that time, all I wanted to play was Lucky in *Waiting for Godot*. I was longing for somebody to ask me to play Lucky. In fact, we were getting together a production, but it all fell through. I didn't want to play Lucky as a woman. I wanted to play it as asexual, of no sex, which I think Lucky is. And I didn't want anyone to know that I was playing Lucky; in fact, we'd worked out that in the program I was going to be Peter Pleasence, so that people wouldn't think of Lucky as a woman. It was not an act of feminism. And Joan, I guess, was sort of a romantic leading lady, which I wasn't really interested in. I wanted to play extraordinary, bizarre, remarkable characters. I was being very idealistic.

Finally I accepted; I would have been an idiot not to accept *Saint Joan*. Then I went and hurled myself into research. I went off to the British Museum and read everything I could possibly get hold of. I knew nothing about Joan of Arc then. I never had girlhood heroines. I read Enid Blyton—a writer of children's books that lots of so-called progressive parents ban from their houses. I stopped with Shadow the Sheepdog. I got stuck at Noddy-land level in my childhood, so I never had romantic ideas about any characters in history; certainly not women.

There's an incorrect historical image of Joan being a large person. I'm not sure about Shaw's play, though he wrote it for Sybil Thorndike, and Sybil Thorndike was my heroine. I was desperately insecure and terrified about doing Joan. I thought, "I'm physically totally wrong for this part, because Joan is always played by somebody bigger," and I was 5′2″ and weighed just over six stone then. Then I started to do research, and was absolutely astounded.

This whole myth of Joan—that the reason everybody was so terrified was that she was this huge, great, butch woman—was just rubbish. It turned out that I was physically her size. That was the first thing that made me think, "Well, it won't be so catastrophically disastrous." It's rather like Electra. Everybody thinks of Electra as being this enormous person, but if you go to see the play in the Greek amphitheatre, she's always this tiny little creature. I thought,

"If I'm her size, that's one thing I've got. Because there's no point in me thinking about Shaw's Joan and Thorndike's performance or anything, because I'm not that size, and nothing in the world can make me seven inches taller and three stone heavier, because I couldn't put that weight on if I ate all day."

I did research into Joan, and decided that I wasn't going to play her in a romantic, poetic way at all, that there was no feasible reason for me to do it like that. That's not denigrating any other actress, because very fine, great actresses have played Joan and been wonderful, and some of them I've seen. But I decided that I was going to be an antihero, that I was going to try and play it medically correctly.

Just before going to the Mermaid, I had played a schizophrenic in this play The Ha Ha, which Richard Eyre adapted from the novel by Jennifer Dawson, and which he also directed. I'd spent three days at Napsbury Hospital, which is one of the biggest mental hospitals. I had been, at that time, very involved in patients who were having revelations, which was fascinating to me. When I came to do St. Joan, all of that research for a totally different character became very, very useful. Also, I had done a prenursing course from a college and had taken my first state prelim, part one, which is the academic examination. I didn't actually go into hospital; I was far too young for that. But when I was reading medical material which applied to The Ha Ha and to Saint Joan, it meant something to me. It helped.

I will try to give whatever details I can, but I have a very serious memory problem—I forget very, very fast. I've said to actresses and actors, "How do you do, we've never met," and they've turned around and said, "We've just done a scene and we've been working together for two months." I played opposite a Romeo and three weeks after the play had finished, I was introduced to this actor and I said, "We've never met." I'm known for my appalling memory. I go into overdrive blank and I don't know what happens. I've been like this since I was a child. I do enormous research for roles, then forget it all very, very quickly.

The first scenes in Saint Joan are very straightforward. Joan is a country girl who has had these revelations, and she really does believe. Whether they are genuine revelations, or a hormonal displacement, or schizophrenic experiences, or whatever, is neither here nor there because the revelations exist. Therefore, I played her

Angela Pleasence in the Mermaid Theatre production.

as a young girl totally, genuinely convinced that what she felt and what she believed was right. I can't see any other way that anybody could play it.

The hearing of the bells—I'm trying very hard to remember—that was played as if she was taking Dunois into her confidence, in the way that you do when there might be someone else listening behind a pillar. It was a secret. When she starts to tell him about it, she thinks he's going to laugh at her because it sounds so ridiculous. She starts to tell him about this extraordinary experience she had that is so private and so secret, and as she starts to tell him, she starts reimagining it herself. And when she goes into this experience of the bells, you then see how terrified she is. It is actually something that takes over. It's not this uplifted, "Dear-child-of-God, Be-brave-go-on" romantic ecstasy. She starts in this very pure, childlike way— the way a child tells you a secret—and it becomes totally terrifying. It's like someone has taken over her body, like a possession.

Dunois is very alarmed by it, and then he tries to brush it off. It did seem to work extremely well that way. Because I've seen actresses play St. Joan wonderfully well, I felt, "I can't imitate somebody doing this performance. I must find another way." And as I read all this research, I thought, "I don't understand why somebody hasn't played it like this before."

I think that the loneliness speech is very angry; that one I presented in a state of sheer, severe anger. She was incredibly young and there was a child quality about her, and I think that is a very petulant time. I'm not saying that's the way Shaw wrote it. I would imagine that Shaw, if he'd seen my St. Joan, would probably have been appalled. One just doesn't know, but I'm very aware that the way I approached and played St. Joan was not following his line, and he would have every right to say, "I didn't write that play, I wrote it in another vein." With the help of Bernard Miles, who was very excited about this idea and gave me free rein to follow it, I chose a completely different emotional approach.

In the trial scene, suddenly this child is thrown into the Inquisition. She has been in prison for a long, long time. The jump in Shaw's play appears to be but a few weeks. In fact, the jump is enormous; it's months and months and months, and Joan is completely changed in that time.

The last person you saw was somebody who was going to be very brave and believed that God would sort everything out for her. I think the fears of that type of person have to be very controlled. She may have moments of insecurity, but they're swept aside quickly. She does have moments of loneliness, but I don't think that they're lasting. The belief in God is—well, we've seen it through history—is all powerful, so I think the change is very dramatic. That's why the Inquisition scene is just remarkable. It's one of the greatest theatrical scenes that has ever been written. The tent scene and the Inquisition, I think, are the two finest scenes in the play, and can stand alone.

When Joan was on trial, historically speaking, she was dying. Had she not burned, she would have died anyway. She had been given the last rites; I'd have to look that up again to be sure, but I think it was three times. She hadn't just been in a prison, she'd been in holes. Those French dungeons are holes in the ground. They're horrendous. The line "to shut me from the light of the sky" says it—you are literally in a hole. In the production, they made a hole in the stage and dragged me up out of it.

Joan was in a pitiable state. She was filthy, disgusting. There was no cleanliness about her at all. I mean, she was living in shit. She was manacled, of course, by her legs and her arms, which would have burned and cut her skin. And she probably was infected with Christ-knows-what. She was very, very ill. And so that whole trial was played in a state of total, utter, deranged exhaustion near death. And terrified, utterly terrified. She signed the recantation out of absolute terror. To tear up her recantation, she had this extraordinary burst of energy, which people sometimes do just before they die.

I played Fantine in a recent film of Les Misérables, and Fantine has just such an extraordinary burst of energy on her deathbed. She's riddled with disease and is just about to die, and she's utterly incapable of doing anything because in physical terms she's like something out of a concentration camp, and she is bereft of all energy. She has this wonderful moment, which Victor Hugo describes, where from this state of almost death, she suddenly hurls herself to an upright position, with her arms across the four-poster bed like the crucified Christ. It is extraordinary when you read it. It's like the German woman who lifted a car off her son a number of years ago—this amazing strength that people have at moments when you don't believe that it's possible. Fantine throws herself up into this position and then falls back dead.

For Joan, that sort of image was very clear, of these extraordinary moments when people are physically incapable of moving, they're so exhausted. So during all of the Inquisition scene, she was in a state of severe shock, panic, illness, and physical degradation because of the totally inhumane existence that she'd had for months in prison. What I did was get up, stagger to the recantation, find her name at the bottom of it—her cross—and tear that off. I didn't actually tear the paper up. I tore the cross off.

Then the "Light your fires" speech was done in a completely unromantic, appalling, agonized way, in the state that she was in. All I was doing was just staggering around this group of people in a circle, like a rat. It was only at the last second, where she has that line—which, of course, I have forgotten—that I threw myself up into the air and landed backwards, flat on my back, on the stage. I was then just picked up and dragged off.

The epilogue I tried to separate completely and make into the most pure, the most simple reading that I was able to do at that time. I tried to make it like a tiny, tiny young child, just saying the lines in the extraordinarily pure way that children speak to you. It was nothing like the rest of the play in that sense. I remembered that when I was at Napsbury Hospital, doing research for The Ha Ha, there was one man who came up to me and said that he was really upset because he hadn't had breakfast that day because the trees had closed up. There was a wonderful tree-lined walk outside the hospital where he always went, and the trees would not let him pass that day.

What I remember is this incredible purity in the way he said it, and that I never questioned anything he said until afterwards, when I thought, "Hey, hang on, just a minute . . . ." That is the quality I wanted to get into the last speech, so that the audience didn't question anything. Whether I got it or not, I don't know, but that is what I tried.

The whole of my performance, and the whole of my research work, was entirely based around the medical, scientific aspect of Joan, really. That state and frame of mind. When I did it, I got letters from the most extraordinary people—two from Sybil Thorndike, who came to see it. I got a letter from these people, John and Isobel-Ann Butterfield, who had written this article in *History Today*.* They're husband and wife, and one of them is a historian and the other is a doctor. They said that they had waited years to see a medically accurate interpretation of Joan, and that mine was.

I didn't know about their article before I did Joan, but I just reread it so that I could remember their ideas, which I think are fascinating. They believe that the historical evidence points to Joan having suffered a form of tuberculosis called bovine tuberculosis. She caught it, as did countless people in the Middle Ages, from the cattle around her village. A special feature of the disease is a tubercular brain tumor, which could have accounted for her visions—though not their content, or her interpretation of them, or her courage and integrity, all of which the Butterfields praise as exceptional. But it may explain, for example, why the executioner couldn't burn her entrails, because calcium deposits or something like that in the abdomen are a result of bovine tuberculosis, and would be next to impossible to burn completely.

I think that probably the reason I got so ill while playing it is that I didn't have the technique, so what I did was emotionally throw myself into it every day, and ended up weighing only five stone. I was very young when I played the part. Technically incredibly inexperienced. I had wild ideas about interpretation. Everything was like a rough cutting of a stone—you could see what I was trying to get, but I would very much like to have another go, before I look too old in the theatre, to try and rework my idea of playing it with the experiences that I've had since.

I have the wonderful advantage of being such a mini-person and having a bone structure such that, if I'm on a stage, I can pass for an absurdly childish age. When I was a child, I remember seeing Ulanova dance Juliet. I thought she was a fourteen-year-old girl, and she was fifty-five years old. Fonteyn is another wonderful example.

I do believe that you have to get older actors. Judi Dench, who I think is one of the most wonderful actresses there is, I've seen on stage when I knew what age she was, and with no difficulty at all she

* "Joan of Arc: A Medical View," September 1958, Vol. 8, No. 9, pp. 628–634.

convinced me and everybody in the audience that she was a child. I think that it's far better that somebody like Judi is playing a younger role, with all her experience and what she has to offer. If Zeffirelli makes a film of *Romeo and Juliet* and wants to take a beautiful, extra-ordinary-looking Olivia Hussey to play Juliet, that's his prerogative. He's a great, great director, and the camera is a different medium. But when he did it on stage, he took Judi Dench. The only time you question actors' ages on stage is if they're bad. If they're wrong and they're bad. And then you question everything.

Laurie Kennedy in the 1976–77 Arena Stage production.

Laurie

Kennedy

Laurie Kennedy was born in Hollywood. She played Joan at the Williamstown Theatre Festival in 1973, and at Arena Stage in 1976.

I was terrified. I was a really young actress, and I was terrified that I wasn't going to be able to play Joan. My acting teacher said, "You don't think Joan's terrified? You don't think she's afraid?" That took away some of the onus for me.

I had worked at the Williamstown Theatre Festival several summers when Nikos Psacharopoulos offered me Joan one May in 1973. I started madly working with my acting teacher, Michael Howard. We worked on the early Joan in the De Baudricourt scene, and on some of her arias—the one to Charlie, "Yes, I am alone," and "Light your fires." I worked on those out of context. So I had a head start by the time I arrived at Williamstown, which is a theatre that is high-pressure quick because it has only two weeks of rehearsals. I knew pretty much what I wanted to do in terms of shaping the role from the early Joan learning and growing up in the world that she's thrown into. I worked on youth getting tougher and tougher; that was my arc.

Nikos directed *Saint Joan* at Williamstown. Martin Fried directed when I played her again at Washington's Arena Stage three years later. That was a much longer experience; at the Arena I think we had four weeks rehearsal and eight weeks of performances. Nikos went more with the spiritual Joan, as I recall, and brought out a softer edge. Marty Fried encouraged a very bold Joan, with a forthrightness that I think is very right for her. He brought out a harder edge in Joan which I rather liked.

For Williamstown, I didn't have time to get involved with the history of Joan. The second time that I played her I did quite a lot of research, and I remember reading books about the real Joan while I was rehearsing. By that time, I was more or less familiar with the play and with different things that I wanted to do with it.

Before Williamstown, I went up to the cathedral of St. John the Divine and just walked around. The cathedral scene was always my favorite in the play. I loved it, and it gave me great nourishment, so I wanted everything in it to be special. I wore little sandals to St. John the Divine, took them off and just padded around. We had wooden floors on stage, but I always remembered the coldness and the sound of walking around on stone.

I did something very weird the first time. I used to work a lot with music as a way of feeding me. There was a Bach cantata that I used for *Pullman Car Hiawatha*, a Thornton Wilder piece. I would rehearse to Bach's music. For *Saint Joan* I used rousing black gospel music. This sounds crazy, but I found it very thrilling and uplifting. It's almost transcendent. You get out of yourself.

When I was a teenager I was fascinated with Southern blues, and my brother and I used to go to the Apollo Theatre in Harlem a lot. We'd watch the Four Nightingales and the Gospel G-Clefs. I still have some of the records. They gave me that sort of extratemporal feeling that Joan sometimes goes into, particularly with the voices, a feeling of not being of this plane. That's what the songs are about.

The first scene was mainly head research. I understood what it was to be a country lass. I'd grown up in the country and run around in bare feet all my life. We lived in Westport, Connecticut, and I went to school in New Hope, Pennsylvania, which has a lot of farms.

My parents also had a home in Nova Scotia, where they had horses, sheep, oxen and other animals, and many of my relatives in Ohio had farms. I'd always been exposed to country life. I wasn't worried about the country Joan because there's a lot of that in me already.

I was a tomboy when I was a kid. There's something very freeing about being one of the guys. I had an older brother and I always wanted to be a part of what he was doing rather than what my peers were doing. When I was growing up in Connecticut and California, I always would try and outdo my brothers' friends, whether we were climbing poles or climbing mountains, and I sometimes did.

The first time I did Joan I made rather an iconoclastic choice for the end of the De Baudricourt scene. I used to play horsey all the time at my girlfriend's house, pretending that I was a horse out in the field. When De Baudricourt told me that I could have a horse and armor and soldiers, I took a huge run around the stage like I was a horse.

Most of the actresses that I've seen in the role have not solved the early Joan. That's a difficult problem. I was fine in the early part because I made silly, youthful choices, particularly the first time that I did it. Things like galloping around the stage, which I'm not sure anybody would really like. I didn't do that the second time. I didn't have the courage. I had gotten a little more cautious of making such crazy choices.

The first two scenes I always refer to as the early Joan. I allowed myself to have moments of fear. In the very first scene, when she comes in and is quite impudent with De Baudricourt, I always took a moment where I feared that he wasn't going to give me what I wanted, that it wasn't going to happen the way my voices had told me and the way I wanted it to happen. It's a combination of total self-assuredness that what she's doing is right and a soupçon of inner doubt: "It will happen this way . . . will it?" I always tried to keep both going. There's a moment in each scene—will she get the horse and armor and soldiers? Will she get the Dauphin to stand by her against his courtiers?

She still has a lot of naiveté when she goes to court. The Dauphin is almost like a playfriend: "Thou't not a king yet, lad." But at the same time the court is working on her, with its strange dresses and strange environment, and Bluebeard and all kinds of things she's never seen before. It has to influence her on some level.

The relationship with the Archbishop and how it changes is fascinating. At first the Archbishop is blushing because she's down on her knees to him in total awe, but by the cathedral scene he's sick and tired of her impudence about what God wants. He's a little hurt, you know, that she thinks she rather than he is the pipeline to God. He is upset by her boldness and her lack of traditional respect. She's not trying to be rude to him, but she gets more confident around these people as things happen.

Each scene has a little epiphany. The first step is De Baudricourt, and she accomplishes her mission there and it almost surprises her. The next steps are getting Charlie to agree to be crowned in Rheims, then getting the wind to blow at Orleans.

She's a different Joan by the time she comes to Dunois—a little more self-assured and cocky. She is what I call the middle Joan. She's been with the soldiers for a period of time, she knows the life, and she comes on in a blazing rage: "What the hell are you doing on this side of the river? Get your act together and get over to the other side. Stop wasting time." She realizes that her reasons are common sense, and she's bar none the most commonsensical person in the world. Then the wind blows, and that's another demonstration that she's on the right path—another little epiphany. The scene with Dunois is wonderful.

Then that magnificent tent scene which she's not involved with at all, but oh, what a wonderful scene that is. Followed by the cathedral scene, where she finally accomplishes crowning Charlie. By this time he has changed and has a different relationship with Joan. By this time she has more or less antagonized everybody in the court, in the army and in the Church.

I certainly empathized with the other characters' caution towards her. Charlie loves money, and now that he's king he doesn't want to drain the realm's coffers on another war. He wants to buy some nice ermine robes for himself and his wife. He wants to stop there. Dunois is very aware of the dangers of war, and he's not prepared for either himself or his men to die in another battle. The Archbishop is, I think, just plain old hurt that this young upstart is overruling his authority.

I always felt that Joan was a very exceptional young girl. I don't think that she had many friends. I think that she was always strange and that her religion became her friend. You see some children having imaginary playmates; she just talked to her voices as she would playmates. The voices initially are driving her to accomplish things. Then they become a source of comfort to her as everybody deserts her.

Anything in the play that makes you wonder "How could she possibly know this?" I felt was something that the voices told her. I just went into an extratemporal state. The Archbishop says "You're in love with religion," and she really is. I think she does carry on conversations with Catherine, with God and everybody. That wonderful cathedral scene where the bells start and she talks about her voices—her voices are usually offstage, she seldom hears them onstage—there was just a button that I was able to push whenever I got to those sections. Some of it was the gospel music. The only thing that I can describe is the result that it had on me. It was like a tingling all over my body.

In the sections where the voices come into play, they're not always quiet and gentle. There is what I would call a pink and baby-blue spirituality. I was going towards a red-hot spirituality with the gospel choice. I didn't suddenly clap and yell "I've found the Lord!"; I don't want to suggest that. It's just a one-mindedness that she has, an obsessiveness.

I am somewhat religious, and I tend to play a lot of parts where characters have an inner calling that transcends this plane. Major Barbara and Hilde Wangel in *The Master Builder* have an extra sense of something they've got to do, and maybe because of my religion or spirituality I can understand that. A button is pushed—I can't describe it as anything other than that.

"Yes, I am alone" is an epiphany speech. In every scene there's a realization for Joan which helps her to move on to the next scene, and when everybody has turned their back on her in the cathedral scene, I think she starts in real despair, "Yes I am alone on earth." She moves into realizing that God is alone too, and that's okay, and France is alone. She gathers momentum and strength through the course of realizing these things as she speaks. So it becomes a speech almost to herself, like someone who has to go out and box the tenth round and has a trainer saying, "Come on, you've got to duck here and you've got to punch there." She's giving herself that kind of advice. It's through these realizations that she comes to "I will dare and dare and dare until I die." I think that's the height of her quest, that aria. That is probably the height of her self-confidence, her belief in herself, her belief in the voices, her belief that she's got a mission in this life and that she's going to go off and accomplish the rest.

Getting captured and being put in prison was a big setback. Shaw doesn't have much about Joan's life in prison, but I got clues from the research that I did. There probably were hundreds of men, guards who were trying to test her—maybe even sexually. I think that she received a lot of abuse during that period of time, and she certainly wasn't fed well. So there's a weakened Joan by the time you meet her in the trial. It's a different Joan from what we've seen up until that time, and it was fascinating to work on how you portray that weakened state. You would say she's physically ill, and through that she recants and double recants and ends up with "Light your fires," which is, even in her weakened physical state, probably the strongest she's ever been.

In the trial scene Joan certainly has fears. Even Jesus Christ said, "Why hast Thou forsaken me?" There's self-doubt by that time as well as fear. Fear that everything she's believed in may not be really so. There's an element of trying to hold on to her faith. The wonderful thing about that scene is that she does have a moment where she recaptures it and is able to tear up the recantation that she was worn down enough to sign.

You are very tired when you get to the trial. The cathedral scene really knocks it out of you because so much happens emotionally and intellectually. She never stops trying in that scene, so by the time you get to the trial you are exhausted. And you use it—you don't have the same scintillating pep that you've demonstrated in the earlier Joan. She's more listless and not physically well. They keep hammering at her, and she's weary of the whole process. She's at rock bottom when she enters, but she gets to sub-rock bottom by the time she recants.

In "Light your fires" another change occurs. I didn't solve this speech the first time that I played Joan. It's a split-second epiphany, even quicker than the four pages between signing and tearing up the recantation, like a sudden shock of electricity. It's such a joyful speech. In rehearsal I often used almost to dance tearing up the recantation. I felt that relief of "Phew, I was right!" In a strange way this aria has a movement from talking to them to just getting into real joy and exaltation.

I never concerned myself with the reality of being burned. Perhaps that was wrong, but she's on stage for a good page after she finishes "Light your fires," and after her doubts, the relief of having her faith returned courses through her veins. She's not about to let it go for a second. The fire is offstage. I think she had a fear, as Christ did, of suffering. But I think that she is so relieved to have refound herself, or refound what it is that she's based her whole life on, that she's never going to let it go.

There is a power that people can have when they concentrate on something other than pain. I get the feeling that her literal burning she was able to transcend. There's no description of her screaming and writhing in pain. She seems very calm, telling the person who holds the cross for her to get away or he'll be burned. There's something almost at peace with her by that time. She knew anyway that she was going to die—there's that reverberating line, "I shall last only a year from the beginning."

I think the epilogue is Shaw's awareness of the ironies of what Jesus had, or Joan, or a lot of the saints. If the Second Coming happened, what would we do? Would we do the same thing that they did to Christ and Joan? I didn't play the epilogue ironically. That's for the audience to question itself about— "Would I accept Joan if she came into my life and told me what to do?" I just very simply asked God when the world would be ready for his saints. She still has the capacity to be hurt. They don't want her to come back, and I dare say the same thing would happen if Jesus returned. People would say, "Are you out of your mind? I'm not going to give up my husband and go off with you and be a fisher of men. I can't think of anything that I'd less rather do."

I think Joan is terrific because she isn't so saintly. I get a little nervous sometimes around stories about Jesus. There's no bullshit about Joan. There's such a practicality, even in her youth and her illiteracy. I really was very fond of her. I liked her boldness and her presumptuousness and her sassiness. I just thought she was terrific. It's a marvelous part to play. Joan gives you back so much. If anybody would give her to me today I'd still play it. I'd love to do it again before I say goodbye to theatre.

Saint Joan has more heart than any other Shaw play. It's much more of an emotional play than *Heartbreak House* or even *Major Barbara*. I think that anybody who plays Joan may have a weird experience. A part of Joan is living in you in a strange way. Something of the real Joan reverberates through the theatre. I'm sure it reverberates whenever there's a production. She's quite a special person.

Lynn Redgrave

The daughter of Michael Redgrave and Rachel Kempson, Lynn Redgrave was born in London. During the 1977–78 season, she played Joan at the Goodman Theatre in Chicago and at Circle in the Square in New York.

I look on my acting as pre-Joan and post-Joan, because what I had to find to play St. Joan changed the sort of actor that I am, and changed my way of working entirely. I found that my old way of working wouldn't do, and I would never have known unless I had played Joan and gone as far into it as I did.

It was a most extraordinary play to work on because its effect on me—and, I'm sure, on all people who play Joan— became deeper and deeper and more difficult to shake off. I think one has to reach a state whereby the reality is so gigantic that it takes you over. Then I think you can play the play. It's such a peculiar thing to make oneself believe truly in seeing the saints and in hearing their voices that when you reach the point that they indeed become real for you, they do some very odd things to you.

It took me months to reach that state. In fact, had we stopped at the end of the Chicago run, I would never have discovered it. During the New York run, I had to find a way of being Joan freshly and totally each night at a level I had never had to explore before, because no other part had made those demands upon me. Early on in my career, I suppose I became fairly adept technically, although I am a very intuitive actress. I would sometimes find that I could go on playing something again and again and it would appear to be just fine. But you can't do that with Joan. You've really got to put yourself through something quite peculiar, I think, in order to play the final half successfully.

When I began, I wanted to visualize very clearly what the voices looked like. Mine had faces that I would recognize anywhere I saw them.

Somebody had told me something which I found very helpful. This person had seen Katharine Cornell playing St. Joan and had always remembered a moment that stood out. In the cathedral scene, at the point where the Dauphin and everyone want to stop, Katharine Cornell looked up, and it was as if she suddenly saw the faces of her saints in the rafters of the cathedral, and from then on said, "Okay. Up yours. I'm doing it my way." It seemed like such a marvelously theatrical thing to do, and I thought it would be great. I had already figured out what my saints looked like and when Joan saw them—when the wind changed, for example, when I signed the recantation, and when I tore it up. It seemed such a good idea also to have them in the rafters of the cathedral.

So that was fine, and they always did the same thing—after all, they were my voices. I imagined them, I put them there, so they reacted the same way every performance. Another place where they would be was when I did indeed decide I was going to burn, and they gave me courage to go through it. By the way, I played the decision to be burned and the being taken off to the fire not with saintly bravery, but with absolute sweating terror. I used to see the saints and I stayed looking at them and I just screamed all the way to the stake.

Then a very interesting thing occurred. This may sound mumbo-jumbo, but I assure you I'm a terribly practical actress, terribly down-to-earth. I get on with it. But something thoroughly peculiar happened to me. A few weeks into the New York run, there was one performance where I really couldn't play it. It was absolutely awful; everything sort of went. I believed in nothing, I saw nothing, I didn't believe myself, I knew the audience couldn't possibly believe me. That was when I thought, "I have to get much deeper into this."

I found that to go on in the trial scene, I had to do much more than put on the outfit and fix my hair so that it looked like I had sores, and walk up to my entrance place where the two guys who played the soldiers put my chains on, and not talk and close my eyes. I found that I had to sort of make myself go back to being four. It was a long and peculiar journey, but if I could make myself four years old when I walked out on stage, it was all right. After that awful performance where nothing worked, I began to discover that I had to take some new impetus each night. It always had to be something slightly different that I would have to think about and believe in to walk on properly.

When I finally began to find that I could walk out there entirely Joan, entirely having been through those months and months and months of prison and filth and chains, one night a very peculiar thing happened. When I signed the paper and recanted, I looked up. The faces were there, and they turned into gargoyles with great big jaws, and they closed them.

From then on, they became totally real, and they always did something different, and they were often in different places, and within the play I never played the moments the same twice. Not moments that ever affected somebody else and depended on interplay, but things like the loneliness speech and tearing up the paper and "Light your fires." From then on I knew that I could play the part eight times a week. I never had another night where I could not play her, and I could have played her for a great length of time.

Believing in the voices so that they had a life of their own—I've never had that experience before or since, I've never been in another play that is open to such a thing happening. The way it made me change as an actor, I think, was that it put me in touch with sides of myself that I had no idea I could drum up, and it made me braver. I had absolutely no idea that I had within me the sort of anger, the depth of the vulnerability, the depth of emotion that came out.

It's helped me enormously in almost every part I've played since. It doesn't matter what the range of the part is, what matters is that I no longer think, "I don't know if I can do that, or if I can find that." I simply set about it, and find it far more accessible. I am totally brave about it now. I don't think "Will this look silly?" and I don't try too hard.

I've far better concentration. It's helped me a great deal on film when there are eight thousand people around you and they suddenly say, "The sun's out, the cattle are running the right direction, now you play the great suicide scene—go!" It's made me able to find whatever it is I have to find and to let it loose at my decision, whether I'm inspired or uninspired. I think before Joan I used to rely a lot on supposed inspiration. It's not enough. You have to make it happen.

St. Joan was sort of a childhood heroine. I kind of knew the Shaw play growing up because I saw my mother play it for a week in a tiny theatre called the "Q" in London. I think St. Joan was a heroine to me—as she is to a lot of young people—because the stand she made was so gigantic, and also because we're lucky to know so much about her. She was so well documented, far better documented than any other person of that period. I guess I did have an admiration of her—one of those few people in history one's heard of as a young child.

As I decided that I wanted to be an actress, I thought—like a lot of young actresses— "I'd like to play St. Joan." One doesn't realize when one's that young how difficult the part is—it just seems amazing.

There are a lot of other great roles, but none that I have that burning desire to play that I had with Joan. I sort of inched up to her and then made it happen. First, I played a lady-in-waiting in Joan Plowright's *Saint Joan* when it got to the National. She was spectacular. Her trial scene was quite wonderful, and through all of it one totally believed in the mixture of her being a peasant and being as strong as she needed to be. She had a real sweetness about her, and yet toughness.

Then I played Joan of Arc in Jules Feiffer's comedy *Knock Knock* on Broadway about a year before I did the Shaw play. I loved *Knock Knock*. It was great fun to do, especially that wonderful final speech when she's levitating up. I played her in a long platinum blonde pageboy

Lynn Redgrave in the Goodman Theatre production.

wig. And a real metal breastplate which I kept bumping into things with. I got that idea from my father.

He told me a wonderful story: years ago, when he was at the Old Vic, they asked him to attend the general audition for new members of the company. He told me that there was this terrible noise offstage, this clunk-clunk-clunk—and up came this young woman who had gone out and rented an entire suit of real armor to do a speech from *Saint Joan*. It weighed tons. Normally on stage you wear fiberglass, which is light. He said she was creaking around the stage because she could barely walk. I remembered that image, and I said to Jose Quintero, who directed *Knock Knock*, "Do you think I can have a real metal breastplate? It's going to be heavy and it's going to be tough for me to get up and down the cabin stairs in, and when anybody touches or bumps into it you'll know it's metal."

So I had one. In fact, I remember being really pissed off at Walter Kerr because he misunderstood what I did on my first entrance. I came on with a spear about twenty-five feet long, and real metal armor, and I had to get down the stairs of this terrible cottage, and the spear caught several times—purposely. He said I had a tough time, but he didn't realize that it was deliberate.

I made her all the things that the real Joan wasn't—terribly innocent, terribly good, terribly saintly, and terribly eager and determined to change everything. It was wonderful fun. I thought, "Well, I guess I'm getting a bit of St. Joan. It's not quite what I had in mind, but if I never get to play Shaw's I'll have done this." Then I decided to make *Saint Joan* happen because I was absolutely determined to play it.

I knew that, like Juliet, she was a part that you cannot play at the correct age. There's no way that you can successfully play Joan or Juliet at seventeen or fourteen—absolutely no way you can have the technique, the stamina or the experience to play those parts successfully then. The qualities that you would bring to them at that age are actually not the most overriding qualities that you need. I knew Joan was something I needed to get some experience to play, and then I reached the point where I realized that to suspend disbelief, I'd better get a move on. I had been asked a couple of times before and I hadn't been able to fit it in, and suddenly I felt time ticking by.

My husband, John Clark, and I very much wanted to do it together because we'd lived through my leading up to playing it, and we understand each other so well. We'd worked together a great many times before, and I didn't honestly trust anybody else to help me through it as my director. So we said, "We're going to do it."

A lovely friend, William Woodman, who was then planning his final season at the Goodman Theatre in Chicago, had said to us many times, "Any time you want to come and do something at the Goodman, let me know." We asked him, "Could you mount *Saint Joan?*" It really has to be done at a subsidized theatre, because it's such a gigantic cast. It's not a commercial proposition. He said, "It's absolutely the sort of play that we like to do, and yes, we could mount it and we'd like it as our opening play of my last season." We were thrilled to bits.

Then, because we wanted it to have a longer life—it's not a part that you can just polish off in eight weeks—I went hustling it. It's the only time I've ever done that, because usually I'm the sort of person who gets excited *after* I'm offered a good part. I very seldom go after things, it's not my nature. We explored the possibility of the BAM season in Brooklyn , of the Vivian Beaumont at Lincoln Center, and then we explored the Circle in the Square on Broadway. I went in and talked to the Circle's producers, Ted Mann and Paul Libin, and thank goodness persuaded them that they would like to do it after the Chicago run.

This is when I went berserk. Once I knew that I was going to do it, I started looking at the play again and realized what I'd taken on. I'm not sure that you can ever come to the end of it. I certainly didn't.

I began reading everything that I could lay my hands on. I reread other plays about her just to see if they had any bearing on Shaw's play,which they don't, mostly. I read Mark Twain's book about Joan, which is just fun because it's so ludicrously romantic, as is the Schiller play. Through historical research, I discovered that Shaw probably wrote the closest to the historically accurate Joan of anybody who wrote fiction about her. I happen to have, thanks to my mother, a transcript of the trial in English. I read that at great length.

The book that I found absolutely inspiring is called *Joan of Arc* by Edward Lucie-Smith. It is a very well-documented, brilliant book which gave me a handle on the part. Edward Lucie-Smith researched all the receipts of money she spent on men's clothes. She wore only the finest, only the very best velvets. She had her hands covered in rings. She wasn't a humble person walking about in leather in that court. She dressed as well as, or better than, the Dauphin. That seemed to fit in terribly well with the sort of person who could walk away at the end of the cathedral scene saying what she does. It allowed dramatically for her downfall, and for the next sight of her in the courtroom to be as devastating as I think it ought to be. That probably was the thing that got me the most. In fact, in the New York production I wore this fabulously rich costume in the cathedral. My coronation clothes were almost as good as the Dauphin's.

What actually went on in prison is also very well documented—how long she was kept chained and what it was like. When I came out for the trial, I tried to look as if I had not been out of those clothes for months. My hair was falling out, I had sores on my head, and bleeding wrists. The concept of Lucie-Smith's of her pride and arrogance goes so well with what Shaw wrote, and allows for the dramatic turnaround when she is weak enough to sign the recantation.

My children used to like to come in for the burning—they rather enjoyed that. They did terrible imitations of me in the trial scene because I got really gross. They still do them, and they're very funny because I reduced myself to this appalling state. I used to sort of dribble a lot, and when they want to do it they say, "Here's Mum"— dribble dribble— "doing St. Joan"—dribble dribble. It's absolutely awful.

They weren't very happy around the time I did St. Joan because they looked on that as a time of my being a rotten mother. You just can't get up in the morning and not gear your entire day to taking your nap in time to play Joan. That was terribly tedious for them. I remember that with my own father, when he was doing some terrific dramatic thing he just sort of completely hid away. I didn't hide away; I used to get up and send them off to school and go back to bed, but by the time they got back from school it was time for my nap and I used to hear, "Shhh. Mum's sleeping."

I found the whole play was one that I both looked forward to and dreaded. I found that I had to take it a bit at a time and not even try to think about the enormity of the job at hand each night, because then

I'm not sure you would do it eight times a week. Not the way we did it anyway; we made a very, very dark and emotional attack on it.

I'd start out, before the first scene, trying to keep myself up and bright and optimistic that I could win people over, and as innocent as possible of the pitfalls ahead. I'd go around and see everybody in the company, and we'd chat and laugh and try to set the tone of the evening so that we weren't playing the end of the play at the beginning. Of course there are lots of funny things in Joan anyway. I think the more one can bring those out, the better the drama of it works.

The audience helped, sometimes unwittingly. Since Circle in the Square is an arena stage, you can see the audience. I remember one day in the cathedral scene, moving down and delivering my final speech, I looked around and there was this young woman in the front row. She was leaning forward and looked as though she was having a great time, and the actor in me went, "Oh, good, it's really working." Then I made a turn, and almost exactly across that space was another woman asleep. It really brought me up. I thought, "Oh. Well, doing well with some, but not so well with others."

The most moving day was when we had a group of blind people in who began shaking and sobbing uncontrollably during the trial scene. It had got to them so much. It happened to be a very good day. I remember thinking afterwards, "Yes, we definitely gave a good one." We met them, and the extraordinary thing was that they knew the staging—they said, "That bit when you got up and moved to the paper"—they knew it all. Of course it's such a strong play verbally.

The company stayed pretty disciplined, but I remember once in Chicago I was sitting offstage in my chains, and the Inquisitor was about to do that long, long speech about heresy. On this particular night, he went blank and said, "Heresy . . . . . heresy, gentlemen, is the name of the game," and sat down. Well, by the time I got onstage there were all these monks' hoods shaking with laughter. "Heresy is the name of the game."

One of the great reasons we got along so well as a company is John's influence. John knows how I work. He knows when I'm on to something; he knows when I'm going down a blind alley and he can save us some time. Most important, he has never said to me anything that I couldn't use, or that in my opinion was not correct. We may have an argument about something—in fact we often do— because he knows me so well. But he's good; I mean, he can come and see me in something and anything he has to say is absolutely bloody right. It won't be a destructive thing; it will be something you can do something about.

He goes straight to the heart of things, and he cast *Saint Joan* brilliantly. Dunois, for example, was not cast at all the way he normally is, which is sort of leading man/juve. John cast Joe Bova, and he was fabulous. When the lights went up on that hill and Joe was sitting waiting for the bloody wind, he'd been in battle for years and years. He made it so real, and he was so wonderful to act with. There was a real sense of comradeship.

I've seen Dunois played gorgeous and vain, and I never thought it worked. I thought it was an impossible part until Joe played it. When he rejected me in the cathedral scene, the audience was really moved. I've always felt that in the scene it would be fine if the audience were thinking, "You idiot woman! Don't go, don't do it— listen to them," so that it doesn't look like a bunch of baddies turning off this lovely saint. They're making a lot of sense. When Joe as Dunois turned his back on me, it almost broke me, because he was the most sensible person.

John also staged the play brilliantly. It all came out of the text and the words and trusting the actors. He makes the sort of atmosphere where actors feel very brave. He has a terrific thing he does with every play if he's got a long-enough rehearsal period. I think it is a Lee Strasberg exercise; John studied with him awhile. It was fabulous for *Saint Joan*. It's very good for a big company where some actors have small parts and can very easily feel left out. It's called the Hot Seat. You do it after you've been rehearsing awhile, say two-and-a-half to three weeks, because you've got to know your characters very well.

What happens is that, in turn, every single actor sits in a chair in the middle of the room, in character. The other people do not have to be in character, and there is no question they can't ask you. They could ask what you eat for breakfast, how well you know so and so, what the house you live in is like. It could be something terribly personal; it could be something very factual. They asked me a lot about my horse.

It makes you know exactly where you haven't done your homework. You must speak in character. You are the character, but you don't have Shaw's words. They can ask you anything, and you must answer. What it does first of all is make you examine how deeply you have gone into your character. Secondly, it opens up for the other performers lots of things that they may not have known which may help them in relating to you.

If you're playing a smaller part, suddenly the part becomes very real to everyone. For example, a page in the Dauphin's court had four lines and played a monk. A lovely actor named Pendleton Brown. We all asked Pendleton Brown about his private life, and we discovered a whole wonderful story. I know that the audience may not get all that, but when he walked on, if you were a character in the court who's supposed to know him, you never looked at him as just the page again. He was a real person who actually had the hots for the Duchess but who was sleeping with the chambermaid. You might choose to ignore him when he walked on with you, but you'll never be unspecific in your attitude towards him or any other person in the play. I tell you, the difference it makes to the group scenes—little things you suddenly notice which are marvelous—is so good.

I don't remember many specifics about what I was asked. I wish I could. I very rarely, when I'm working, use the technique of substituting something else. I don't find it valid. I'm not criticizing anybody who does. To reach the point of entering the trial in the correct state of mind, somebody might well take a personal experience. But I'm not sure then how much one walks out as Joan and how much as oneself. I think perhaps it comes down to basic differences of actors. When I say I'm a character actor, I like to turn into somebody who is not me. I think that's why I became an actor. Obviously my experience is useful. The more experience I have, the more I can understand or sympathize. But if I haven't experienced something, that doesn't mean I can't play it.

With almost any part—and I think most actors find this—probably the day after it ends you're still a little bit in that world, but usually, even when you've loved something, there's a sense of relief. Sometimes there's a sense of disappointment if it didn't work out quite as well as you hoped. Usually when you end it you're already thinking, "What's next?"

When *Saint Joan* ended I'd been playing it, counting from first rehearsal in Chicago to the end of the run in New York, for about six months. It was the first and only time in my life when I didn't want to work afterwards. I felt completely washed out. I was terribly emotional about it ending, as were all the members of the company. We all loved it so, because it grew and grew, and in the final months we felt it reach something we didn't think it would reach. We were very sentimental about it and terribly sad to see it go. I personally went into quite a decline for about three months. It's never happened to me before; it may never happen again.

I was terribly relieved not to wake up to the role every day, and also felt as if I'd lost something. I think I became so entrenched in it that it wasn't possible just to let it drop. It's very rare, however deeply or thoroughly you work on a role, that it needs to alter you to that extent. There aren't very many parts like that.

Eileen
Atkins

Born in London, Eileen Atkins played Joan with the Prospect Theatre Company,
at the Old Vic and on tour, between 1977 and 1979.

I was rather keen on heroines altogether. I remember I had a book about Florence Nightingale, Grace Darling and St. Joan. But I was terribly put off by productions I'd seen of *Saint Joan*. I thought she was a very, very boring woman. Just goody-goody and pie-in-the-sky. Nothing to do with anything I might believe in myself. I did play, when I was very young, Shakespeare's Joan La Pucelle. I did it out of perversity, because she is such a bitch that I was really pleased to be doing another kind of Joan, screaming as she's taken to the stake. I thoroughly enjoyed that, and that was all—I'd given my St. Joan.

I was offered Shaw's play five, if not seven times. One of the offers came when I was about thirty-five, from the Oxford Festival, and I turned it down flat, saying I was now far too old, really, what were they thinking? And then, when I was thirty-nine, I literally trapped myself into doing it.

It was when they thought the Old Vic was going to be lost forever, and a friend of mine, Toby Robertson, was running it as part of the Prospect Theatre Company's season. I was very fond of Toby, who said, "I'm really in a state. I need a play to open the season. Will you do a play for me?" I said, "All right. I trust you, Toby." The next thing, he told me, "We've settled on *Saint Joan*," and I nearly died. I said, "Toby, I've turned that down five, six, seven times. And I hate it. And now I really am too old." And he said, "Oh, rubbish. Absolute rubbish." And he'd done it by then, so I couldn't really do anything about it. It was a *fait accompli*.

I said I would do it only if they cut the line in the first scene, "How old are you, Maid?" "Seventeen, or maybe nineteen, sir." It was a horribly young age. And I said, "I am not standing on stage"—I remember sitting in the audience when a certain actress said that and I died of shame for her. And he said, "All right, we'll cut that."

Then he proceeded to tell me he wasn't directing himself. He'd got a director in who didn't want to direct me, because most of the young, new directors hate directing anybody who is very experienced. He wanted to bring in one of his young girls from up North. So, *he* didn't want to do it with me, I didn't want to do it with him, and I didn't want to play it anyway. And as soon as we started rehearsing we were crazy about it, and each other, and everything. In fact, once I started working on it, I couldn't believe I'd ever not liked it.

We really shoved it on, and the production was awful the first time we did it. John Dove, the director, wasn't quite onto it, and the sets weren't right, and we had a terrible supporting cast except for Cauchon and Warwick. And, my God, we toured one-night stands all over Europe for two weeks because you had to do all that for the Prospect to get the money. Then we toured England, but it was still a mess.

All the same, it was a success, parts of it, and Toby said, "Please come back again next year," because I just opened the season, did three weeks, and that was it. So I said "Yes." Then John Dove said he didn't want to do it. I rang him up and just gave him hell. I said, "How many times are you going to get this opportunity in your life to have messed up something and then get the chance to do it again? How *dare* you not do it again!" I sort of browbeat him into doing it.

Absolutely like Joan. You do get like the parts you're playing, there's no doubt. It was a lot better; I was better the second time round.

I only ever go from the script. I'm not somebody who has an idea about a part separately and then fits it on. I just take the script and do it and think, in this case, "Now what is Shaw trying to say through her?"

One thing that was crucial to my interpretation was a great friend who's a very weird man. Well, I'm saying he's weird—he's an excellent clairvoyant. Now, he's extremely fat; very unprepossessing to look at. He comes from the north of England, and he's very practical. He will say to me, "I've put the potatoes on to boil, and you come up over the steam as Charlotte Bronte. It will come into your aura; you'll be offered Charlotte Bronte." And I'll say, "No, Kenny. Really, if I were offered any of those Bronte sisters, it would be Emily and not—." "Ah-ah! I'm telling you. That's what it is."

He gets very angry if you don't believe him. And he's nearly always right. I mean, he can give you the news. He is clairvoyant. He does believe in spirits, but it is immensely practical. And one of the key things, I thought, for Joan when she speaks to God, is that to her God is a very present person. He's absolutely real. Therefore, she doesn't have to go into another voice, or suddenly go all pie-in-the-sky. He's there. He's someone who talks to her and helps her.

But Joan also experiences an ecstasy which, of course, Kenny doesn't have. One knows ecstasy all too rarely, but I certainly think I've known it, so therefore I can use the two things, the practical and the ecstatic.

The beginning of the cathedral scene, when Joan talks about her bells, I found difficult for a long time. Because she's very practical then, and you don't really see the ecstatic side of her. She's really got to start going, because Dunois has got to say, as he enters the door, "Now stop it. I'm with you when you're practical, but when you start doing all this, I don't believe it."

She has got to do those bells— "Dear-child-of-God/Be-brave-go-on." And at the end of that speech, when she's done all of them— "But it is at the hour, when the great bell goes after 'God-will-save-France,' it is then that St. Margaret and St. Catherine, and sometimes even the blessed Michael will say things that I cannot tell beforehand"—there's a broken line, "Then, oh then—." Well, if you're saying "Then, oh then," you know you're way beyond being practical.

You know from the pure text that it's comic if you make "Then, oh then" practical. So you know that she's got to be gone by then. Now, how does one do that? I don't know. I can't tell you. You see, this terrible thing about actresses is that you have enormous imaginations. In fact, I was taken to the doctor by my mother when I was three because I couldn't sleep. I've had insomnia all my life. Nowadays I'd be sent to a psychiatrist, I suppose. But the doctor just said to my mother, "This child has an abnormal imagination, and there's nothing I can do about it. She's going to lie awake at night."

It's not difficult for me to imagine a religious ecstasy on "Then, oh then." Maybe you call upon your own earthly loves to help you through it. Passions that you have had, and reminding yourself of when your body didn't matter—the whole of you is infused, is caught up, you can only think, dream, talk of one thing, one person, one whatever-it-is. And certainly I've had plenty of examples of that. Well, not plenty. But two or three examples of that in my own life.

But it isn't as clear as that. If you imagine that you are someone who is utterly transported at the thought of an angel talking to you— I think that if an angel talked to me, I would be totally transported. I can conjure that; it may not be Joan's ecstasy, but it's an ecstasy that will do. We don't know what hers was, so it's the nearest I can come to it, and if that conveys itself to an audience, then that's fine.

But you do feel strange. I'd always remember on that line, "It's then that St. Catherine"—I can remember almost feeling like I was lifting off. I was discussing it with Albert Finney the other day. Somebody as prosaic as that. You think, "Ah, yes, we all feel the same way," and you feel so relieved. It sounds so camp, and actors, I think, are very nervous about talking about it.

There are some parts—and I suppose if you were totally a nonbeliever this couldn't happen—where you're standing on stage, and you feel you are the vessel through which this person is talking. You have become—as far as you can—somebody else. You feel as if— well, this is how I feel, Albert gave me another version which was the same thing—I feel that the back of my head is opening up. There is an energy, a god, whatever you like to call it, a great energy coming through the back of my head, and it is for getting it across to the

Eileen Atkins in the Prospect Theatre Company production.

audience, for making them see some raw, some impossible thing. It's like saying, "Yes, I'm the vessel; it's coming from somewhere back there, and I have to get it to you, and I will be filled with it so you will get it." And, on lines like "Then, oh then," it's wonderful if you can get it.

Then the desolation of when you say, "Yes, I am alone on earth." She's thinking her way through that, and it's just the most wonderful speech. It is, I think, to know utter desolation and look it in the face, and then to find God. Before, when I'd heard of Saint Joan, the only speech anybody ever talked about was the trial speech. I couldn't believe the loneliness speech. It is just wonderful.

It's very much like Celia Coplestone's "awareness of solitude" in The Cocktail Party. It's the same thing. It's like getting rid of everything. I'm afraid I'm probably, as a person, much more like Lavinia. You know, when Eliot's Sir Henry Harcourt-Reilly says, "Well, there's a way of life. You can agree to read the paper and chat. It's a very nice life. Quite lucky if you get that. But, if you are more than that . . . ." I can imagine more than that, but I'm not living a life more than that.

I love playing things like The Cocktail Party and Saint Joan. I love playing anything that says something which is to me so uplifting. It seems to me, whether you believe or not, you make people feel a sort of hope. Even nonbelievers come out of Saint Joan feeling "Ye-e-s."

Alec Guinness came to see Joan, and was very nice indeed about my performance, but he said, "Oh, I wish you would say 'How long, oh Lord, how long' at the end without having that accent on it." I said, "Well, you can't suddenly drop your accent." I think some people didn't like me being so prosaic about it. But I think she would have been—she isn't starry. She is very depressed that they've all gone off there, and I think "O God, that madest this beautiful earth, when will it be ready to receive thy saints?" is a genuine question. I don't think it's in the air. I think it's "How much longer have we got to bear people being such idiots and ruining what He's given us?" It is a direct question. Well, not totally direct; it's comic if it's totally direct.

You tread a very fine line when you try and make her prosaic. The beginning of the play, obviously, should be very funny, and I considered it a disaster if we didn't get a lot of laughs in the first scene. But I think you should say "Oh God that madest this beautiful earth" with

Joan really meaning how she thinks about the earth, which all comes in the "Light your fires" and which everybody in the audience can understand. Young lambs crying, and stars, the clatter of horses' hooves—all that is available to them. Then as she says the line "that madest this beautiful earth" they're all going to think—or it's what they should think— "I'm on it. I'm here, now. He has made a beautiful earth." So they're sitting thinking about that, and then the actress says, with real appeal and sadness, to herself, "How long." I think they have a feeling of, "Well, I can enjoy it tomorrow. I can make it all right tomorrow." I think they should go out thinking, "You can do anything." They've seen somebody do anything. They've seen a young girl who had nothing do everything. And I think it's in the back of their minds that it has sprung from a true story.

I suppose it's a philosophy of mine that it would be wonderful if you could endlessly pare away things that are taught, layers of stuff, and just try to be pure and direct. I can't work on my life like that; I wish I could. But that's how I work on a part. I always imagine, when I start, that the whole body inside me is covered in barnacles that are received things or whatever, and somewhere in the middle is just the sheer, steel rod of the part, and I've got to chip away and chip away and chip away until I get to the essence each time. Which Joan gets to as a person in her life. She doesn't take in any of those outside things. She just says what she feels and knows to be true.

I think you have never to have any self-pity. Self-pity is a bore, anyway—that's why I would hate to play Blanche Dubois. But, you see, I'm not drawn to things like that, though they're good parts. But there's no self-pity in Joan. She's like a clean arrow. I do find it, on the whole, wonderful if you meet someone who can speak from a still center.

I am very attracted to parts that are very direct, and say what they think. I long to do a lot of Greek tragedy. I did Electra on the television some years ago. The interesting thing, when I worked on Electra, was that the line is what she means. In the same way that Joan is saying what she means. There's nothing underneath, she's not being crafty; what she says is what she means. And I have a tremendous feeling for those parts. Now, I happen to be able to play the devious ones rather well, and I think that's maybe more like I am really. But there is something *wonderful* about somebody who just goes out there and says it. With passion. Because I loathe people who don't have passion. Well, I don't loathe people, I feel sorry for them. But I think to lead a passionless life must be terrible.

You must have got by now that I'm not a very intellectual actress. I leave the intellectualizing, really, to people to discuss when I've done it. But I endlessly go back to scripts. I drive people potty by just going back all the time and saying, "Well, it's no use your all talking. What do we actually say?"

I started out knowing that there had got to be an accent and trying to see, just by reading what Shaw had written, what came up off the page. And I was going along on the top of a bus one day, and I was going over a speech—it was the trial scene—and I was suddenly absolutely convinced it had to be Glaswegian. What was attracting me about the Glaswegian is that it's extremely aggressive. It suddenly felt right for Joan, because it wasn't your posh English, which makes you immediately feel tur-ri-bly tight and proper; it was a loose accent, but it had *attack*.

Most English actresses use Mummerset. That means anything, really, west of England, which to our ears is country-life-like. It's not real Somerset, it's a mummer's Somerset. It's all kind of rolley, and I couldn't get any attack on it. And I knew that Joan was an attacker. So I turned up at rehearsals and said, "Right. I'm doing it Glasgow." And the director very carefully didn't say anything, and I stuck with it for ages. At the end of the second week, I said, "You know, it's not altogether right, is it?" And he said, "No. I'm very relieved to hear you say that."

The whole cast used to laugh at me, because they said I kept it for one line: "I will darrre and darrre and darrre again." They said, "You were so addicted to it, Eileen." With Glaswegian you can get hold of a word and you can *shove* it.

Really, the accent comes out of trying what will suit you best as an actress, and I'm quite prepared to believe that other actresses will find another. The Midlands country accent still has attack, because all northerners have more attack than southerners; their whole way of speaking has more attack. So I settled on that, because when I'm playing a part, I just keep going around saying, "Now why can't I get that right? It doesn't sound right." I go back and think how they're thinking, and suddenly . . . suddenly it did all seem to gel.

I think Joan doesn't think about sexuality. Now that came out of a very interesting question I had from a publicity woman after a film. She was trying to get me going, asking "What are your favorite parts?" And I said a list of them, and then she asked, "Don't you want to do anything else in Shakespeare?" And I said, "No. I've played the two. There's only one other. The breeches parts are the best. Rosalind and Viola. I would quite like to have a go at Portia, but I've got a bit too old now, and it doesn't worry me. I don't want to play any of the others."

She asked, "What else?" and I said, "I played St. Joan," and she said, "Oh, you seem to like it only when you're dressed as a man." I could see her getting at something, and I thought, "Well, maybe she's right; maybe I do like getting into drag." I went back and thought about it. Then I saw her again the next day and I said, "No. I've worked out what it is. And I think I've come across the really interesting thing about writers. All the parts that I've enjoyed playing are when the man writing them has not bothered about writing a feminine woman. Sex hasn't come into it, so he isn't having to bother about 'This is a woman now speaking.'"

Certainly Shakespeare is *released* as soon as his heroines go into the male clothes. He stops having to worry about them being frightfully feminine, and he writes as he'd write for a boy. And it's wonderful.

I don't want to play Cleopatra. I think it's a nightmare to play, though some of the stuff between Antony and Cleopatra is wonderful. Cleopatra is helped by the fact that she's a ruler, so they give her a lot of . . . balls, I suppose.

But Joan—sexuality is something you didn't have to take into consideration. I don't think she ever flirts. I think it's a wonderful bit when she says to Dunois that she likes babies, but as a soldier.

Joan's intelligence didn't bother me. But, then, I come from a working-class family, very ordinary. In fact, my father was a terrific simpleton in a way. But he could say the most amazing things. And that was just my father, who was nothing in particular. And I myself think there's an enormously wrong way of thinking, that the intellectuals are the only ones who can say things. It seems to me that intellectuals often frighten people into being quiet and not saying anything. But when quite ordinary people are left to it, there's amazing wisdom there. And this girl obviously had a lot more than most people.

I think that Rosalind is the only other role that's comparable to Joan. *As You Like It* is a comedy, but with great depth, actually, behind the comedy. But you can't get going with the emotion, the tragic side as you can with St. Joan. I guess Hamlet is the part to end all parts and has everything. You even have sexuality with Hamlet. I suppose Hamlet is a complete man and Joan is not a complete woman. But I think it's the greatest challenge there is for an actress.

Roberta Maxwell

Born in Toronto, Roberta Maxwell played Joan at the Seattle Repertory Theatre during the 1979–80 season.

John Dexter was the reason I wanted to play Joan. He directed me on Broadway as Jill in *Equus* and Portia in Arnold Wesker's *The Merchant*, and then as Eliza in *Pygmalion* with Robert Stephens at the Ahmanson in Los Angeles. Dexter said, "St. Joan is a part you must play, and I would like to direct you."

Working with John Dexter is always a great experience. You can't imagine anything better happening to you as an actress. He prepared me mentally for the role of Joan, and he gave me this copy of the Constable edition of *Saint Joan* with the illustrations by Ricketts. When we talked about it, he always referred to the soldierly qualities of Joan, her physicality, and the bravery, the courage and the nonfeministic feminism about the part.

Nonfeministic feminism means that Joan wasn't making a statement about being a woman or being involved in a society that didn't allow women to do anything. She simply had a job to do, and a calling, and she never questioned her right to do that. She saw it as a task that she could not *not* have done—she couldn't have lived unless she'd done it. And so there were no sides to her, there was no psychology; it was pre-Freudian. She listened to her own voices—listened to her own voice, as they say now, and followed that. That was compelling to me, to do something unquestioningly. Simply, in a way, to follow orders. I found that a very interesting challenge, not to ask questions.

Dexter and I had planned to do *Saint Joan* together, and then I got offered the part at the Seattle Rep by John Hirsch while Dexter was off working on other projects. Hirsch said, "This is a good part for you. Would you be interested in opening my season?" I'd worked with Hirsch, but not in depth, in Stratford, Ontario, and in his theatre in Winnipeg many, many years before.

I'd read lots of histories about Joan and opinions about her, but finally I found them to be like anecdotes. As Dexter always said, "It's in the text; if you can't find it in the text, it isn't a great play." I found questions in the histories, but the answers always came from the text.

For example, part of the myth that surrounds Joan is her youth. However, nineteen wasn't young in those days. Dunois was twenty-four. I know he says he's twenty-six, but he was actually twenty-four. People didn't live very long then. So you don't need to worry about trying to be very young as Shaw's Joan—for her time, she was a woman.

You also don't need to worry about her being illiterate. She was eloquent because people talked in those days. If you go to Ireland, the most simple people can engage you for an hour in conversation—and no doubt will, especially if you want to catch a train—and simply blow you away with their ability to use words. America's language is poor in words now. It's television. We don't speak; we watch, we deal with visual images. In Joan's day, they conversed, they communicated ideas through words.

One of the questions that you really want to answer is: how could a girl go from Domremy to the battlefield? I think the answer is that the society in which she lived was one of tremendous upheaval and suffering and hunger. She saw that, and she listened to her voices.

She listened to herself, and what she heard sent her out to do something about those problems.

The voices weren't difficult for me, because I think that anyone who is in tune with themselves and their own godhead must go inside. If you actually do go in there, you can have a dialogue with God and His manifestations in yourself. She believed in God. She was also at one with nature. In fact, that's what eventually broke her. Take her away from that, and there are no voices. This I understood, that she felt herself to be a part of it all and thus, although she was lonely, she wasn't alone. Being a person who, at the best of times, has dialogues with the different aspects of my own character and voices, I felt that this was a completely natural thing. I felt very secure in choosing a path that told me she was not hearing anything unnatural. I think other people misunderstood, because they hadn't heard their voices. They were corrupt people, by and large, and used the word God in a very different way from the way she used it.

I had a Catholic upbringing, and I was well informed about the morals of the Church, the dress code, and the importance of virginity. In the cathedral scene, I felt that Joan didn't want to go back. She really was a soldier. She didn't want to go back to wearing women's clothes. I left my own convent school; I literally packed my bags and left because they wouldn't let me do a play in men's clothes. They said I could do the man's role, but I'd have to play it in a skirt. Rubbish! You know, to dress up in men's clothes, to deny your femininity, is a very frightening thing for the Catholic church. You don't see any nuns walking around in trousers even now.

I was aware of the power of the Catholic church, but I don't think you have to be Catholic to understand that. Joan was a mystic. She wasn't a priest; she was a Christ figure. For that reason she was martyred. She had to be martyred, finally, because she was antimaterialism. I don't know how you can understand Joan if you aren't religious. Religious is a very dangerous word, but she was. She believed in God. She didn't believe in a god; she believed in God.

Joan was like Etty Hillesum. She was a woman who kept diaries of her spiritual life in Holland for two years, before she went to a concentration camp. Her book is called *An Interrupted Life*, and it's the most extraordinary, amazing book. There are also Simone Weil and Bernadette Devlin. These woman weren't political; they were hu-

Roberta Maxwell with John de Lancie as Brother Martin in the Seattle Repertory Theatre production.

man, and they were spiritual. They understood that their values were in their own development, and in their at-oneness with God, rather than in a political party.

I think the journey that Joan has to travel from being the person in the first scene to the soldier is difficult. Especially if she is portrayed as being very feminine for theatrical contrast. That was a problem in our production. John Hirsch, in terms of energies, is very theatrical and flamboyant. He had me come in with long, curly hair, and Carrie Robbins designed the costumes wonderfully, but that didn't stop me from playing the nonfeminine aspects of her character, at the risk of people saying, "My goodness, that girl is a bit boyish, isn't she?"

I simply wasn't intimidated by the sexuality of the male actors and the characters around me. I never played passive. I was always active, and always felt and believed that it wasn't their will that I was doing but the will of God, and that I would do it no matter what they said. It was God and I, and it was way beyond sex. I think that's something that people want reassurance about in Joan: was she a lesbian, or was there something peculiar about her sexuality? She was not a sexual person as portrayed in the play, nor do I see that in any of the histories, although there's a very amusing incident where she spent the night with a woman.

There was a kind of local traveling show going around in which a monk named Brother Richard tried to involve Joan with a kind of magic-mystical phenomenon. She was already famous, and people were starting to accuse her. Brother Richard wanted to become part of her life, and she wasn't having any of it. She was not interested in anything to do with publicized mysticism. She was like Bernadette Devlin; she saw the future and the destiny of her country and she wasn't interested in tricks.

When Joan was trying to raise money for what became her last campaign, Brother Richard brought into the arena a woman who was married and had two children, but who said that she could foresee who would give money to Joan and who wouldn't because she had extrasensory perception. They dithered about and, obviously, it was very dangerous to become involved because of heresy, as Joan knew. This woman had said that a lady in white came to visit her at night in bed, so Joan said fine, she would spend the night with this woman and see for herself. She spent not one night but two nights, and the "lady" never appeared. The woman went back to her family and was never heard of again. I thought that was a very amusing incident in Joan's life. She was very smart.

I was aggressive in the part, very much encouraged by Hirsch. I'm pretty fierce, and there was a stridency about my performance, as people have who are committed to something. They see only one thing. I remember a story about Bernadette Devlin when she was brought here to do her book. She'd never been to New York before. She got off the plane. The publisher met her. She got into the limousine, and she never stopped talking. He couldn't get over it. She looked neither to the left nor to the right. She was not interested in being in New York, seeing the Empire State Building; she had something to say and she never wasted one moment in saying anything else. I think Joan was like that.

I was in a rage for "Light your fires." I signed the recantation because I didn't want to die. I wasn't ready to die. I was terrified of these people, as one would be. And I doubted. I doubted; that's how I was broken. I think I would have been much more broken but Hirsch wouldn't allow it. He didn't want me to give way. I think there was a sort of animal cunning, with the fear of the fire, "How am I going to get out of this?" And then, when I was betrayed again, the feeling of exaltation: saved!

I loved the last scene. I thought it was so wonderful that there she was, a saint, and she said, "Is all this going to get me back to my body, so I can go back to earth?" She loved the earth. She didn't want to be a saint. She didn't want to be elevated above everybody. And I had the opportunity to do that wonderful last line. It was the quietest line that I said in the entire play.

I was tired when I played Joan, and I didn't feel that, within the context of the production, all the questions had been solved. But perhaps they're not solved in the play. The saint, for instance. Shaw was a very logical man, and he believed Joan, but there was a quality of irreverence. Mother Teresa eats only a teaspoon or tablespoon of honey a day. She's one of those people who lives on air. She's very highly evolved. I think that Joan must have been the same, and I couldn't realize that part of her character to my satisfaction. I don't know if that's Shaw or not.

We had a wonderful design in Seattle. It was a Ming Cho Lee set. There was nothing to it, yet you could feel when the wind changed. You could feel the wind moving the water; you felt that the grasses were rippling. It was so still. It was so simple. The image within your own mind was of a bird flying across against the stillness and simplicity of the set. It was extremely helpful because of Joan's feeling for the country, and the emptiness, and the quiet that you have to have around you if you are going to hear your voices.

I had a wonderful Dunois, Jack Ryland. He had great humor, and tremendous love and respect for the character of Joan. That was so helpful. I could just stand there and know that whatever happened, he would be there with me. He was very humorous about me and awed by the strength and the power, and filled with admiration. But he was a soldier.

Phillip Piro, the Dauphin, was great. He was kind of loose—a unique sense of timing, and a great softness to him. Very appealing, lovable, and sad in spots. Not a man who connived or had anything going for him other than his own kind of need to be what he felt it was his right to be. Her challenge was convincing him that he was legitimate; he always knew it, but he was surrounded by people who were so mean to him. I wanted to embrace him, to build him. I really loved him—I loved him as an actor and I loved him as the Dauphin. Cauchon—Louis Turenne—was just terrifying.

I don't consider that I have a career. I consider that I'm a working actress. And as such, yes, I was influenced by Joan by just getting to know the woman, the character, the courage, and the journey she took. I took that journey, as best I could, with her, under the guidance of a very great playwright. And so to have asked myself those kinds of questions makes me a bigger and better person, because when I'm in my own time of questioning, I can always refer to her. But that's true of many roles that I've played. I feel very much at one with Stevie Smith and with the woman in *Ashes*.

I'd like to get into all the mature women in Shakespeare, all the mature women in Chekhov. Those are the classics. I think I'm probably just beginning a whole new level in my work, but I don't know about that because I'm just at the threshold now. I've always played ingenues, although I did play Hedda Gabler. Very poorly. I hadn't a clue what she was about. But I put on a good show.

I played ingenue roles until a very late age, actually. I played Nina only five years ago. I've just been offered Arkadina. I had a very early start when I was first at the Stratford, Ontario Festival as an apprentice. I think I had my fourteenth birthday the very first year. And before that I worked in the theatre and on television.

Shakespeare was the greatest playwright ever, and I have had two opportunities to play Hamlet. I was once asked by John Hirsch, and subsequently by Nikos Psacharopoulos. When I read the part of Hamlet, with that in mind, I was so astounded and thrilled and honored. But I think for me to play Hamlet would be a distortion, whereas for me to play Joan is quite natural.

Hamlet is the greatest role ever written, because of the dimensions, the size, and the language. Hamlet may not be playable, but Joan is. He can't make up his mind. Joan doesn't seem to have that problem. Except for a slight hiccough in her trial scene, the line for Joan is very straight. I don't think that Shakespeare meant Hamlet to be played by a woman. Simple, bottom line. Now Oscar Wilde, perhaps, wouldn't have minded Lady Bracknell being played by a man, but I don't think that it ever crossed Shakespeare's mind that a woman would play Hamlet.

Joan is undoubtedly one of the great roles for women. It's Shaw, and she stands out because the play is called *Saint Joan*. It's not *Misalliance* or *Pygmalion*. As a historical figure, Joan of Arc couldn't be better represented than by the clear decisiveness of Shaw.

The part required enormous physical stamina, and I run on a very short and thin wire in that respect. John Hirsch filled me with chicken soup. It must have worked, because I went on at top volume from the moment I stepped on the stage. And whenever I went over to his place, he would always say, "Just sit down." "Oh God, John, not another cup of chicken soup." "It's going to work, you're going to feel much better." Before every performance I had an enormous bowl of John Hirsch's chicken soup. So I can attribute a great deal of my success to chicken soup.

My direction from John Hirsch complemented what I'd learned about *Saint Joan* from John Dexter. They both believed in the importance of being able to say the words of the playwright, that he is the primary interpreter of the character and of the situation. They believe that you just have to get out of the way, and if you just say

Shaw's words, you're at least three-quarters of the way there. The trick is, do you have enough strength and mental agility and courage just to say those words?

I was in a voice class with Diana Sands at the time that she was rehearsing Saint Joan at Lincoln Center. Diana came into class one day totally devastated because John Hirsch, who was directing, had threatened to tie her to the stool in his zeal to make her say the words of the text as simply as possible and not to do any "acting." If I had tried to do any embroidering on the text, I think that John Hirsch might have poured his chicken soup over my head.

Nora McLellan in the Shaw Festival production.

Nora McLellan

Born in *Vancouver*, Nora McLellan *played Joan at Canada's Shaw Festival in 1981.*

I had about eleven months before the first day of rehearsal, and I read so much that I knew more about Joan of Arc than any other person in our theatre. At one point during rehearsals of the Loire scene, they were discussing whether the wind should be blowing stage left or stage right. I was sitting there with a smug "I'm not saying a word" look on my face. Christopher Newton, our director, knew that I'd done all this research, and he finally turned to me and said, "I'll bet you know which way." I went, "Well, as a matter of fact, I happen to have a map," and I brought out this huge document, because I was so desperate. I mean, I knew all this stuff.

I think what amazed me the most was that while Shaw had written a fantasy, basically, and condensed events, so much in the trial scene was from the real transcripts. I found myself some nights just wanting to turn to the audience and say, "Ladies and gentlemen, do you realize that this was actually said by this person?" That was what gave me such a thrill—that Shaw couldn't write this any better than Joan herself.

When I was asked to do *Saint Joan* I was twenty-five, and usually you play it when you're older. I'd been working since I was a kid, and I'd acted for Christopher when he had a company in Vancouver when I was seventeen and eighteen. I came to the Shaw Festival in 1980 to do a Brecht play called *Respectful Wedding*, and one night Christopher asked, "Would you like to play St. Joan next season?" I laughed and said, "Of course. That's cute. Let's get you another drink."

The next day I called him up and asked, "Were you serious?" He said yes, and I went, "Ub dub dub dub." I kept phoning him up and saying, "Are you serious?" Christopher had an idea for the kind of person he really wanted. I think he wanted someone who was not afraid of just lumbering out on the stage and being aggressive and masculine. It's funny—this is the longest my hair has been since then, and it's not even shoulder length. It seems I've gone through a period of transvestites. I did *Two Gentlemen of Verona*, *The Club* and *The Singular Life of Albert Nobbs* after Joan. I said, "I've got to start playing girls," and they gave me Sabina in *Skin of Our Teeth* this season so that I could go back to wearing dresses.

When I was cast in the show nobody in Canada could believe it. There was a great "Are you kidding?" because I was known as a singer. I was working hard on being an actress, but I was noted for musicals. There was a famous director in Canada who tried to talk me out of doing Joan. He said, "I think it's the worst thing that's ever happened to you." But I think it was the first time that I was able to take all the things I knew and use them.

Luckily I had studied acting with Uta Hagen in New York. I couldn't have gotten through the first day of rehearsal without her. She taught that you work from yourself, so actually playing Joan for Christopher was a good lesson. It was the first time after studying with Miss Hagen that I was able to apply everything I learned from her, starting from myself and asking, "How would I react to this?" then recognizing it within Joan's political and historical venue. It made an enormous amount of sense.

In my research, I found all sorts of information that I could know and then just throw away and concentrate on doing the play. There are so many speculations about Joan. I think the most valuable biography I read was by Vita Sackville-West. She wrote about the religious fanaticism a person would have fasting for three weeks on end, if the person did have a power. I actually tried going for about four days without eating, just to see what it was like. Well, I can see where it would be very easy to hear things. Joan would fast for three or four weeks at a time, and if she had anything it would be maybe a small glass of wine, a tiny crust of bread. There's a thing that happens with the brain after a certain point.

Because I have no real religious background, I thought, "Oh boy, this is going to be a hardbone." It is very difficult, I think, to act. You cannot anticipate hearing voices. I did an awful lot of reading. I wanted to know who her voices were, why they were important to her. It was difficult for me to be able to really mean it when I said, "I've been told," but when Vita Sackville-West talked about long periods of not eating and having mass three times a day and being consumed with faith—I really do believe that the voices came to her. Maybe it is true that visionaries of our time like Gandhi put their bodies into a physical state that enabled them to be very open to outside influence.

There's a wonderful sequence in Skin of Our Teeth. We are all discussing why the hours of the night come out as Aristotle and Spinoza. I say, as Sabina, "I think it means that when people are asleep they have all those lovely thoughts, much better than when they're awake." That doesn't make any sense, so another character steps forward and says something like, "No, what the author meant was that all of the philosophers and great thinkers are in the air around us and they're working on us all the time. Only we don't know it." Like those thoughts are all there, just out there.

I think there might be something in that—that when you put yourself into a physical state you become very open, like a medium. Possibly Joan was a medium for an enormous amount of knowledge. It is difficult to understand how she would have known the things that she knew, coming from where she did, and that's what makes the mystery. That's what makes the saint, I suppose.

I think what interested me the most in modern terms—and this is something that we were trying to say in our production—was the parallel to someone like Lech Walesa. In the souvenir program we had a quote from Mr. Walesa saying, "I'm just a peasant. I'm just an ordinary man with ordinary desires in life, but I have this mission." Statements that he and Joan made are very, very similar.

When the powers that be figure that it's convenient for somebody like Lech Walesa to be doing what he's doing, it's fine. But when they have no use for him anymore, they just wait for him to screw up, and when he does they get rid of him. Not by killing him—he's out on the street and walking around. The biggest mistake that the English made was having Joan burnt, thereby creating the great martyr. They're not going to do that in Poland now, but Lech Walesa's power was taken away.

The speech at the end of the cathedral scene— "I shall dare and dare"—is generally downstage center. I can see it as a speech that would end with great applause, but Christopher said to me, "If you ever get applause there, you've missed the point of this production." I asked why, and he said, "Because that's the moment we as an audience want to feel, 'You've just blown it.' You've actually said, 'I will go out into the common people and they will love me.' But that is the moment that everybody in political power is going, 'We've got her, and it's just a matter of time.'" Aside from the fact that just her hair and her dress would have done it, I could almost see that feeling of people collecting information and chuckling, "This is great. She's digging her own grave."

When I played Joan, I could not for the life of me see how any of the people in the trial were trying to help me, ever. I would sit on the stage when they were talking to me, and I'd think, "I can't see it. I really can't see that you're trying to do anything but hurt me." And I really wanted to see it. I think that there's a naiveté to a person who's that young and from that small a village and who wants to believe. She wants to believe that Cauchon is trying to help her in the trial scene. I think a person does.

I was also frustrated that Bernard Shaw didn't write in so many of the things that I thought were very important. The fact, for example, that they examined her and took depositions when she was first in Poitiers, after she connected with the Dauphin. She kept saying during the trial, in fact it was relentless when you read the transcripts, "Check that. You check that. I've answered all this, and everybody bought it then. You check that."

Their taking away her rings that were given to her by her family was very, very, very important to her. They wouldn't let her hear mass when she was in prison. To go from hearing mass three times a day to being without for so long must have been devastating. Those were the things that almost killed her. I kept thinking, "I understand that you can't make a play seven hours long, but why doesn't he touch upon the agony that she want through in prison?" Shaw only does the thing about "I ate some fish."

Also I found amazing that Mr. Shaw would have Joan go from "I know what I'm saying," to recanting, to recanting her recantation in a space of a few pages. I figured that that was what he had to do; condensing ten or eleven months of trials into forty minutes is, I imagine, a playwright's nightmare. But the result, I think, is an actress's nightmare.

I found I had to build myself up to saying, "You're right. I must have lied about the voices. I must have," and then to actually recanting. The confusion and the illness had to start much earlier than the lines suggest. I found myself playing the character becoming very confused much earlier on, approximately after the section about the Archangel Michael being clothed and their asking, "Why were you in men's clothes?"

After that there was the huge uproar, and I would just start having great fears and doubts, thinking, "I'm not sure," until I recanted from just being beaten down to the point of really believing, "Yes, I have sinned, and now because I've said I have sinned and I'm a good Catholic, you'll set me free." And finding out, of course, that that means "No, you're going to be put away forever." Then there's a snapping point of just saying, "No, I would rather burn." Because the interesting thing about Shaw's last speech about the lambs and the trees and everything is that it has very little to do with God. It is basically a statement about life— "without these things I cannot live, and by your wanting to take them away from me" . . . it's making me weep thinking about it . . .

What she's saying in that speech is "I have lived, no matter what." I found that to be the most moving thing of all. Chris and I had talked about what do you do if you know you are going to die? After I said, "That is my last word to you," I used to find myself being terribly benevolent. I guess it is the feeling you get after the anger stops, when all of a sudden you realize that they will never understand. You think, "You're putting me to death, but that's because you don't know what I know. I love you, but you don't understand, so that is my final word to you."

I used to think about what I'd just said, and I'd be looking at my hands, and I remember I'd just listen to Cauchon, and I used to smile at him. The first time that happened the actor playing Cauchon went "Oh, oh, my God." He just about fell over. Not that it was intentional. I wasn't doing it for effect. I just started thinking that somebody who had lived with such zeal all of a sudden realizes, "This is the third-to-last breath I'll take. This is the last time I'll see that," and I'd be thinking about my trees and the farm that I grew up on, and obviously—well, I'm crying again right now.

God, do you hear the Muzak they're playing in the bar? "Come On, Baby—Light My Fire"! From tragedy to farce. We were going to have "The Shaw Festival Saint Joan Cookbook." Everything was flambéd. The biggest joke we had was everybody standing around the stake going, "Phew, phew," trying to blow out the fire. You can get very disrespectful, but sometimes I think it's the only way to keep your sanity.

You have to understand that Saint Joan had never been done at the Shaw Festival in its twenty-nine-year history. Our production was fairly controversial. As a matter of fact, the Shaw estate tried to close it down before it opened. My nerves were—well, I was quite hysterical.

In the Loire scene with Dunois—I'll never forget Chris doing this to me. At first I really did think he was doing this to me. He said, "Dunois and his page have been sitting by the river for six weeks, and the page has been in the water swimming and is naked when you make your entrance. He has no idea that you're a woman, and he's drying himself off and all of a sudden realizes that you are Joan of Arc and there's a great—" and I said, "Christopher, I have the text, and there's somebody naked on the stage?" Finally I said, "Okay, while he's naked stage right, I'll be masturbating stage left," because I just couldn't believe it.

But I came to realize that actually Christopher had a very good point—that Joan of Arc lived with and was indistinguishable from soldiers. But I knew that as an actor I had to get the audience away from "Oh my God, there's a naked boy on the stage." So as I said, "I do not want to be thought of as a woman. I will not dress as a woman. I do not care for the things women care for," I used to point right at the page's crotch on "the things women care for." Everybody had a good laugh, and we could get on with the play. I thought, "Why is Christopher doing this?" but actually it was a big help for the play. Not only did the soldiers not realize I was a girl, but also once they did they were instantly put at ease because they realized that I really didn't care.

The play is called *Saint Joan*, but I think Christopher's play was *Joan*. Not a saint at all. You're not a saint until you die, first of all. We have a tendency to think of St. Joan as Ingrid Bergman walking around to saintly music being a saint. Our Joan was a peasant girl who wasn't very nice a lot of the time. Historically you read that Dunois used to be simply furious with her, that sometimes they refused to listen to her. She was very stubborn, as someone is who knows she's right. I think that was something that our audiences were a little upset with. They wanted that saintly person to be there. I used to joke about it with a RADA-trained voice: "I shall dahre, and dahre, and dahre, until I die, and I shall now goooh out into the mahrketplace—you know it's teddibly lohvely," whereas I was actually very Canadian—a flat tone, very peasantish.

In the opening scene of our production, there was a trap door. All the soldiers were downstairs singing a song, being very loud, and De Baudricourt was trying to get them to quiet down. Joan was down there with the soldiers at first, and one day in rehearsal I came up the stairs and I said, "Good morning, Captain Squire." They were all singing, and I just leaned down and yelled, "Quit it," and they all shut up. Chris said, "Well, why not? Why not?" So I used to come out and go, "Good morning, Captain Squire. Quit it," and Chris said to me, "You know, Nora, if they buy that they're going to buy the rest of this production."

Well, on the opening night I knew there were eight hundred people with pens and papers in hand, and I came bounding up the stairs and went, "Good morning, Captain Squire. Quit it," and I heard eight hundred voices do this— "Ohhhh, Ohhhhhh!" I wanted to turn at that moment and say, "Chris, they didn't buy it." I just wanted to die. I wanted to say, "We'll take the curtain down and

I'll come back up and do 'Good morning, Captain Squire' in a RADA voice." I'll never forget that opening night, because people were quite stunned.

I never read any of the press notices, and I don't ever intend to. I think that they were very unkind, but I think it's interesting that a lot of people have thought of our production for a number of years, and now they come to me—some always did come—and say, "You know, I was terribly moved."

We originally cut the epilogue, which Shaw's estate asked us not to do. Then Christopher said, "All right. We'll read the epilogue." It was a lovely choice which came out of a moment of anger— "All right, we'll read the damn thing." He put a notice in the program saying, "At the end of the play there will be a brief intermission and the actors will read the epilogue."

I would say about seventy percent of the audience stayed. Many of the people I've talked to said they just didn't want to stay. It wasn't for a bad reason. They wanted to leave with what they were thinking about, which was Warwick's line "I wonder." A very, very large actor who must have been thirty feet up on the set was the Executioner, just walking away as Warwick spoke. It was absolutely stunning.

So we ended the play with "I wonder," took a curtain call, a ten-minute intermission, and then we stood at lecterns. Actually it was beautiful—twelve people, each with a candle and a little spotlight. We read the lines, and then one by one the others said, "Oh, no, I'm not dealing with this," blew their candles out, and their spotlight would go out. Then "How long, oh Lord, how long," and it was gorgeous. I said to Christopher, "If I ever do this production again, or if I direct it, I would read the epilogue." Because it didn't have that slapstick quality. I loved it being read, because it was so simple.

One other thing in our production that I think was really important is that the company work here is extraordinary. Christopher has managed to get an incredible ensemble. In Saint Joan there were people in the cast who didn't agree with my playing the part, but I had twenty-five actors who all gave me the moon. I never had anything but the feeling that we were all playing together. Around about September, somebody would come up and say, "Well, you know, you won me over," and it amazed me that I'd never felt his resistance.

I think that's a true tribute to actors. Not only were they professionals, they were just great. I also realized that the play is very much the sum total of everyone. Joan can be as good as she can be, but I learned what everybody else gives to that play. I used to find myself incredibly moved by the energy that the cast would give me, just when I needed it, and there were an awful lot of times that I really needed it. I needed help because I didn't know what it was like to carry that kind of a piece. I'd carried plays before, but not anything like Saint Joan. I needed people, and everybody was extraordinarily supportive. That was one of my nicest experiences, so even when a lot of people were negative about it, that never bothered me. I just had such a wonderful time with the company.

I think about the role a lot. I don't know—I don't think I'm very much what people would like to see in Saint Joan, but I'm hoping that someone will give me the opportunity to play it again. We did the show for seven months, and the last performance was like somebody taking off my right arm. I could still be doing that play. I could easily do it for years. I thrill to everything about it.

Biographical Information

Jane Alexander

EDUCATION: Sarah Lawrence College; University of Edinburgh.

PROFESSIONAL STAGE DEBUT: Long John Silver in *Treasure Island*, Boston.

NEW YORK THEATRE: Eleanor Bachman in *The Great White Hope* (Tony, Drama Desk and Theatre World awards); Ann in *6 Rms Riv Vu*, Jacqueline in *Find Your Way Home*, Judge Ruth Loomis in *First Monday in October* (all Tony nominations); Gertrude in *Hamlet*, Natalia in *Goodbye Fidel*, Catherine in *The Heiress*, Annie Sullivan in *Monday after the Miracle*, Joanne in *Losing Time*, Anna in *Old Times*.

OTHER THEATRE: Arena Stage and Kennedy Center (Washington, D.C.), American Shakespeare Festival (Connecticut), Alliance Theatre (Atlanta), Hartman Theatre (Connecticut), Spoleto Festival/USA.

FILMS: *The Great White Hope*, *All the President's Men*, *Kramer vs. Kramer*, *Testament* (all Oscar nominations); *The New Centurions*, *Brubaker*, *Night Crossing*, *City Heat*, *Sweet Country*; co-producer: *Square Dance*, *Common Scents*, *Jaguar*.

TELEVISION: *Eleanor and Franklin* (Television Critics Circle award), *Eleanor and Franklin: The White House Years* (both Emmy nominations); *Death Be Not Proud*, *Mourning Becomes Electra*, *The Time of Your Life*, *Find Your Way Home*, *Hamlet*, *Playing for Time* (Emmy award), *Dear Liar*, *Kennedy's Children*, *Calamity Jane*, *A Circle of Children*, *Malice in Wonderland*.

Co-author: The Bluefish Cookbook, The Master Builder (translation).

Honors: Helen Caldicott Leadership Award for work in WAND (Women's Action for Nuclear Disarmament); St. Botolph Club Achievement in Dramatic Arts; Israel Cultural Award; Honorary Doctor of Humane Letters, Wilson College.

Eileen Atkins

Training: Guildhall School of Music and Drama.

Professional stage debut: Nurse in Harvey, Repertory Theatre, Bangor, Ireland.

London theatre: Royal Court Theatre: Juliette in Exit the King (Derwent award), Joan Middleton in The Restoration of Arnold Middleton, Joan Shannon in The Sleeping Den; Old Vic: Miranda in The Tempest, Lady Anne in Richard III, Viola in Twelfth Night (SWET nomination); Royal Shakespeare Company: Rosalind in As You Like It, Nell in Passion Play (SWET nomination); National Theatre: Hesione in Heartbreak House; Other: Jacquenetta in Love's Labor's Lost, Eileen in Semi-Detached, Lady Brute in The Provok'd Wife, Childie in The Killing of Sister George (London Standard award), Celia in The Cocktail Party, Elizabeth I in Vivat! Vivat Regina! (Variety award), Jennet in The Lady's Not for Burning, Mrs. Hitchcock in Serjeant Musgrave's Dance, Medea.

New York theatre: Lika in The Promise, The Killing of Sister George (Tony nomination), Vivat! Vivat Regina! (Tony and Drama Desk nominations), Marie David in The Night of the Tribades (Drama Desk award).

Other theatre: Bristol Old Vic, Edinburgh Festival, Chichester Festival, American Shakespeare Festival (Connecticut), Long Wharf Theatre (New Haven), Ravinia Festival (Illinois), Mark Taper Forum (Los Angeles).

Films: Inadmissible Evidence, The Baby, Equus, The Dresser.

Television: The Age of Kings, The Lady's Not for Burning, The Three Sisters, Party Games, Electra, The Heiress, The Duchess of Malfi, Major Barbara, Oliver Twist, A Midsummer Night's Dream, The Lady from the Sea, Double Bill, The Letter, Titus Andronicus, Smiley's People, She Fell among Thieves, A Better Class of Person, Sons and Lovers, Breaking Up.

Elisabeth Bergner

Training: Vienna Conservatory.

Professional stage debut: A small role at the City Theatre, Zurich; in same season acted Ophelia to Alexander Moissi's Hamlet.

Berlin Festival: Rosalind in As You Like It, Katherine in The Taming of the Shrew, Miss Julie, Nora in A Doll's House, Viola in Twelfth Night, Juliet in Romeo and Juliet,

Marguerite in *The Constant Nymph*, Portia in *The Merchant of Venice*, Hannele, Queen Christina, Nina in *Strange Interlude*, Alkmena in *Amphitryon 38*.

OTHER GERMAN THEATRE: Burgtheater (Vienna); Deutsches Volkstheater, Koeniggraetzer Theater and Staattheater (Berlin).

LONDON THEATRE: David in *The Boy David*, Toinette in *The Gay Invalid*.

NEW YORK THEATRE: Gemma in *Escape Me Never*, Sally in *The Two Mrs. Carrolls*, The Duchess of Malfi, Ellen in *The Cup of Trembling*, Mrs. Pat in *Dear Liar*.

EUROPEAN TOURS: Hester in *The Deep Blue Sea*, Mary Tyrone in *Long Day's Journey into Night*, *Dear Liar*, Aurelia in *The Madwoman of Chaillot*, Deborah in *More Stately Mansions*.

OTHER THEATRE: Opera House (Manchester), Arnaud (Guildford), Oxford Playhouse, Malvern Festival.

FILMS: *Der Evangelimann*, *Ariane* (Blue Ribbon 1934), *Dreaming Lips*, *Catherine the Great*, *Stolen Life*, *As You Like It*, *Paris Calling*, *Escape Me Never*.

HONORS: First actress to receive the Schiller Prize "for outstanding contribution to the cultural life in Germany, 1963; Goldeneband (Gold Ribbon) of the International Film Festival, Berlin, 1963 and 1965.

Marjorie Brewer

TRAINING: Montreal Repertory Theatre School.

STAGE DEBUT: Good Deeds in *Everyman*, Everyman Players.

MONTREAL THEATRE: Everyman Players: Chorus Leader in *Murder in the Cathedral*, Madalena in *The Spanish Miracle*, Salome and Kundry in *The Holy Grail*; Sixteen-Thirty Club: Louisa in *Festival in Time of Plague*, Sarah Bernhardt in *Divinity in Montreal* (both Best Actress Award at the Dominion Drama Festival); Ella in *Judge Lynch*, Elizabeth in *Dark Lady of the Sonnets*, Hesione in *Heartbreak House*, Arkadina in *The Seagull*; Montreal Repertory Theatre: *Dark Lady of the Sonnets*, *Lady Precious Stream*, Edna in *Waiting for Lefty*, *Mary of Scotland*, Lydia in *Judgment Day*, *Joan of Lorraine*, Eve in *Back to Methuselah*.

RADIO: Canadian Broadcasting Corporation: *Way of the Spirit* (series); drama productions of Rupert Caplan.

Zoe Caldwell

EDUCATION: Methodist Ladies College, Melbourne.

STAGE DEBUT: *Major Barbara* and Shakespeare roles with the Union Theatre Repertory Company, Melbourne.

AUSTRALIAN THEATRE: Ophelia in *Hamlet*, Bubba in *Summer of the Seventeenth Doll*, other roles with the Elizabethan Theatre Trust.

BRITISH THEATRE: Memorial Theatre, Stratford: Daughter of Antiochus in *Pericles*, Margaret in *Much Ado about Nothing*, Bianca in *Othello*, Helena in *All's Well that Ends Well*, Cordelia in *King Lear*; Royal Court Theatre: Ismene in *Antigone*, Whore in *Cob and Leach*, Isabella in *The Changeling*, Jacqueline in *Jacques*; West End: Lady Hamilton in *A Bequest to the Nation*.

NEW YORK THEATRE: Sister Jeanne in *The Devils*, Polly in *Slapstick Tragedy* (Tony and New York Drama Critics awards), *The Prime of Miss Jean Brodie* (Tony and New York Drama Critics awards), Eve in *The Creation of the World and Other Business*, *Colette* (Drama Desk award), Mary Tyrone in *A Long Day's Journey into Night*, Alice in *The Dance of Death*, *Medea* (Tony and Drama Desk awards), *Lillian*.

CANADIAN THEATRE: Stratford Festival: Rosaline in *Love's Labor's Lost*, Sonia Downfahl in *The Canvas Barricade*, Cleopatra in *Antony and Cleopatra*, Lady Anne in *Richard III*, Mistress Page in *The Merry Wives of Windsor*; Manitoba Theatre Centre, Shaw Festival.

OTHER THEATRE: Adelaide Festival of the Arts, Goodman Theatre (Chicago), Kennedy Center (Washington, D.C.); founding member, Guthrie Theater (Minneapolis).

DIRECTOR: *Richard II* (Stratford Festival), *The Taming of the Shrew* (American Shakespeare Festival), *An Almost Perfect Person* and *These Men* (New York).

TELEVISION: *The Apple Cart*, *The Lady's Not for Burning*, *Macbeth*, *Witness to Yesterday*, *The Seagull*, *Sarah*.

HONORS: O.B.E. 1970.

Ann Casson

PROFESSIONAL STAGE DEBUT: At age six as Tiny Tim in *A Christmas Carol*, Lyric Theatre, London, and as Astyanax in *The Trojan Women*.

LONDON THEATRE: Vivie in *Mrs. Warren's Profession*, Hilda in *Because We Must*, Leonora Strozzi in *Night Candles*, Gladys in *George and Margaret*, Cassandra in *The Trojan Women*, Regan in *King Lear*, Olivia in *Twelfth Night*, *Electra*, Perdita in *The Winter's Tale*, Violet in *Man and Superman*, Ann in *Man and Superman*, Duchess of York in *Richard II*, Margery in *The Shoemaker's Holiday*.

OTHER THEATRE IN ENGLAND: O.U.D.S., Macdona Players, Cambridge Arts Theatre, Streatham, Tewkesbury Festival, C.E.M.A. tour with Old Vic, E.N.S.A. tour, Pilgrim Players tour, Bristol Old Vic, Birmingham Rep, Citizens' Theatre (Glasgow), Theatre North and Crucible (Sheffield).

CANADIAN THEATRE: Stratford Festival: Mrs. Peachum in *The Beggar's Opera*, Duchess de la Plaza Toro in *The Gondoliers*, Constance in *King John*, Lady Capulet in *Romeo and Juliet*, Mrs. Railton-Bell in *Separate Tables*; Canadian Players, Bastion (Victoria), Northern Light and Citadel theatres (Edmonton),

Neptune (Halifax), Centaur (Montreal), Huron Country Playhouse (Ontario), Theatre London, Shaw Festival.

U.S. THEATRE: Guthrie Theater (Minneapolis), Goodman Theatre (Chicago).

DIRECTOR: Theatre North.

FILMS: *Dance Pretty Lady, Number 17, The Marriage Bond, George and Margaret.*

TELEVISION: *Family Reunion, Peer Gynt, The Gondoliers, A Gift to Last.*

Constance Cummings

EDUCATION: St. Nicholas School, Seattle.

PROFESSIONAL STAGE DEBUT: Chorus of *Treasure Girl*, Broadway.

NEW YORK THEATRE: Chorus of *The Little Show*, Carrie in *This Man's Town*, Linda Brown in *Accent on Youth*, Regina in *Young Madame Conti*, Racine in *One-Man Show*, Antiope in *Rape of the Belt*, Gertrude in *Hamlet*, Emily Stilson in *Wings* (Tony and Drama Desk awards).

LONDON THEATRE: Old Vic Company: Juliet in *Romeo and Juliet*, Miss Richard in *The Good Natured Man*; National Theatre: Volumnia in *Coriolanus*, Leda in *Amphitryon 38*, Mary Tyrone in *Long Day's Journey into Night*, Ranevskaya in *The Cherry Orchard*, Agave in *The Bacchae*, *Wings*; Other: Alice in *Sour Grapes*, *Young Madame Conti*, Katherine in *Goodbye, Mr. Chips*, Kate in *The Jealous God*, Lydia in *Skylark*, Gabby in *The Petrified Forest*, Jane in *Clutterbuck*, Anna in *Happy with Either*, Madeline in *Don't Listen, Ladies!*, Laura in *Before the Party*, Martha in *Return to Tyassi*, Georgie in *Winter Journey*, Ann in *The Shrike*, Andrea in *Trial and Error*, *Rape of the Belt*, Sarah in *J.B.*, Katy in *The Genius and the Goddess*, Martha in *Who's Afraid of Virginia Woolf?*, Liza Foote in *Public and Confidential*, Julia in *Justice Is a Woman*, Jane in *Fallen Angels*, Mother in *Children*, Dodie in *Stripwell*, Amanda in *The Glass Menagerie*, *Fanny Kemble at Home*.

OTHER THEATRE: Oxford Playhouse, Westport Country Playhouse (Connecticut), Malvern Festival, Citizens' Theatre (Glasgow), Arnaud (Guildford), Bristol Old Vic.

FILMS: *The Criminal Code, The Guilty Generation, Movie Crazy, Channel Crossing, Broadway through a Keyhole, Glamour, Looking for Trouble, Remember Last Night?, Seven Sinners, Busman's Honeymoon, This England, The Farmer Went to France, Blithe Spirit, John and Julie, The Intimate Stranger, The Battle of the Sexes, Sammy Going South, In the Cool of the Day, A Boy Ten Feet Tall.*

TELEVISION: *Cyrano de Bergerac, Touch of the Sun, Clutterbuck, The Last Tycoon, Ruth, Late Summer, Long Day's Journey into Night.*

HONORS: C.B.E. 1974.

Judi Dench

TRAINING: Central School of Speech Training and Dramatic Art.

PROFESSIONAL STAGE DEBUT: Ophelia with the Old Vic Company at the Royal Court Theatre, Liverpool.

LONDON THEATRE: Old Vic Company: Juliet in *Measure for Measure*, First Fairy in *A Midsummer Night's Dream*, Maria in *Twelfth Night*, Katherine in *Henry V*, Phebe in *As You Like It*, Cynthia in *The Double Dealer*, Cecily in *The Importance of Being Earnest*, Anne Page in *The Merry Wives of Windsor*, Juliet in *Romeo and Juliet*, Kate in *She Stoops to Conquer*, Hermia in *A Midsummer Night's Dream*; Royal Shakespeare Company: Anya in *The Cherry Orchard*, Dorcas in *A Penny for a Song*, Viola in *Twelfth Night*, Perdita and Hermione in *A Winter's Tale*, Grace Harkaway in *London Assurance*, *Major Barbara*, Nurse in *Too True to Be Good*, Adriana in *The Comedy of Errors*, Beatrice in *Much Ado about Nothing*, Lona in *Pillars of the Community*, Millamant in *The Way of the World*, Lady Macbeth (SWET award), *Juno and the Paycock* (SWET and Evening Standard awards), *Mother Courage*; National Theatre: Deborah in *A Kind of Alaska* (SWET nomination, Evening Standard award), Lady Bracknell in *The Importance of Being Earnest* (SWET nomination); Other: Josepha in *A Shot in the Dark*, Lika in *The Promise*, Sally in *Cabaret*, Vilma in *The Wolf*, Miss Trant in *The Good Companions*, Sophie in *The Gay Lord Quex*, Barbara in *Pack of Lies* (SWET and Plays and Players awards), Carrie Pooter in *Mr. and Mrs. Nobody*.

OTHER THEATRE: Memorial Theatre at Stratford-upon-Avon, Nottingham Playhouse, Oxford Playhouse, Edinburgh Festival, Old Vic and British Council tours.

FILMS: *He Who Rides a Tiger*, *Study in Terror*, *Four in the Morning*, *A Midsummer Night's Dream*, *The Third Secret*, *Dead Cert*, *Wetherby*, *A Room with a View*, *84 Charing Cross Road*.

TELEVISION: *Major Barbara*, *Hilda Lessways*, *Talking to a Stranger* (Television Actress of the year), *An Age of Kings*, *Village Wooing*, *Luther*, *On Approval*, *Days to Come*, *The Comedy of Errors*, *Macbeth*, *On Giant's Shoulders*, *Love in a Cold Climate*, *A Fine Romance* (series), *The Cherry Orchard*, *Going Gently*, *Saigon*, *Ghosts*, *Make and Break*.

HONORS: O.B.E. 1970; Honorary Doctor of Letters, Warwick University, 1978, and York University, 1983.

Joyce Ebert

EDUCATION: Carnegie Institute.

TRAINING: Uta Hagen, Actors Studio.

PROFESSIONAL STAGE DEBUT: In *White Sheep of the Family*, Pittsburgh Playhouse.

NEW YORK THEATRE: Julie in Liliom, Alithea in The Country Wife, Emmanuele in Asmodee, Flora in Sign of Winter, Cordelia in King Lear, Camille in No Trifling with Love, Ophelia in Hamlet, Twelve O'Clock in Pullman Car Hiawatha, Rosie/Gossamer/Polly/Bessie/Mrs. Cherry Owen in Under Milk Wood, Vittoria in The White Devil, Stepdaughter in Six Characters in Search of an Author, Andromache in The Trojan Women (Derwent and OBIE awards), Mariane in Tartuffe, Wife/Barbara in Solitaire/Double Solitaire (Variety Arts award), Matron in The National Health, Maggie in The Shadow Box (Drama Desk nomination), Sara Muller in Watch on the Rhine, Golda in Requiem for a Heavyweight, Kate in All My Sons.

OTHER THEATRE: Long Wharf Theatre (New Haven), Ashland Shakespeare Festival (Oregon), San Diego Shakespeare Festival, American Shakespeare Festival (Connecticut), Mark Taper Forum (Los Angeles), Arena Stage (Washington, D.C.), McCarter Theatre (Princeton), Williamstown Theatre Festival (Massachusetts).

FILMS: Stardust Memories, Mrs. Soffel, The Young Doctors.

TELEVISION: Frontiers of Faith, Suspense, Kraft Television Theatre, Theater in America, St. Elsewhere.

Pat Galloway

TRAINING: RADA; Conservatoire d'Art Dramatique, Paris.

PROFESSIONAL STAGE DEBUT: The Tommy Trinder Show, Moss Empire tour of England and Scotland.

THEATRE IN BRITAIN: No. 1 tour of Guys and Dolls, Lincoln Repertory Players, The Penguin Players.

STRATFORD FESTIVAL, CANADA: Hippolyta in A Midsummer Night's Dream, Valeria in Coriolanus, Anne Bullen in Henry VIII, Dorine in Tartuffe, Lady Sneerwell in The School for Scandal, The Duchess of Malfi, Lady Macbeth, Lorenzo in Lorenzaccio, Goneril in King Lear, Kate in The Taming of the Shrew, Kate in She Stoops to Conquer, Toinette in The Imaginary Invalid, Rosaline in Love's Labor's Lost, Gwendolen in The Importance of Being Earnest, Gertrude in Hamlet, Natasha in Three Sisters, Olivia in Twelfth Night, Tamora in Titus Andronicus, Masha in The Seagull, Mrs. Malaprop in The Rivals, Arsinoe in The Misanthrope, Mistress Ford in The Merry Wives of Windsor, Queen Elizabeth in Mary Stuart, Ruth in The Pirates of Penzance, Alice in A Man for All Seasons.

OTHER THEATRE IN CANADA: Manitoba Theatre Centre: Little Mary Sunshine, Amanda in Private Lives, Eliza in Pygmalion, Polly in Threepenny Opera, Ranevskaya in The Cherry Orchard; Shaw Festival: Hesione in Heartbreak House, Mrs. Pat in Dear Liar, Lady Cicely in Captain Brassbound's Conversion; Theatre London, Crest and Royal Alexandra theatres (Toronto), Vancouver Playhouse, Bastion (Victoria), National Arts Centre (Ottawa), numerous musical revues.

OTHER THEATRE: Stratford tours to Europe and Russia, Guthrie Theater (Minneapolis), Pasadena Playhouse (California), Alley Theatre (Houston).
DIRECTOR: *Le Magicien* (Stratford), *The School for Scandal* (National Theatre School).
FILMS: *Triangle, Hey Cinderella.*
TELEVISION: *Le Treflea Quatre Feuilles, Ile aux Tresors, Playdate, Festival, McQueen, The National Dream* (all series); *She Stoops to Conquer, Meet Mr. Chopin, Tartuffe.*

Ellen Geer

TRAINING: American Shakespeare Academy.
PROFESSIONAL STAGE DEBUT: First Fairy in *A Midsummer Night's Dream,* American Shakespeare Festival, Connecticut.
NEW YORK THEATRE: APA: Maria in *The School for Scandal, A Midsummer Night's Dream,* Nina in *The Seagull,* Sally in *The Tavern,* Gertrude in *Fashion,* Jessica in *The Merchant of Venice,* Queen in *Richard II;* Other: *Alice in Wonderland.*
GUTHRIE THEATER, MINNEAPOLIS: Laura in *The Glass Menagerie,* Mrs. Fainall in *The Way of the World,* Rosalind in *As You Like It,* Ophelia in *Hamlet,* Irina in *Three Sisters,* Lady Anne in *Richard III,* Marianne in *The Miser,* Dunyasha in *The Cherry Orchard,* Gladys in *The Skin of Our Teeth.*
OTHER THEATRE: American Shakespeare Festival (Connecticut), American Conservatory Theatre (San Francisco), San Diego Shakespeare Festival, Mark Taper Forum (Los Angeles).
WILL GEER THEATRICUM BOTANICUM (TOPANGA, CALIFORNIA): Artistic director since 1978; actor: many roles; director: *Twelfth Night, The Merry Wives of Windsor, The Tempest, A Midsummer Night's Dream, Romeo and Juliet, Cymbeline, As You Like It, The Taming of the Shrew, A Winter's Tale, Three Sisters, The Seagull, The Skin of Our Teeth, Lysistrata, The Trojan Women, The House of Atreus, Gammer Gurton's Needle, The Glass Menagerie, Voices, Americana.*
FILMS: *Memory of Us, Harold and Maude, On the Edge, On the Nickle, Something Wicked This Way Comes, Kotch, Abraham and Isaac, Petulia, Silence, Hard Traveling, The Creator, Heart like a Wheel.*
TELEVISION: *Jimmy Stewart Show* (series), *Quincy, Night Cries, Code Red, The Lindbergh Kidnapping, The Babe Didrikson Story, A Shining Season, Dark Side of Love, Dallas, Trial of Lee Harvey Oswald, Fantasy Island, The Car, Strike Force, The Waltons, Ghost Story, Name of the Game, Dynasty, Falcon Crest, King Fu: The Movie.*
AUTHOR: *Memory of Us* (Atlanta Film Festival Gold Medal, 1973), *Dory* (musical biography); co-author: *Americana—Saints and Sinners* (play), *The Labor Story* (musical recitation), *Silence* (film).

Lee Grant

TRAINING: High School of Music and Art; Art Students League; Juilliard School of Music; Metropolitan Opera Ballet School; Neighborhood Playhouse School of the Theatre; Actors Studio.

PROFESSIONAL STAGE DEBUT: At age four as Hoo-Chee in *L'Oracolo*, Metropolitan Opera.

NEW YORK THEATRE: Shoplifter in *Detective Story* (New York Drama Critics Circle award), Mrs. Rodgers in *A Hole in The Head*, Gittel in *Two for the Seesaw*, leads in *Plaza Suite*, Edna in *The Prisoner of Second Avenue*, *Electra*, Solange in *The Maids* (OBIE award).

DIRECTOR: *A Private View* (Drama Desk nomination).

FILMS: *Detective Story* (Cannes Best Actress and Oscar nomination), *Middle of the Night*, *The Balcony*, *The Landlord* (Oscar nomination), *Plaza Suite*, *Portnoy's Complaint*, *Shampoo* (Oscar award), *In The Heat of the Night*, *Voyage of the Damned* (Oscar nomination), *Tell Me a Riddle*, *Nobody's Child* (Golden Globe nomination), *When Women Kill*, *What Sex Am I?*, *Down and Out in America* (Oscar nomination). Director: *The Stronger*.

TELEVISION: Guest appearances on many major series, Stella Chernak on *Peyton Place* (Emmy award), *The Neon Ceiling* (Emmy award), *The Gates of Cerberus* and title role in series *Fay* (Emmy nomination). Director: *The Shape of Things*, *For the Use of the Hall*, *Lt. Shuster's Wife*.

Uta Hagen

EDUCATION: One semester at the University of Wisconsin.

TRAINING: One term at RADA.

PROFESSIONAL STAGE DEBUT: Ophelia to Eva Le Gallienne's Hamlet, Cape Playhouse (Dennis, Massachusetts).

NEW YORK THEATRE: Nina in *The Seagull*, Edith in *The Happiest Days*, Alegre D'Alcala in *Key Largo*, Desdemona in *Othello*, *Vicki*, Olga in *The Whole World Over*; (in German) Margaret in *Faust* and Hilda in *The Master Builder*; Bella in *Angel Street*, Blanche in *A Streetcar Named Desire*, Georgie in *The Country Girl* (Tony and Drama Critics Circle awards), Tatiana in *Tovarich*, Hanna in *In Any Language*, Grace in *The Magic and the Loss*, Agata in *Island of Goats*, Natalia in *A Month in the Country*, Shen Te in *The Good Woman of Setzuan*, Angelique in *Port Royal*, Martha in *Who's Afraid of Virginia Woolf?* (Tony, Drama Critics and Outer Critics Circle awards), Ranevskaya in *The Cherry Orchard*, Charlotte, *Mrs. Warren's Profession*, Mrs. Clandon in *You Can Never Tell*.

LONDON THEATRE: *Who's Afraid of Virginia Woolf?* (Plays and Players award).

OTHER THEATRE: Westport Country Playhouse (Connecticut), Paper Mill Playhouse (New Jersey), Ann Arbor Drama Festival (Michigan), Mt. Kisco and Bucks County playhouses (Pennsylvania), Vancouver International Festival.

FILMS: The Other, The Boys from Brazil, A Doctor's Story.

TELEVISION: Macbeth, A Month in the Country, Out of Dust.

AUTHOR: Respect for Acting, Sources, Love for Cooking.

HONORS: Theatre Hall of Fame, 1983; Wisconsin Hall of Fame, 1984; Honorary Doctor of Fine Arts, Smith College and Wooster College; Doctor of Humane Letters, De Paul University, 1982; The Mayor's Liberty Medal of New York City, July 4, 1986.

Wendy Hiller

EDUCATION: Winceby House School, Bexhill.

PROFESSIONAL STAGE DEBUT: Maid in The Ware Case, Manchester Repertory Theatre.

LONDON THEATRE: Old Vic Company: Portia in Julius Caesar, Mistress Page in The Merry Wives of Windsor, Hermione in A Winter's Tale, Emilia in Othello, Helen in Troilus and Cressida; National Theatre: Gunhild in John Gabriel Borkman, Mrs. Whyte in Waters of the Moon; Sally in Love on the Dole, Sister Joanna in The Cradle Song, Princess Charlotte in The First Gentleman, Tess of the D'Urbervilles, Ann Veronica, Catherine in The Heiress, Evelyn in Waters of the Moon, Margaret in Night of the Ball, Isabel in Flowering Cherry, Carrie in Toys in the Attic, Mary Kingsley in Mr. Rhodes, Susan in Wings of the Dove, Nurse Wayland in The Sacred Flame, Enid in The Battle of Shrivings, Queen Mary in Crown Matrimonial.

NEW YORK THEATRE: Love on the Dole, The Heiress, Josie in A Moon for the Misbegotten, Flowering Cherry, Miss Tina in The Aspern Papers.

OTHER THEATRE: Wartime C.E.M.A. tour as Viola in Twelfth Night, Bristol Old Vic, Gaiety (Dublin), Birmingham Rep, Edinburgh Festival, Cambridge Arts Theatre, Chichester Festival.

FILMS: Lancashire Luck, Pygmalion, Major Barbara, I Know Where I'm Going, Outcast of the Islands, Single Handed, Something of Value, Uncle George, Separate Tables (Oscar award), Sons and Lovers, Toys in the Attic, A Man for All Seasons, David Copperfield, Murder on the Orient Express, Voyage of the Damned, The Elephant Man, Making Love.

HONORS: Honorary Doctor of Letters, Manchester University, 1984; O.B.E. 1971, D.B.E. 1975.

Frances Hyland

EDUCATION: University of Saskatchewan.

TRAINING: RADA.

PROFESSIONAL STAGE DEBUT: Stella in *A Streetcar Named Desire*, Aldwych Theatre, London.

BRITISH THEATRE: London: Esther in *The Same Sky*, Mary in *The Step Forward*, Hester in *A Woman of No Importance*, Fleur-Therese in *A Time to Laugh*, Gertie in *Little Idiot*; Chichester Festival, Edinburgh Festival.

CANADIAN THEATRE: Stratford Festival: Isabella in *Measure for Measure*, Bianca in *The Taming of the Shrew*, Portia in *The Merchant of Venice*, Ophelia in *Hamlet*, Olivia in *Twelfth Night*, Perdita in *A Winter's Tale*, Phebe in *As You Like It*, Desdemona in *Othello*, Lucile in *Le Bourgeois Gentilhomme*, Goneril in *King Lear*, Margaret in *Henry VI* and *Richard III*, Mistress Ford in *The Merry Wives of Windsor*; Shaw Festival: *Candida*, Florence in *The Vortex*, Prola in *The Simpleton of the Unexpected Isles*, Mrs. Higgins in *Pygmalion*, Gunhild in *John Gabriel Borkman*, Lady Utterword in *Heartbreak House*, Francine in *The Chemmy Circle*, Oracle/Serpent/Ghost of Lilith in *Back to Methuselah*; Toronto Arts Productions: Jessica in *The Sea*, Elizabeth I in *The Shoemaker's Holiday*, Blanche in *A Streetcar Named Desire*, *The Ecstasy of Rita Joe*; Vancouver Playhouse; Citadel and Northern Light theatres (Edmonton); Victoria Playhouse, Bastion and Belfry theatres (Victoria); Crest Theatre and Bayview Playhouse (Toronto).

U.S. THEATRE: New York: Laura in *Look Homeward Angel*, Young Actress in *Moby Dick*; American Shakespeare Festival (Connecticut), Goodman Theatre (Chicago; Joseph Jefferson award for Mary Tyrone in *Long Day's Journey into Night*).

FILMS: *The Changeling*, *Pygmalion*, *The Sight*.

TELEVISION: *The Great Detective* (series); Hostess on *Tuesday Night Dreams*.

DIRECTOR: *Othello* (Stratford Festival), *Black Coffee* (Shaw Festival), *Private Lives* (Manitoba Theatre Centre), *Playboy of the Western World* (Theatre Calgary).

HONORS: Member of the Order of Canada; Honorary Doctor of Law, University of Saskatchewan and University of British Columbia; John Drainie Award of ACTRA, 1981; Silver Ticket Award for ongoing contribution to the theatre, 1985.

Barbara Jefford

TRAINING: Hartly-Hodder Studio, Bristol; RADA (Bancroft Gold Medal).

PROFESSIONAL STAGE DEBUT: Walk-on in *Our Town*, Dolphin Theatre, Brighton.

LONDON THEATRE: Old Vic Company: Imogen in *Cymbeline*, Beatrice in *Much Ado about Nothing*, Portia in *The Merchant of Venice*, Julia in *Two Gentlemen of Verona*,

Tamora in *Titus Andronicus*, Courtesan in *The Comedy of Errors*, Lady Anne in *Richard III*, Queen Margaret in *Henry VI*, Isabella in *Measure for Measure*, Regan in *King Lear*, Viola in *Twelfth Night*, Beatrice in *The Cenci*, Rosalind in *As You Like It*, Gwendolen in *The Importance of Being Earnest*, Lavinia in *Mourning Becomes Electra*, Lina in *Misalliance*, Stepdaughter in *Six Characters in Search of an Author*, Nan in *Ride a Cock Horse*; Royal Shakespeare Company: Patsy in *Little Murders*, Mother Vaujou in *Mistress of Novices*; National Theatre: Gertrude in *Hamlet*, Zobina in *Tamburlaine*; Prospect Company at the Old Vic: *Hamlet*, Thetis in *War Music*, Cleopatra in *Antony and Cleopatra* and *All for Love*, The Nurse in *Romeo and Juliet*, Anna in *The Government Inspector*; Other: Bertha in *Frenzy*, Rose in *Trelawney of the 'Wells'*, Andromache in *Tiger at the Gates*, Margaret in *The Dark Horse*, *Filumena*, Millie in *The Browning Version*, Grace in *The Winslow Boy*.

MEMORIAL THEATRE AT STRATFORD-UPON-AVON: *Measure for Measure*, Anne Bullen in *Henry VIII*, Calpurnia in *Julius Caesar*, Hero in *Much Ado about Nothing*, Lady Percy in *Henry IV*, Queen of France in *Henry V*, Juno in *The Tempest*, Desdemona in *Othello*, Helena in *A Midsummer Night's Dream*, Katherine in *The Taming of the Shrew*, Helen in *Troilus and Cressida*.

NEW YORK THEATRE: *Tiger at the Gates*; Old Vic tours: Ophelia in *Hamlet*, *Twelfth Night*, Lady Macbeth.

OTHER THEATRE: Dundee Repertory Company, New Zealand Players Company, Paris Festival, Oxford Playhouse, Nottingham Playhouse, Arnaud (Guildford), Arts Theatre (Cambridge), Bristol Old Vic, Edinburgh Festival, Chichester Festival, Brighton Festival, national tour of *Veronica's Room*.

FILMS: *Ulysses*, *A Midsummer Night's Dream*, *The Shoes of the Fisherman*, *And the Ship Sails On*.

TELEVISION: *Edna*, *The Inebriated Woman*, *The Visitors*, *Skin Game*, *Walter*, *Porterhouse Blue*.

HONORS: O.B.E. 1965; Jubilee Medal 1977.

Laurie Kennedy

EDUCATION: Sarah Lawrence College.

TRAINING: Michael Howard, Joseph Chaikin, David Craig.

PROFESSIONAL STAGE DEBUT: Irina in *Three Sisters*, Williamstown Summer Theatre, Massachusetts.

NEW YORK THEATRE: Paula in *End of Summer*, Sheila in *A Day in the Death of Joe Egg*, Violet in *Man and Superman* (Derwent and Theatre World awards), Esther/Anna in *Remembrance*, *Major Barbara*, Helen in *Ladyhouse Blues*, Ann Herford in *He and She*, Silvia in *The Recruiting Officer*, Harriet in *Isn't It Romantic*, Hilda in *Master Builder*, Holga in *After the Fall*, Lady Macbeth.

OTHER THEATRE: Long Wharf Theatre (New Haven), PAF Playhouse (Huntington, New York), North Shore Music Festival Theatre (Massachusetts), Ahmanson Theatre and Mark Taper Forum (Los Angeles), Arena Stage (Washington, D.C.), Massachusetts Center Repertory Company, Hartman Theatre Company (Connecticut), BAM Theater Company (Brooklyn), Buffalo Studio Arena, Hartford Stage, Williamstown Theatre Festival, Edinburgh Festival.

TELEVISION: *Edge of Night* (series), *President Kennedy, Sherlock Holmes, Choices, St. Elsewhere, Twisted.*

Roberta Maxwell

TRAINING: Kristan Linklater, Judy Leibowitz.

PROFESSIONAL STAGE DEBUT: Ursula in *Much Ado about Nothing*, Stratford Festival, Canada.

CANADIAN THEATRE: Stratford Festival: Olivia in *Twelfth Night*, Marya in *The Government Inspector*, Anne Page in *The Merry Wives of Windsor*, Lady Macbeth, Rosalind in *As You Like It*, Elmire in *Tartuffe*, Nina in *The Seagull*, Heloise in *Heloise and Abelard*; Shaw Festival: Vivie in *Mrs. Warren's Profession*, Raina in *Arms and the Man*, Orinthia in *The Apple Cart*; Stevie (YPT in Toronto, Dora award); Manitoba Theatre Centre.

NEW YORK THEATRE: Chorus in *The House of Atreus*, Mrs. Dullfeet in *The Resistible Rise of Arturo Ui*, Desdemona in *Othello*, Katherine in *Henry V*, Lucienne in *There's One in Every Marriage*, Nora in *The Plough and the Stars*, Jessica in *The Merchant of Venice*, Jill in *Equus*, Portia in *The Merchant*, Betty in *A Whistle in the Dark* (OBIE award), Sorel in *Hay Fever*, Joanne in *Slag* (Drama Desk award), Anne in *Ashes* (OBIE award), *Stevie, Mary Stuart* (Villager award), Beaty in *Lydie Breeze*, Irina in *Before the Dawn.*

AMERICAN SHAKESPEARE FESTIVAL (CONNECTICUT): *Henry V*, Maria in *Twelfth Night*, Hero in *Much Ado about Nothing*, Natasha in *Three Sisters*, Ophelia in *Hamlet, Othello*, Juliet in *Romeo and Juliet*, Helena in *All's Well that Ends Well.*

OTHER THEATRE: Everyman Theatre (Cheltenham), Guthrie Theater (Minneapolis), Long Wharf Theatre (New Haven), Old Globe Theatre (San Diego), Charles Playhouse (Boston), Philadelphia Drama Guild, Center Theatre Group (Los Angeles).

FILMS: *Rich Kids, The Changeling, Popeye, Psycho III.*

TELEVISION: *As the World Turns, Airwaves* (both series); *Antigone, Uncle Vanya, Mourning Becomes Electra, St. Elsewhere.*

Siobhan McKenna

EDUCATION: National University of Ireland (scholarship and first honors).

PROFESSIONAL STAGE DEBUT: Wife in *Tons of Money*, An Taibhdhearc Theatre, Galway.

IRISH THEATRE: An Taibhdhearc, in Gaelic: Lady Macbeth, Mrs. Gregson in *Shadow of a Gunman*, Bessie in *The Plough and the Stars*, Mariamne in *Winterset*, Bella in *Gaslight*, *Mary Rose*; Abbey Theatre: *The Countess Cathleen*, Monica in *The End House*, Mabel in *Marks and Mabel*, Nicole in *The Bourgeois Gentilhomme*, Marian in *The Far-Off Hills*, Nano in *The Railway House*, Eileen in *Thy Dear Father*, *The Plough and the Stars*, Juno in *Juno and the Paycock*, *Here Are Ladies*, Julia in *Fallen Angels*; Gate Theatre: Josie in *A Moon for the Misbegotten*; Gaiety Theatre: Beauty in *The Love of Four Colonels*, Louka in *Arms and the Man*, Pegeen Mike in *The Playboy of the Western World*, *Anna Christie*.

LONDON THEATRE: Nora in *The White Steed*, Helen in *Berkeley Square*, Maura in *Fading Mansion*, Regina in *Ghosts*, *Heloise*, *The Playboy of the Western World*, Anna in *Play with a Tiger*, Joan Dark in *Saint Joan of the Stockyards*, Marie-Jeanne in *The Cavern*, Pearl in *A Foggy Day*, Josie in *Best of Friends*, *Here Are Ladies*, *Juno and the Paycock*, Agrippina in *Britannicus*, Sarah Bernhardt in *Memoir*.

NEW YORK THEATRE: Miss Madrigal in *The Chalk Garden*, Margaret in *The Rope Dancers* (both Tony nominations), *Hamlet*, *Here Are Ladies*, *The Plough and the Stars*, Margaret in *A Meeting by the River*.

OTHER THEATRE: Memorial Theatre at Stratford-upon-Avon, Stratford Festival (Canada), Edinburgh Festival, Dublin Festival, New York Shakespeare Festival, Cambridge (Massachusetts) Drama Festival, Guelph Festival (Canada).

DIRECTOR: *Saint Joan*, *The Playboy of the Western World*, *Daughter from over the Water*, *I'm Getting Out of This Kip*, *The Tinker's Wedding*, *In the Shadow of the Glen*, *Riders to the Sea*, *Juno and the Paycock*, *The Golden Cradle*.

FILMS: *Hungry Hill*, *The Adventurers*, *King of Kings*, *Doctor Zhivago*, *The Playboy of the Western World*, *Of Human Bondage*, *Philadelphia, Here I Come*.

TELEVISION: *The Letter*, *The Cradle Song*, *What Every Woman Knows*, *The Winslow Boy*, *Don Juan in Hell*, *The Woman in White*, *The Rope Dancers*, *Cuckoo Split*, *A Cheap Bunch of Flowers*, *The Landlady* and *Lady Gregory*.

HONORS: Honorary Doctor of Humane Letters, Wilson College; Gold Medal of the Eire Society of Boston.

Nora McLellan

TRAINING: HB Studio.

PROFESSIONAL STAGE DEBUT: At age nine in *La Boheme*, Vancouver Opera Association.

CANADIAN THEATRE: Shaw Festival: Bride in *A Respectable Wedding*, Mrs. Lunn in *Overruled*, Charlotte in *The Magistrate*, Ida in *See How They Run*, Albert in *The Singular Life of Albert Nobbs*, Proserpine in *Candida*, Mrs. Hyerling in *The Simpleton of the Unexpected Isles*, Sabina in *Skin of Our Teeth*, Mary Haines in *The Women*, Jane Marryott in *Cavalcade*, Louka in *Arms and the Man*, Parlor Maid/Mrs. Lutestring in *Back to Methuselah*; Vancouver Playhouse: Who in *Waterfall*, Daphne in *Paraphranalia*, Scrooge in *A Christmas Carol*; Arts Club, Vancouver: Bobby in *The Club*, Kathy in *Vanities*, Principal in *Bistro Car* and *Starting Here, Starting Now*; Heritage Festival, Vancouver: Principal in *Tribute to Theatre under the Stars*; Toronto theatres: *Jennie's Story*, Miss Prue in *Love for Love* (St. Lawrence Centre), Ellen/Mrs. Saunders/Lin in *Cloud Nine* (Bayview Playhouse), Sonya in *Uncle Vanya*, May in *Farther West* (Tarragon Theatre; both Dora Mavor Moore award nominations); Belfry Theatre, Victoria: Jessie in *'night, Mother*, Barbara in *Children*; National Arts Centre, Ottawa: Eve in *A History of the American Film*, Blue Fairy in *Pinocchio*; Citadel Theatre, Edmonton: Maria in *Twelfth Night*, Mrs. Potiphar in *Joseph and the Amazing Technicolor Dreamcoat*.

U.S. THEATRE: Seattle Repertory Theatre: Gladys Bump in *Pal Joey*, Billie Dawn in *Born Yesterday*, Julia in *Two Gentlemen of Verona*, Susannah in *Bedroom Farce*.

Sarah Miles

TRAINING: RADA.

PROFESSIONAL THEATRE DEBUT: *Dazzling Prospect*, Globe Theatre, London.

LONDON THEATRE: Royal Court Theatre: Anna in *Kelly's Eye*; National Theatre: Abigail in *The Crucible*; Other: Marina Oswald in *The Silence of Lee Harvey Oswald*, Woman in *World War 2½*, Mary, Queen of Scots in *Vivat! Vivat Regina!*

OTHER THEATRE: Chichester Festival, Ahmanson Theatre (Los Angeles), American Conservatory Theatre (San Francisco).

FILMS: *Term of Trial*, *The Servant*, *The Ceremony*, *Those Magnificent Men in Their Flying Machines*, *Blow Up*, *Ryan's Daughter* (Oscar nomination), *Lady Caroline Lamb*, *The Hireling*, *The Man Who Loved Cat Dancing*, *The Sailor Who Fell from Grace with the Sea*, *The Big Sleep*, *Ordeal by Innocence*, *Priest of Love*, *Venom*, *Steaming*, *Six-Sided Triangle*, *Hope and Glory*.

TELEVISION: *Great Expectations*, *James Michener's Dynasty*, *Harem*.

AUTHOR: *Sarah Miles Is Me* (musical).

Sian Phillips

EDUCATION: University of Wales.

TRAINING: RADA (Bancroft Gold Medal).

PROFESSIONAL STAGE DEBUT: Touring for the Arts Council in Welsh plays.

LONDON THEATRE: Royal Shakespeare Company: Julia in *The Duchess of Malfi*, Bertha in Ondine; National Theatre: *Major Barbara*; Other: *Hedda Gabler*, Princess Siwan in *King's Daughter*, Arlow in *The Lizard on the Rock*, Penelope in *Gentle Jack*, Yolande in *Maxibules*, Hannah in *Night of the Iguana* (London Standard nomination), Myra in *Ride a Cock Horse*, Ann in *Man and Superman* (Standard nomination), Strange Lady in *The Man of Destiny*, Edwina in *The Burglar*, Ruth in *Epitaph for George Dillon*, Virginia Woolf in *A Nightingale in Bloomsbury Square*, Duchess of Strood in *The Gay Lord Quex*, Myra in *Spinechiller*, Mrs. Clandon in *You Never Can Tell*, Aunt Alicia in musical of *Gigi*, Vera in *Pal Joey* (SWET nomination), Mrs. Pat in *Dear Liar*.

OTHER THEATRE: Belgrade Playhouse, Nottingham Playhouse, Oxford Playhouse, Ashcroft (Croydon), Arnaud (Guildford), Palace (Watford), Chichester Festival.

FILMS: *Becket*, *Laughter in the Dark*, *Goodbye, Mr. Chips* (3 Best Supporting Performance awards), *Murphy's War*, *Clash of the Titans*, *Dune*, *A Painful Case*, *Return to Endor*.

TELEVISION: *How Green Was My Valley* (BAFTA award), *I, Claudius* (BAFTA and Royal Society of Television awards), *Crime and Punishment*, *Shoulder to Shoulder* (all series); *The Orestia*, *The Achurch Papers*, *Lady Windermere's Fan*.

HONORS: Governor, St. David Trust, Wales; elected to the Honorary Order of Druids of the National Eisteddfod of Caernarvon in recognition of service to Welsh drama; Fellow of Cardiff College, University of Wales; Honorary Doctor of Letters, University of Wales.

Angela Pleasence

TRAINING: RADA.

PROFESSIONAL STAGE DEBUT: Titania in *A Midsummer Night's Dream*, Birmingham Repertory Theatre.

LONDON THEATRE: Juliet in *Romeo and Juliet*, Josephine in *The Ha Ha* (West End Critics award), Miranda in *The Tempest*, Electra in *You Were So Sweet when You Were Little*, Jean in *The Entertainer*, Miss Cutts in *The Hothouse*, Marlene in *The Bitter Tears of Petra von Kant* (West End Critics award), Charlotte in *The Cherry Orchard* (West End Critics nomination), Water Sprite in *Better Days, Better Knights*, Girl in *The Square*, Belzer in *When She Danced*.

OTHER THEATRE: Chichester Festival, Edinburgh Festival, Ludlow Festival, Nottingham Playhouse.

FILMS: *Tales from Beyond the Grave, Here We Go Round the Mulberry Bush, Hitler—the Last Ten Days, Symptoms* (Cannes nomination), *The Godsend.*

TELEVISION: *Six Wives of Henry VIII, Marching Song, Breath, Murder at the Wedding, Charlotte Bronte, Mansfield Park, Les Misérables, Barchester Chronicles, Christmas Carol, Anastasia, Silas Marner.*

RADIO: Twice nominated as Best Actress BBC Radio.

Joan Plowright

TRAINING: Laban Art of Movement Studio; Old Vic Theatre School.

PROFESSIONAL STAGE DEBUT: Hope in *If Four Walls Told*, Grand Theatre, Croyden.

LONDON THEATRE: English Stage Company at the Royal Court Theatre: Mary Warren in *The Crucible*, Baptista in *Don Juan*, Mrs. Shin in *The Good Woman of Setzuan*, Margery in *The Country Wife*, Old Woman in *The Chairs*, *Major Barbara*, Beatie Bryant in *Roots*, Daisy in *Rhinoceros*; National Theatre: Sonya in *Uncle Vanya*, Maggie in *Hobson's Choice*, Hilde in *The Master Builder*, Masha in *The Three Sisters*, Dorine in *Tartuffe*, Rosaline in *Love's Labor's Lost*, Portia in *The Merchant of Venice*, Mistress Anne in *A Woman Killed with Kindness*, Silla in *The Rules of the Game*, Beatrice in *Much Ado about Nothing*, Stella in *Eden End*, *Mrs. Warren's Profession*; Other: Donna Clara in *The Duenna*, Young Actress in *Moby Dick*, Jean Rice in *The Entertainer*, Rosa in *Saturday Sunday Monday*, *Filumena* (SWET award), Alma in *The Bed before Yesterday* (Variety Club award), Arkadina in *The Seagull*, Ranevskaya in *The Cherry Orchard*, Lady Wishfort in *The Way of the World*, Poncia in *The House of Bernarda Alba* (Drama Magazine award).

OTHER BRITISH THEATRE: Bristol Old Vic, Belgrade (Coventry), Nottingham Playhouse, Old Vic Company South African tour, Chichester Festival, Edinburgh Festival.

NEW YORK THEATRE: *The Chairs* and *The Pupil* in *The Lesson*, *The Entertainer*, Jo in *A Taste of Honey* (New York Drama Critics Circle and Tony awards).

DIRECTOR: *Rites*, co-director: *An Evasion of Women* and *The Travails of Sancho Panza* (all National Theatre); *A Prayer for Wings* (Edinburgh Festival).

FILMS: *Moby Dick, The Entertainer, Three Sisters, Equus, Britannia Hospital, Brimstone & Treacle, Wagner, Revolution 1776.*

TELEVISION: *Odd Man In, The Secret Agent, The School for Scandal, The Diary of Anne Frank, Three Sisters, Daphne Laureola, Merchant of Venice, Saturday Sunday Monday, A Dedicated Man, The Birthday Party, The Importance of Being Earnest.*

HONORS: C.B.E. 1970.

Lynn Redgrave

TRAINING: Central School of Speech and Drama.

PROFESSIONAL STAGE DEBUT: Helena in *A Midsummer Night's Dream*, Royal Court Theatre.

LONDON THEATRE: National Theatre: Rose in *The Recruiting Officer*, Barblin in *Andorra*, Margaret in *Much Ado about Nothing*, Kattrin in *Mother Courage*, Miss Prue in *Love for Love*, Jackie in *Hay Fever*; Other: Sarah in *The Tulip Tree*, all the women's roles in *The Two of Us*, Joanne in *Slag*, Billie Dawn in *Born Yesterday*.

NEW YORK THEATRE: Carol in *Black Comedy*, Vicky in *My Fat Friend*, Vivie in *Mrs. Warren's Profession* (Tony nomination), Joan of Arc in *Knock Knock*, Sister Mary Ignatius Explains It All for You, Margot in *Aren't We All?* (Drama Desk nomination), Sue Too in *Sweet Sue*.

OTHER THEATRE: Edinburgh Festival, Gate Theatre (Dublin), American Shakespeare Festival (Connecticut), Goodman Theatre (Chicago), Academy Festival Theatre (Chicago; Sarah Siddons and Joseph Jefferson awards for Hypathia in *Misalliance*); Drama-Logue awards (Los Angeles) for *Thursdays Girls* and *Sister Mary Ignatius* (also Robby award).

FILMS: *Tom Jones*, *The Girl with the Green Eyes*, *The Deadly Affair*, *Georgy Girl* (New York Film Critics and Golden Globe awards, Oscar nomination), *Smashing Time*, *The Virgin Soldiers*, *Last of the Mobile Hotshots*, *Don't Turn the Other Cheek*, *Every Little Crook and Nanny*, *Everything You Always Wanted to Know about Sex*, *The National Health*, *The Happy Hooker*, *The Big Bus*, *Sunday Lovers*, *Home Front*.

TELEVISION: *The Fainthearted Feminist*, *House Calls* (Emmy and Golden Globe nominations), *Teachers Only*, *Not for Women Only*, *The Weightwatchers Magazine Show* (all series); *Pygmalion*, *Vienna 1900*, *A Midsummer Night's Dream*, *Daft As a Brush*, *Centennial*, *Gauguin the Sauvage*, *The Turn of the Screw*, *The Seduction of Miss Leona*, *Beggarman/Thief*, *The Shooting* (Emmy nomination), *Rehearsal for Murder*, *Antony and Cleopatra*, *The Bad Seed*, *My Two Loves*.

Janet Suzman

EDUCATION: Kingsmead College, University of Witwaterstand.

TRAINING: LAMDA.

PROFESSIONAL STAGE DEBUT: Liz in *Billy Liar*, Tower Theatre, Ipswich.

LONDON THEATRE: Hester in *Hello and Goodbye* (Evening Standard award), *Vassa*, Masha in *Three Sisters* (Evening Standard and Plays and Players awards), *Hedda Gabler* (SWET nomination), Shen Te in *The Good Woman of Setzuan*, Lena in *Bozeman and Lena*.

ROYAL SHAKESPEARE COMPANY (STRATFORD AND LONDON): Iris in *The Tempest*, Joan

La Pucelle in *Henry VI*, Lady Anne in *Richard III*, Lady Percy in *Henry IV*, Luciana in *The Comedy of Errors*, Ophelia in *Hamlet*, Rosaline in *Love Labor's Lost*, Portia in *The Merchant of Venice*, Katharina in *The Taming of the Shrew*, Celia in *As You Like It*, Rosalind in *As You Like It*, Beatrice in *Much Ado about Nothing*, Lulu in *The Birthday Party*, Cleopatra in *Antony and Cleopatra* (London Standard award), Lavinia in *Titus Andronicus*, Clytemnestra/Helen in *The Greeks*.

OTHER THEATRE: Edinburgh Festival, Oxford Playhouse.

FILMS: *A Day in the Death of Joe Egg*, *Nicholas and Alexandra* (Oscar nomination), *The Black Windmill*, *Nijinsky*, *Priest of Love*, *The Draughtsman's Contract*, *The Boat Sails On*.

TELEVISION: *Three Sisters*, *Hedda Gabler*, *The House on Garibaldi Street*, *Miss Nightingale*, *Clayhanger*, *Mountbatten: The Last Viceroy*, *The Singing Detective*, *Twelfth Night*, *Macbeth*, *Antony and Cleopatra*, *The Family Re-Union*.

Selected

Bibliography

Joan of Arc in History, Legend and Art

France, Anatole. *The Life of Joan of Arc.* Trans. Winifred Stephens. 2 vols. London: John Lane, 1908.

Gies, Frances. *Joan of Arc.* New York: Harper and Row, 1981.

Lucie-Smith, Edward. *Joan of Arc.* New York: Norton, 1977.

Michelet, Jules. *Joan of Arc.* Trans. Albert Guerard. Ann Arbor: University of Michigan Press, 1957.

Mouton, Janice Malmsten. "Joan of Arc on the Twentieth Century Stage: Dramatic Treatments of the Joan of Arc Story by Bertolt Brecht, George Bernard Shaw, Jean Anouilh, Georg Kaiser, Paul Claudel, and Maxwell Anderson." Diss. Northwestern, 1974.

Munitz, Barry. "Joan of Arc and Modern Drama." Diss. Princeton, 1968.

Murray, T. Douglas, ed. and trans. *Jeanne D'Arc, Maid of Orleans, Deliverer of France, Being the Story of Her Life, Her Achievements, and Her Death, as Attested on Oath and Set Forth in the Original Documents.* London: William Heinemann, 1902.

Pernoud, Regine. *Joan of Arc: By Herself and Her Witnesses.* Trans. Edward Hyams. New York: Stein and Day, 1982.

Rakhem, Ingualet. *Joan of Arc in History, Legend and Literature.* New York: Columbia University Press, 1972.

Sackville-West, Vita. *Saint Joan of Arc.* Boston: G.K. Hall and Co., 1984.

Sun, Shirley Sui-Nin. "Joan of Arc: A Re-Evaluation of the Figure Between History and Legend." Diss. University of California at Berkeley, 1979.

Twain, Mark. *Personal Recollections of Joan of Arc.* New York: Harper and Brothers, 1896.

Voltaire, Francois Marie Arnout de. *The Virgin of Orleans or Joan of Arc.* Trans. Howard Nelson. Denver: Alan Swallow, 1965.

Warner, Marina. *Joan of Arc: The Image of Female Heroism.* New York: Vintage Books, 1982.

Reflections on and Interpretations of Shaw's Saint Joan

Boas, F.S. "Joan of Arc in Shakespeare, Schiller and Shaw." *Shakespeare Quarterly,* 2. January 1951.

Devlin, Diana. *A Speaking Part: Lewis Casson and the Theatre of His Time.* London: Hodder and Stoughton, 1982.

Dukore, Bernard F. *Bernard Shaw Director.* Seattle: University of Washington Press, 1971.

———. *The Collected Screenplays of Bernard Shaw.* London: George Prior Publishers, 1980.

———. *Saint Joan: A Screenplay by Bernard Shaw.* Seattle: University of Washington Press, 1968.

Johns, Eric. *Dames of the Theatre.* New Rochelle: Arlington House, 1974.

Langer, Lawrence. *G.B.S. and the Lunatic.* London: Hutchison, 1964.

Laurence, Dan H., ed. *Bernard Shaw's Collected Letters 1911–1925.* New York: Viking, 1985.

Mosel, Tad, with Gertrude Macy. *Leading Lady: The World and Theatre of Katharine Cornell.* Boston: Atlantic Monthly Press, 1978.

Morley, Sheridan. *Sybil Thorndike: A Life in the Theatre.* London: Weidenfeld and Nicolson, 1977.

Patch, Blanche. *Thirty Years with G.B.S.* London: Victor Gollancz, 1951.

Pearson, Hesketh. *Bernard Shaw: His Life and Personality.* London: Collins, 1942.

Peters, Margot. *Bernard Shaw and the Actresses.* New York: Doubleday and Co., Inc., 1980.

Sprigge, Elizabeth. *Sybil Thorndike Casson.* London: Victor Gollancz, 1971.

Tyson, Brian. *The Story of Shaw's Saint Joan.* Montreal: McGill-Queens University Press, 1982.

Weintraub, Stanley, ed. *"Saint Joan" Fifty Years After.* Baton Rouge: Louisiana State University Press, 1973.

Plays about or Inspired by Joan of Arc

Anderson, Maxwell. *Joan of Lorraine*. Washington, D.C.: Anderson House, 1946.

Anouilh, Jean. *The Lark*. Adapt. Lillian Hellman. New York: Random House, 1956.

Brecht, Bertolt. *Saint Joan of the Stockyards*. Trans. Frank Jones. Bloomington: Indiana University Press, 1969.

Claudel, Paul (text) and Arthur Honegger (music). *Joan of Arc at the Stake*. Trans. Dennis Arundell. Paris: Editions Salabert, 1939. (English version available through Gus Schirmer, Inc.).

Feiffer, Jules. *Knock Knock*. New York: Samuel French, 1976.

Kaiser, Georg. *Gilles und Jeanne*. Potsdam: G.K. Kiepenheuer, 1923.

Mueller, Lavonne. *Little Victories*. New York: Dramatists Play Service, 1984.

Schiller, Friedrich von. *The Maid of Orleans*. Trans. Charles E. Passage. New York: Frederick Ungar, 1961.

Shakespeare, William. *Henry VI, Part One*. Baltimore: Penguin Books, 1966.

Shaw, George Bernard. *Saint Joan*. New York: Penguin Books, 1957.

Index

:

Opposite page: GBS at the dress rehearsal of the 1936 Malvern Festival production of Saint Joan, featuring Wendy Hiller. Everything has come to a halt while a problem with getting the banner to change direction is corrected.

The photographs in this book are reproduced with the kind permission of the following: p.16 Herbert Whittaker; cover, p.48, 140 Billy Rose Theatre Collection, The New York Public Library at Lincoln Center, Astor, Lenox and Tilden Foundations; p.62 photo by Peter Smith, Metropolitan Toronto Library Board; p.80, 109 photo by Angus McBean, Harvard Theatre Collection; p.88 photo by Robert Ragsdale, Stratford Shakespearean Festival Foundation of Canada; p.95 Adelaide Advertiser; p.98 photo by Otto Rothschild, Music Center Operating Company; p.118 The Guthrie Theater; p.134, 170 photo by George de Vincent, Arena Stage; p.146 The Williamstown Theatre Festival; p.155 BBC Enterprises, British Broadcasting Corporation; p.183 The Goodman Theatre; p.204 photo by Greg Gilbert, Seattle Repertory Theatre; p.210 photo by David Cooper, The Shaw Festival, Canada. All uncredited photographs are by the kind permission of the individual actresses.

ABOUT THE AUTHOR

Holly Hill is New York theatre correspondent for *The Times* of London and theatre critic for the *Stamford Advocate/Greenwich Times* in Connecticut. A professor of speech and theatre at John Jay College of the City University of New York, she is associate editor of the two-volume *Encyclopedia of the New York Stage 1920–30*. Her arts reviews and features have appeared in such publications as the *Wall Street Journal, Christian Science Monitor, American Theatre, Soho News, Westchester-Gannett Newspapers, Houston Chronicle, Horizon, American Arts Magazine, Theatre Journal* and *Contemporary Review*.